Examining
Sociology

Examining Sociology

Jane L. Thompson

Hutchinson
London Melbourne Sydney Auckland Johannesburg

Hutchinson & Co. (Publishers) Ltd
An imprint of the Hutchinson Publishing Group
17–21 Conway Street, London W1P 5HL

Hutchinson Group (Australia) Pty Ltd
30-32 Cremorne Street, Richmond South, Victoria 3121
PO Box 151, Broadway, New South Wales 2007

Hutchinson Group (NZ) Ltd
32-34 View Road, PO Box 40-086, Glenfield, Auckland 10

Hutchinson Group (SA) (Pty) Ltd
PO Box 337, Bergvlei 2012, South Africa

First published 1980
Reprinted 1981, 1982

© Jane L. Thompson 1980
Illustrations © Hutchinson & Co. (Publishers) Ltd 1980

Set in Century Schoolbook

Printed in Great Britain by The Anchor Press Ltd
and bound by Wm Brendon & Son Ltd
both of Tiptree, Essex

British Library Cataloguing in Publication Data
Thompson, Jane Lindsay
  Examining sociology.
  1. Sociology
  I. Title II. Sociology for schools
  301   HM66

ISBN 0 09 141061 4

Contents

1 What is sociology?

There was a time when explaining human behaviour was a fairly straightforward business. Whether you were intelligent or stupid, rich or poor, good or bad was all put down, more or less, to 'human nature' or 'fate'. But very few people these days believe that explanations like these will do when it comes to understanding the varied and complex behaviour of individuals and groups of people in a fast-moving society like ours.

Certainly we are more conscious about 'what makes people tick' these days. All kinds of experts – psychologists, psychiatrists, philosophers, biologists, theologians, economists, political scientists, not to mention sociologists – all claim to have some kind of special insight into the reasons why people behave as they do. And of course, the 'man in the street' and the 'woman next door' all have their own personal theories and opinions to explain everything from bingo-mania to wife battering.

So why has the interest in human behaviour become so widespread in recent years? Well, of course, there are many reasons. But an important one is to do with the side-effects of living in a modern, technological and rapidly changing society, with huge numbers of people living and working together in towns and cities, and new developments quickly making yesterday's ideas and attitudes seem out of date.

In the days before the industrial revolution, the pace of life went on much the same for generations. The lives of the rich people and the poor people were vastly different and people seemed to accept things as they were - or were not able to do very much about changing them. People did not live so long, they were more vulnerable to disease, most of them knew very little about what was going on in different parts of the country, let alone in other parts of the world. But industrialization, developments in medicine, education and mass communications have changed all that. Today society is a highly sophisticated and highly organized set of relationships, in which people's behaviour is subject to countless influences and experiences, and in which the state - in the form of the government, the civil service, the law, welfare organizations and education - has a much more intricate control over people's lives than at any time in the past.

On the other hand, people are not as prepared, as they once were, to accept everything that happens to them as 'fate' or as 'the will of God'. An important by-product of increasing wealth, education and political democracy is the concern to find out more about why things are as they are, to try to influence what happens and even to change things.

This sort of interest in human behaviour and the characteristics of different social groups, organizations and institutions in society is very much the 'meat and drink' of sociology.

Sociology has often been called the 'science of society', and at its most simple level it is a way of studying scientifically why people in society behave as they do. Unlike biologists, however, sociologists are not particularly interested in the physical and genetic make-up of human beings. Unlike psychologists and psychiatrists, sociologists are not particularly interested in the workings of the individual mind. Unlike philosophers and theologians, sociologists do not usually look for clues in abstract ideas or beliefs. Sociologists are mainly concerned with the ways in which people are influenced by their experiences in life - by the families they grow up in, the friends and neighbours they come into contact with, the ways in which they are affected by the state, the jobs they do, the groups they belong to. But sociologists do not just see all these influences as impersonal forces, busily moulding 'helpless infants' into 'fully automatic' human beings. There has never been a time when any one individual, or even God, has suddenly waved a magic wand and said, 'Let there be families' or rugby clubs or comprehensive schools or a National Health Service. All of these phenomena, and the countless others which help to influence the way individuals behave, are themselves man-made. The other great interest of sociologists, therefore, is to discover how over time men and women have come to create and organize and give meaning to social institutions like the family and the law and the system of work and production. Sociologists also want to know how these organizations have become part and parcel of the things we all take, more or less, for granted in our everyday lives.

'So what else is special about sociology?', you might ask. Most of what I have said already could be applied to the work of journalists and writers. They are interested in human behaviour and what makes people tick. This is where the 'scientific' side of the sociology comes in. Clearly sociology is not a science in the same way as physics or chemistry is a science. You cannot do experiments on people in quite the same way as you would do experiments with chemicals in a laboratory. But scientists do have a special way of working. They try to explain things by:
1   having some idea of what they want to find out;
2   carefully and methodically collecting evidence, sifting through it and recording it in a way which is as foolproof as possible;
3   on the basis of their findings, trying to formulate explanations and

interpretations of the evidence they have uncovered so that others can learn from it too.

Sociologists try to work in a similar way, although their raw material is people and human behaviour. In identifying a problem to study, collecting evidence and offering explanations, they try at all times to be as systematic and methodical as possible. You cannot explain 'soccer hooliganism', for example, by observing one or two soccer hooligans at work, or talking to three angry policemen on a particularly bad afternoon at a local derby. You cannot explain why drug-taking is illegal in Britain merely by getting the views of one or two judges. You cannot explain poverty by assuming that some people do not work as hard as others. There are many factors involved and sociologists try in their investigations to look at as many aspects as possible, collect as much evidence as they can and then attempt to come to some conclusions and try to offer explanations.

Of course, there is one big difficulty when the subject of study is human behaviour and not chemicals in test tubes. It's much more difficult to be dispassionate. Scientists claim that science is 'objective' - it is to do with neutral experiments, calculations, scientific laws and special formulae. I am not sure whether that is altogether true, but I am sure that humans studying humans can never be 'objective'. All people have, as a result of their own upbringing and experiences, certain assumptions, attitudes and prejudices, some of which they are not even aware of. And even when they are, they can never be completely set aside by 'putting on the sociologist's hat' for a while. It might be, for example, that if, as a person, an individual has a certain amount of sympathy for unemployed teenagers, as a sociologist he or she might produce a very different set of proposals about the best ways of helping them than if he or she considers that unemployed teenagers deserve to be without jobs because they are lazy or stupid.

To be fair, though, most sociologists now recognize the danger of their own bias. Most of them do not try to deny that it exists. But in an attempt to be as scientific as possible, they try to arrive at fair and logical conclusions and to make sure that the evidence they collect is there for others to examine and to interpret differently if they choose to. The attempt to be as scientific as possible is the main difference between journalists and sociologists. Journalists and writers do not usually try to be objective or set out to research all facets of a story. They are more interested in what is 'newsworthy' or dramatic or unique. They would not claim to be making generalizations about human behaviour that could be used as a guide to policy-making. Their job is a different one - it is to entertain, to inform, to persuade and to influence. So, although the subjects they write about are often the same as those chosen by sociologists the approach they use is completely different.

Another characteristic of sociology is the interest in groups rather than individuals. This is not to say that sociologists are not interested in individuals. Nor does it mean that the roles individuals play in the family, or at work, or in a group of friends is not important to sociological understanding. But there is a sense in which every individual is quite *unlike* anybody else in the whole world. The study of countless unique individuals, however interesting, does not in itself tell you very much about anybody else or why society is the way it is. Sociologists are much more concerned with the similarities between people, the generalizations that can be made about the behaviour of whole numbers of individuals who share the same sex, religion, educational background, social class or leisure interests. And not only the similarities, but the differences too: why some groups, for example, often have noticeably different behaviour patterns to others. Sociologists, therefore, are more interested in the 'general' rather than the 'particular' when it comes to human behaviour. They are concerned, first, to identify general trends; secondly, to explain them; third, to try to account for how and why they change over time. They try to explain why, for example, the behaviour of young people is more permissive today than it was thirty years ago, how the roles of men and women in the family have changed, and what has brought about the obvious increase in the power of trade unions in comparison with the beginning of the century when they were very weak and shaky organizations.

The study of human society, therefore, although it may not seem to be so at first, is quite a complex business. It is not just a question of looking at an incident or an individual, but also trying to 'place' what you see into some kind of context. It is not enough to go on 'face value', you also need to know what has gone before, what other 'invisible factors' are influencing the situation and how your own appearance on the scene might indirectly be affecting what is happening or colouring your interpretations. As you will soon discover, although there is a fair amount of unanimity, there is also a good deal of disagreement between different sociologists on almost everything they set out to investigate!

What kind of methods, then, do sociologists find useful in taking on such a daunting task?

Different methods of investigation

When sociologists set out to investigate some aspect of social behaviour, they obviously have available the kind of background information that is generally accessible to any commentator on social life - official records, government statistics, previous reports, newspaper articles, etc. They may treat them with a fair degree of scepticism, but use them as starting-points. Sociologists will probably set the subject being studied into some kind of historical perspective, and possibly make comparisons with the behaviour of other groups in other societies, if it seems relevant. They will certainly be conscious of whether they are investigating something in an urban or a rural setting, and in an industrial or a pre-industrial society. And they will probably make some kind of assessment of the political, economic and social characteristics of the group they are studying or the environment in which they are at work.

After establishing this general background, the sociologist has to build up a more detailed picture using a variety of methods.

Surveys, questionnaries and interviews

Surveys and questionnaires are the techniques most often associated with sociology. They provide the opportunity for large numbers of people to be questioned, either in person, according to a carefully worked out schedule of questions, or by leaving a questionnaire to be filled in by the respondent, returned by post, or collected later by the researcher. The responses are then 'analysed' and turned into statistics, often with the help of a computer, so that sociologists are able to say, '57 per cent of our sample were . . .' or '49 per cent of the women questioned agreed that. . .'. Sometimes this approach is used with relatively small samples of people, to compare their experiences of marriage, for example, or their views on religion, and is usually followed up by personal interviews. But it is a technique which best lends itself to large-scale investigations in which the researcher wants to contact as many as several thousand people.

Obviously the ways in which the questionnaires are compiled and the surveys are conducted are quite central to the success of these methods. Postal questionnaires are relatively cheap, but they risk the failure of respondents neglecting or forgetting to return them. A personal collection of the forms, and even the presence of the researcher while the questionnaire is being filled in, is often more efficient, but is also more time-consuming, costly and perhaps more intimidating for the respondent. He or she may well choose to put down what he/she thinks the researcher wants to know, or will approve of, rather than what he/she really believes.

Interviewing respondents personally is usually thought to be the most reliable way of getting questionnaires completed, and making sure the respondent knows what he or she is expected to do. Interviewers are trained by sociologists to be as neutral and objective as possible but, as I have indicated earlier, this is an almost impossible ideal.

The questions themselves have to be simple enough to be understood by the respondents, they have to be phrased in as straightforward a way as possible, and they have to be capable of being analysed and turned into statistical presentations. A question which is badly worded like, 'Do you read books very often?' may produce the response 'Yes' or 'No' but give no indication of what the respondent means by 'often' or how different individuals' understanding of 'often' varies. It may also disguise the fact that individuals may mean different things by 'books'. Some may mean hardback or paperback novels; others, magazines.

Questions which are so simple and straightforward that there can be no mistake about them are usually only capable of providing the most simple and obvious information. If sociologists want to find out about feelings, opinions or patterns of behaviour, they must frame their questions in a more 'open-ended' way and encourage their respondents to reply at length. But again, if the sociologist wants to put people at ease and get them talking naturally about what they really believe, it is unlikely that an interviewer with a clipboard and set of inflexible questions or a bureaucratic-looking form will remove the barriers between them!

Another problem is deciding whom to question. Since it is obviously impossible to interview *all* divorced women or *all* juvenile delinquents, for example, the sociologist has to draw up a representative *sample* which he or she assumes is a fairly typical cross-section of the group he/she is studying. In some cases sociologists prefer to take a 'random sample' on a kind of 'first-come-first-served' basis as being as good a way as any of getting a cross-section of the population. Others try to balance their sample in terms of age, sex, social class and other characteristics that might be important. If you were doing a study of marriage, for example, and you questioned only men, it is likely that your findings would be rather one-sided!

Sociologists try to get over some of these problems, before they begin their main research, by carrying out a small *pilot study* first. This means drawing up a questionnaire, selecting a small sample of people and trying out the questions on them first. If, as a result, any of the questions are proved to be confusing, or the results seem unduly biased, or the method of giving out and getting back the forms does not work, the sociologist can make modifications and changes before undertaking the main survey.

Clearly this approach does have a number of advantages, especially if sociologists want to contact a lot of people, but it also presents many problems. And, of course, the biggest criticism made by sociologists from opposing camps is that 'it's just not a good way of understanding the complexities and idiosyncracies of human behaviour'.

Attitude scales and clinical tests

If surveys, questionnaires and interviews are regarded sceptically by many people, attitude scales, clinical experiments and statistical analysis present even more problems. Again the aim is to be as scientific as possible and to apply the best tried methods of natural science to social science. All of them are ways of 'measuring' human behaviour in an effort to relate 'individual' reactions to 'general' categories. A sociologist investigating racial prejudice, for example, might present a subject with a list of statements about black people, to agree or disagree with. He would then give their replies a rating on a scale which ranged from 'extremely prejudiced' to 'totally unprejudiced'. Another sociologist may set up an experiment, under controlled laboratory conditions, to test the reaction of 'sexual deviants', for example, to photographs of the naked human body. Both of these methods owe much to the influence of clinical psychology and are used most by sociologists who have a commitment to psychological explanations of human behaviour. The problems involved in the two methods are probably clear to you. What is meant by 'prejudice' and 'sexual deviance', first of all? Surely these can mean different things to different people. They are not terms which can be taken for granted as 'commonly agreed upon'. So whose definitions are being used in experiments like these? Equally, there are so many different social, emotional, personal, historical and economic factors influencing people's prejudices and their definitions of 'normal' and 'deviant' sexual behaviour that they cannot easily be measured in clinical or laboratory conditions which are shut off from the 'real world'. The success of laboratory-based experiments, therefore, often depends upon preventing outside influence interfering with the experiment. But in understanding human behaviour it is likely that these 'outside influences' are the very ones which provide the important insights into the behaviour being studied.

Statistics

Statistical analysis always gets a bad press. The notion that you can 'make statistics prove anything you like' dies hard. But, ironically, a great deal of emphasis is placed on official statistics when recommendations are being made and new policies introduced. You are more likely to be allowed to build 10,000 new council houses if you can show that 20 per cent of a city's population is living in substandard housing than if you provide five or six detailed, but personal, accounts of living in damp and decaying conditions.

Official statistics drawn up by government departments, trade unions, the census office and other organizations are obviously a useful source of information for sociologists, but they need to be used carefully. One problem is that official categories are not always the ones sociologists would use. Sociologists are interested in the *social* causes of crime or suicide, for example, but these are not the sort of things which are recorded on police records or death certificates.

Equally, some kinds of statistical information that would be useful just are not recorded. We no longer have any accurate records about the numbers of children from racial minorities in British schools, for example. The reasons why such information is not kept is open to speculation, but its absence enables all kinds of conflicting beliefs about the 'numbers involved' and the 'problems posed' to be both magnified and underestimated.

A third difficulty is that statistics are not always available in a way that is useful to sociologists. Figures may be presented separately from each other - for example, the number of people owning the largest amounts of wealth in Britain, and the numbers of people involved in different occupations. It might be that the relationship between these two circumstances is the one which is of interest to sociologists, but the link is not made in the original collection of statistics.

In providing their own statistics from the findings of surveys and questionnaires sociologists are on surer ground, because they can cross-reference and interrelate different categories to fit in with what they are trying to find out or to prove. But so long as popular cynicism about the accuracy of statistics continues, they must ensure that their sources and procedures are as sound as possible.

Interpretive research

Some sociologists have become disillusioned with the usual 'scientific' methods of carrying out research. They argue that those approaches treat people as 'things' to be studied like 'objects', and not as individuals capable of thinking and reacting in a varied and complex way. These sociologists are more concerned with finding out *why* people do things, rather than collecting a mass of 'inhuman' facts and figures.

To do this the sociologist must 'get into a relationship' with the individuals and groups he is studying, a relationship that isn't 'cluttered' or 'distorted' by the paraphernalia of questionnares and tightly structured interviews. His aim is to be more informal, to meet people on their own territory rather than in a university or a special interview room, for example, to 'observe' things as they happen, and to allow enough time to enable confidence and trust to be built up between the researcher and his or her subjects. Interviews are most likely to be 'unstructured', 'open-ended' and 'in-depth' discussions, in which subjects are encouraged to expand at length, and in their own words, about their experiences. A tape-recorder is often used so that the sociologist has an accurate record of what is said without having to remember or note down specific responses.

Meanwhile the sociologist's interpretation of what is happening has to pass through three phases. He must first try to identify the attitudes and feelings which influence the behaviour of those he is studying and try to 'see things from their point of view'. The second stage is to observe, analyse and interpret what they say and do, in an attempt to find the reasons for and the causes of their behaviour. The third phase is to recognize that the sociologist's participation in the discussion, and observation of the action, in some senses changes it, as he in turn is changed by it. There can be no question of the 'objectivity' in the scientific sense so if his conclusions are to be taken seriously he must ensure that the stages in his analysis are logical and consistent. If his procedures are seen to be sound and his deductions convincing, the results will speak for themselves.

Ethnography

Ethnography is a term that means quite literally a 'picture' of the way of life of a social group in relationship together, and comes originally from studies carried out among people living in pre-industrial societies. A group's 'total way of life' or culture is considered to be 'ongoing' and 'ever-changing' and the methods of ethnography aim to capture this as thoroughly as possible, in all its various shades and nuances, in as much detail, and with full recognition of the 'many levels' at which relationships function. The ethnographer tries to begin with no preconceived ideas about people's roles or positions or about what is happening, but waits for these to become revealed over time.

The main method of ethnography is 'participant observation', which clearly puts the researcher right into the middle of the action. The starting-point for the study of a family group, for example, would not be to assume that 'two happily married adults were looking after and bringing up a number of dependent children in a more-or-less successful kind of way'. The researcher would begin by asking rather different questions like, 'What's going on here?', or, 'What are these people doing to each other?', and he would try to 'build up a picture' of the family group by building in what each of them says about it. Now, obviously there are problems here. The individuals' accounts may differ, they may not know why they do things, they may not be able to put into words what they feel without being misleading. And how is the sociologist to make sense of it all? Ethnographers take the view that from 'participation' the sociologist gains insight which an outsider or a detached scientist would not. They do not merely 'sit in on' an unstructured group discussion, but actually 'take on a role' within the group or the institution and make some contribution to its day-to-day activities. Some sociologists have actually joined street-corner gangs, spent time in prison, become 'hippies' or taught in classrooms. As a member of the group, with a role to play, they can gradually begin to analyse their own behaviour and feelings and their relationship with others.

Here again the problems are obvious. If you join a gang, for example, do you reveal to the members that you are a sociologist? And what if you develop loyalties to the gang which prevent you from being detached enough to see clearly what is happening? You may find yourself defending the gang behaviour rather than 'studying' it. Being a teacher may present fewer problems, except that gaining the confidence of colleagues to get their views of the situation may prevent the researcher getting close enough to the pupils to be trusted by them. Alternatively, a researcher who is not 'identified with the teachers' by the pupils may be mistrusted by the staff.

In the last resort a great deal will depend on whether or not members of groups believe in the researcher. If the researcher's motives and behaviour are in any way suspect, he or she will 'have difficulty in continuing with the work, and his/her access to information will be blocked. Often the most revealing information is not disclosed because the researcher feels it would be a betrayal of the trust he or she has built up.

Ethnographers claim that this 'deep involvement in the action' over a considerable period of time is the best way of building up a picture of social behaviour in a given group. But it is obviously not the only way. Social relationships exist on a variety of levels and are influenced by many interconnected factors. It makes sense, therefore, to 'cross-check', to get as many different accounts of the 'same' experience as possible, and to recognize that in any situation there will be not only one but many versions of what is happening.

Part of the picture might include more structured interviews, a review of 'official' sources of information, a detailed analysis of the legal factors involved, or a reference to what has been learned from similar studies elsewhere. To fully understand the behaviour of the family group mentioned earlier may also require an analysis of its economic circumstances, an account of the jobs the family members do, their educational experience, the social characteristics of the environment they live in and the links between all of these and the wider society. In all of these respects the ethnographer has much to learn from other sociological methods, but whereas other sociologists may take a broad view of society as a starting-point, and explain families' behaviour in terms of how it fits in with what society demands, the ethnographer is more likely to start from the family group itself and work outwards.

In practice different methods of investigation are decided both by what is being studied and on the confidence of sociologists in different techniques. It would be wrong to assume that one method is always right, or that another is always wrong. In some circumstances surveys and questionnaires will be more appropriate than participant observation. In others unstructured interviews and the personal involvement of the researcher will be more revealing. They are all, to some extent, versions of the same practice - the attempt by sociologists to make their studies as accurate as possible, and to provide the evidence which will allow them to explain why human beings living in societies behave the way they do.

2 Social class

1 Background information

Who says the class system doesn't exist? I mean, it's all right for people like Maggie Thatcher to say the class system doesn't exist. Sure it doesn't - for her. She doesn't belong to the working class! But it's got to... well, it hasn't got to exist, but the way this country's run, it's bound to. Because the people that are doing well out of it are running the country. You couldn't have everybody in the middle class, cos you'd have no working class then. If everyone was middle class, some of the middle classes would have to work down the local motor firm or they'd have to be stevedores or coalmen! OK, so a lot of the working class can't do the so-called middle-class jobs, but I think a lot of them could - if they were given the opportunity. And it doesn't just boil down to money. If you're not in the right class, there are loads of things you can't do. But you could be as poor as a church mouse, so long as you come from the right family, then you'd be accepted.

RON PACK, assembly line worker at Ford

One of the first things sociologists want to know when they are studying the way of life of people in our society is: 'What social class do they belong to?' Most of us use terms like 'working class', 'middle class' and 'upper class' quite frequently, but what do we mean by them?

Some people feel very proud to be a member of the working class or the middle class. Others use the terms almost as a kind of insult and talk about 'middle-class attitudes' in a way which suggests snobbish people, or 'working-class behaviour' to suggest people who are rough and uncouth. The upper class are often made fun of as 'snooty types' with 'posh accents' and leisurely lives. Some people try to suggest that social class does not exist any more in Britain, that the days of landed gentry and penniless workers are over and no one 'looks up to' or 'looks down on' others as they used to. But sociologists would argue that this is not true. Certainly a lot of the characteristics of different social classes have changed over the years as society has changed, and the divisions between different classes are perhaps not as clear as they used to be. But it is just as possible to find hundreds of ways in which the lifestyles, behaviour and opportunities of people are still greatly influenced by the social class they belong to. Later in the book we shall be considering some of these in more detail.

Definitions of social class

When sociologists are deciding people's social class they generally go by the kind of job they do and the amount of money they have.

Jobs

The kind of jobs people do vary enormously. Some provide much higher wages than others, demand more education, skill or training and give much greater prestige, power and influence in society. Some jobs like politician, doctor or manager in industry allow their holders to make decisions which affect the lives of lots of other people. Others like labourer or factory worker could be done by more or less anyone and give their holders very little influence or power over anyone else.

Security

Some jobs are much more secure than others. Most people in professional occupations like lawyer, civil servant, banker and architect can be sure of a job for life. They have no need to worry about redundancy, unfair dismissal or firms closing down and making them unemployed. Workers in manual jobs are much more vulnerable. When industry and the economy is doing well, there is plenty of work, but in times of economic crisis, the jobs of shop-floor workers in factories and those who are unskilled and semi-skilled labourers are the first to be cut back to save money and protect profits.

The class pyramid

So far, we have been discussing the difference between middle-class occupations which are largely 'professional' and 'white collar', and working-class ones which are usually manual. Not only are these two categories different but they are also unequal. The class system in Britain is shaped a bit like a pyramid - there are more people at the bottom than in the middle and at the top, and the higher up you go the more wealth, power and prestige the people have.

But what about those at the top? Who are they?

Ideas of aristocracy may seem to be a bit old fashioned in today's Britain, although people with titles do still exist. They are still extremely wealthy compared to most other people, and many of them live in large country houses on vast rural estates as their fathers and forefathers did

before them. In more recent times they have been joined by a slightly
different group. The people in this group may not have inherited titles but
they do have enormous amounts of wealth. Their money comes from
industry, either from the profits made by industries which they own
directly, or in income from investments in the stocks and shares of large
profit-making companies at home and abroad. This 1 per cent of the adult
population owns one-quarter of all the wealth in Britain. The richest 10
per cent owns two-thirds of it.

Income and wealth

Accurate information about income and wealth is quite difficult to get. In
practice we know who the rich people are but it is very difficult to find out
just how wealthy they are. This is because there is a distinction made
between income and wealth. Income is defined as the money earned from
paid employment and the dividends received from investments. Incomes
have to be declared to the Inland Revenue and income tax has to be paid.
But there are all kinds of perfectly legal ways in which people can get tax
relief on things like mortgages, life assurance, school fees and business
expenses. In practice a person who earns an average wage and does not
have any of these things on which to claim tax relief is likely to pay more
of his income in tax than a wealthier person who owns his own house,
sends his children to public school and employs a secretary or cleaning
woman to help at home. He might be earning more money but not so much
of it will have to go in tax because he is allowed to claim relief on all of
these things.

Wealth refers to people's other financial assets like land, property,
stocks and shares. No tax has to be paid on any of these except when they
are passed on to someone else when their owner dies. But even in this
case, there are legal ways of transferring wealth before death to avoid
paying death duties. Since rich people do not have to divulge the extent of
their wealth to anyone, it is almost impossible to find out just how much
they own.

What is known is that the majority of income and wealth is
concentrated in the hands of a relatively small section of the population,
as Figures 1–4 (page 22) show. And things have not altered very much,
despite the apparent changes in British society over the last 100 years.

Lifestyles

In defining social class sociologists take other things into account as well,
like educational background, the kind of houses people live in, their
interests, hobbies and leisure-time activities, and their attitudes to life. Of
course, these other factors are still bound up with jobs and money. For

Figure 1   *Inequality of incomes*

total incomes

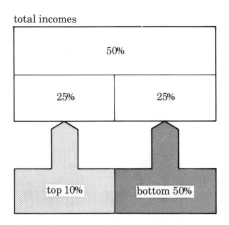

About 25 per cent of all the income
earned goes to the *top 10 per cent* of
wage earners.
Another 25 per cent goes to the *bottom
50 per cent* of wage earners.

Source: Royal Commission on the
            Distribution of Income and Wealth
            (1975)

Figure 2   *No progress*

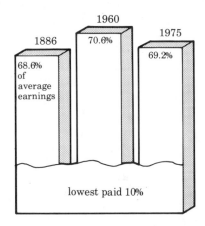

The lowest paid 10 per cent of men doing
manual jobs earned 69.2 per cent of the
average earnings in 1975. Not much
progress since 1886.

Source: PIB Report on New Earnings
            Survey (1975)

Figure 3   *Who is rich?*

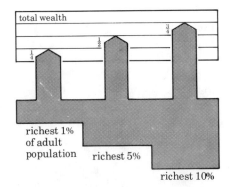

The richest 1 per cent of the population
own about one-quarter of all wealth.
The richest 5 per cent owns one-half.
The richest 10 per cent owns two-thirds.

Source: Royal Commission on the
            Distribution of Income and Wealth
            (1975)

Figure 4   *Who owns shares?*

Those with a total wealth of
more than £10,000 own 95 per cent of
all personally held shares.

Source: TGWU evidence to the Royal
            Commission on the Distribution of
            Income and Wealth (1975)

instance, a person is much more likely to live in a large and expensive home if he is earning a good salary in a highly valued profession than if he is on a low income with periodic bouts of unemployment. To do such a job he is likely to have had a university or college education. He is more likely to see that his children go to good schools, even if he has to pay for their education, rather than put up with whatever happens to be available locally, as most working-class people have to do. His leisure-time interests and social life are more likely to be influenced by his education and his ability to afford more costly activities than his opposite number on a low wage with less education and less money to spend. So, while housing, educational experience and spare-time activities are all useful indications of different social class lifestyles, it is important to remember that the most important factors which influence them are still wealth and occupation.

Social class categories

Information about wealth, occupation and lifestyles is used by sociologists to put people into one of seven categories. Their edges may be a little blurred, and obviously there are exceptions to every rule, but in general it is thought that people in the same group tend to have the same kind of jobs, amount of money, education, interests, attitudes and way of life in common.

These are the seven categories:

Upper class   Aristocracy and large property owners
Upper middle class Professional occupations, like lawyers and
    architects
Middle class Managerial and technical jobs, like shop managers and
    computer operators
Lower middle class Non-manual, white-collar and clerical jobs, like
    office workers and supervisors
Upper working class Skilled manual jobs, like electricians and vehicle
    mechanics
Working class Semi-skilled manual jobs, like machine operators and
    trawler men
Lower working class Unskilled manual jobs, like road sweepers and
    canteen assistants

Sometimes you will find only five categories used and the divisions referred to on the Registrar General's scale. In practice though, as we have already seen, both the seven and the five categories get simplified into three – upper class, middle class and working class.

Social status

Social status is not the same as social class although in practice the two
terms are closely linked. Status is more concerned with the way in which
people are respected and valued in the minds of others. But 'value' is still
largely decided by the jobs people do and the ways in which different
occupations are rated by society. In general professional skills are
thought to be more important than manual skills even though society
clearly depends on the contributions made by manual workers. Some of
the most respected occupations are not necessarily the best paid; for
example, nurses have quite high status but do not earn the kind of wages
or have the kind of power and influence that would put them into the
upper middle class. Also, people's social status can change as society
shifts its admiration from one group to another. Miners at one time had
quite high social status because of the dangerous jobs they do, but now
they are more often thought of as greedy and troublesome workers. But
although their status has changed, their social class has not.

Status can also vary depending on which groups in society are
expressing their respect. Young people are much more likely to give pop
stars high status than older people. Football fans are more likely to rate
footballers more highly than those who have no enthusiasm for the game.
Social class definitions are not as flexible as this. Whatever different
groups of people think about businessmen or politicians they are still
middle class. Whatever different people think about hospital porters or
postmen, they will always be working class because their jobs are only
regarded as semi-skilled.

Social mobility

Although society is changing and more women work these days, social
class definitions are still influenced by 'chauvinist' ideas! As I am sure
you have realized by now it is the wealth and occupation of the man in the
family which is still most often used to decide a family's social class.
Children are put in the same category as their parents until they are able
to support themselves, and married women are put in the same class as
their husbands. In the majority of cases people stay in the same group all
their lives. Middle-class children get middle-class jobs, marry middle-
class people and become middle-class adults. Working-class children get
working-class jobs, marry working-class people and become working-
class adults.

But it is possible for children to alter the level of their original class by
their own efforts during their lifetimes. This movement is called social
mobility and it is usually a movement up the social scale from a lower to a
higher position.

The opportunity most often comes through education. A working-class child may well stay on at school, go to university and qualify as a lawyer or a doctor. A second way is through marriage. A working-class girl may marry a bank clerk or a local boy who has qualified as a teacher. As her husband gets more responsibility in the bank or takes up his first teaching post she will move with him into the middle class. A third way is by increased wealth. High wages or a win on the football pools can enable working-class people to buy the kind of house and possessions which are more often typical of middle-class living. But if the person's job is still regarded as manual and his attitudes and values do not alter very much, money alone will not change his class position.

Evidence of social mobility is often used to suggest that the class system is breaking down and that rigid divisions between groups no longer exist. But it is important to remember that, while almost everyone's living conditions are better these days than they were, say fifty years ago, there are still tremendous gaps between the wealthy and the poor, and the numbers of people in the upper class are still very small and exclusive. While there is some movement for some individuals up the social scale, the majority of people do not move very much at all. The proportion of working-class youngsters going on to university has not changed in fifty years. The proportion of girls has been reduced. One in three children in Britain comes from a family whose income is below the average national wage, and the vast increases in unemployment over the last few years has hit working-class adults and their children leaving school considerably more than people from the middle class.

2 Looking at the evidence

Who's who in the class system?

What do we mean by workers when we speak of the working class? What distinguishes them from others who work, for in the wider sense of the word there have been workers as long as there have been men on this earth. If we look at the social structure of any country today, we find no stratum, group or class in which people do not work. Nonetheless, the working farmer or university professor, the newspaper reporter or factory owner, and the child working at school are none of them called workers.

How do workers differ from their contemporaries?

The difference between them and those who own businesses is obvious. It is a question of property. Workers toil in the places of work where they neither own the buildings nor have a hand in the organization. They are not, perhaps, without property, like slaves: for their clothes, furniture and everything else of a personal nature belongs to them. But at work nothing belongs to them. They are to a certain extent doubly free: free to move around where they wish compared to their ancestors who were serfs and virtually tied to the soil. They are free, too, from responsibility for the means of production, and therefore different from the capitalists, who own these means of production.

If we disregard slaves, who do not even own themselves, there has been, in the history of men who work with their hands, no group, stratum or class which has not owned at least a substantial portion of its tools. Workers in the modern sense of the word are the first class not to own tools.

JÜRGEN KUCZYNSKI, *The Rise of the Working Class*

In everyday language, class is often used as an evocative term with undertones of social prejudice. Expressions such as 'middle class' or 'working class' frequently imply a value judgement; and this judgement is influenced by one's view of society or one's political standpoint. Occasionally these views are explicit as in the terms the 'upper classes' or the 'lower classes'. Many people in our society - some much more intensely than others - think socially in terms of 'them' and 'us'; and 'class' is often a part of this thinking.

In this general context class carries some implications of a person's standing - or even his worth - within a hierarchical society. It is this element which adds the emotive flavour.

In Britain one of the most frequently used classification of occupations is that adopted by the Registrar General for census purposes. This is modified in detail from time to time but the general outline remains. The basic framework is of five occupational groups which are termed social classes 1 to 5. Social class 1 consists of occupations which require the highest professional qualifications, usually a university degree or its equivalent. Occupations in social class 2 also often demand a professional qualification and, for example, school teachers and many higher civil servants are in this group; it also includes managers and others of similar position in industry or commerce even if they are 'unqualified'. Virtually all the occupations in these two groups are of a non-manual nature.

Social class 3, by far the largest single group, is usually sub-divided into a manual and a non-manual section. In the latter are placed almost all the remaining non-manual occupations, such as foremen in industry, shop assistants and clerical workers. The occupations in the other section are all regarded as skilled manual. Social class 4 consists almost exclusively of semi-skilled manual occupations and social class 5 contains the unskilled manual occupations. The

Great Britain, social class structure

Social class	Proportion of the population (%)
1	2.9
2	14.6
3	49.1
4	22.3
5	8.0
Not classified	3.0

classification is summarized in the table together with the proportion who fall
into each group. If there is no father or male head of the household the members of
the family are not classified. With very few exceptions the first two groups in
in the table contain non-manual and white collar jobs and these groups are
described as middle class. The occupations in the other three groups are almost
exclusively of a manual nature and are referred to as working class.

In our society a man's occupation tends to be related to the way he lives outside
his work situation. At the most obvious level it is linked to his income and hence to
the kind of house he can afford and often to the kind of neighbourhood in which he
chooses - or has - to live. The classification of occupations is directly related to
qualifications, training and skill; and therefore it is often linked to the level of
education. A less direct but still quite marked association can be shown between
social class and attitudes. For example, the middle class family is more likely to
take a keen interest in the children's formal education and have higher career
aspirations for them than the working class family. Social class differences can
also be seen when physical attributes are studied: children of middle class parents
are in general taller and heavier than those of working class parents. But it should
be stressed that social class is only of relevance when looking at *group*
differences. An individual working class child may well be taller and more
intelligent than an individual middle class child, or even than most middle class
children.

A. DAVIE *et al., From Birth to Seven*

The notion put about by many sociologists is that we live in a two-class society.
Education, for example, reflects this division. The working class, on the one hand,
show only a limited interest in education and aren't much good at it. The parents
fail to encourage the children at school or provide the right setting at home for
educational successes. They don't read many books and they watch the wrong
sort of television. Their language, too, we are told, is all wrong. The working class,
except for a small group trying to get their children a better start in life, are, in
fact, born educational failures.

The middle class, so the theory goes, are the other group in society. They take
good care that their children succeed at school - so much so that when it comes to
higher education, eight out of ten students are still from middle class homes. By
and large, schools are designed for the middle class and run by their
representatives, the teachers. The way people are supposed to behave in schools, a
large part of what they are supposed to learn, the goals they are supposed to strive
for, all these things and more are custom-made for middle class children.

No wonder working class people aren't interested in education, say the
sociologists: they can see the game is rigged against them. Failure for the working
class is built into the system just as surely as success is for the middle class.

These Jeremiahs, however, miss one vital point. A class system which has a
bottom and a middle but no top makes nonsense. How strange that we hear so
much of the 'working class' and the 'middle class' whilst we hear almost nothing
about any 'upper class'. There is no argument about the existence of a working
class although most sociologists tend to underestimate both its size and its

significance. The working class is really, in a sense, nearly all of us. Our society is a capitalist one - a society in which the ownership and control of industry, property and trade belongs to a relatively small number of individuals. These capitalist owners are the really dominant class in our society - the 'upper class'. Compared to them the rest of us are all 'workers', in the sense that we all of us have to sell whatever labour-power we have in return for a wage or salary.

But, whilst the vast majority of people are actually employed in producing things to make profits for the owners, there is a largish group engaged in managing this process on behalf of the owners and controllers, making day to day decisions, studying and organizing technology, looking after health, culture, entertainment and legal problems and - not the least important - running the education system at its different levels. This is the well known middle class. Although it tends to be a little fuzzy at the edges, its way of life is sufficiently different from that of either the ruling class or the working class to form a distinct group.

DOUG HOLLY, *The Invisible Ruling Class*

1 How does Kuczynski distinguish between the working class and their contemporaries?
2 What is meant by the term 'serf'?
3 What is the main difference between working-class people today and their ancestors who were serfs?
4 Discuss with your teacher the meaning of the terms 'stratum', 'capitalist' and 'means of production'. Explain what they mean in your own words.
5 What is the significance of working-class people not owning the 'means of production', do you think?
6 What does Davie mean by a 'hierarchical society'?
7 Explain the ways in which people's general use of the terms 'middle class' and 'working class' might be influenced by their 'view of society' or their 'political standpoint' as Davie suggests.
8 Find out who and what are the Registrar General and the census and explain them in your own words.
9 How do the Registrar General's social classes 1 to 5 differ from the seven categories described on page 23? Which list of categories do you think is better? Give reasons for your answer.
10 What does the category 'Not classified' in the Registrar General's scale tell you about the way in which social class is defined in our society?
11 In what ways does social class affect a person's life outside of work, according to Davie?
12 How far do you agree with Davie about the differences between middle-class and working-class attitudes to education? Give full reasons for your answer.

13 Suggest reasons why middle class children are generally taller and heavier than working class children.
14 Do you think that Holly agrees with Davie's view of the class system? Give as many illustrations as you can to support your answer.
15 What does Holly mean by a 'capitalist society'?
16 Which is the dominant class according to Holly?
17 How does Holly's definition of class differ from the Registrar General's?
18 How does Holly distinguish between the working class and the middle class?

The professions

To have a profession is a sure enough sign that one is a member of the middle class. But the concept of a profession is not very precise and there are no comprehensive definitions of what a profession really is. The term usually conjures up an image of someone in the older professions of medicine, law and the church, but from the end of the last century there has been a steady growth not only in the old professions, the clergy excepted, but also in the new professions connected with science and technology; the engineers of various kinds, the metallurgists, physicists, chemists, as well as a host of new arrivals called into being by the development of government services, and by the new welfare services. The term profession has a curiously old fashioned air about it. While some retain the traditional independent role, selling their skill for a fee, others are increasingly employees earning salaries. While some groups remain small and exclusive such as lawyers, teachers correspond more in size with other major occupational groups like miners and shop assistants.

Most professions both old and new do have certain common characteristics. Generally, we can say that to become a member of a profession entails a period of specialized training in order to master a body of knowledge at the end of which a qualification is obtained. It generally involves following a code of conduct, either written or unwritten, which applies not only to relationships with clients but also to the profession itself.

When one comes to analyse the professions in terms of their work, market and status situations, then the difference between the members of the older professions and the new professional employees become clearer. So far as the work situation is concerned, membership of one of the older professions allows for a high degree of independence; traditionally they sell their skills to a client for a fee and work individually or in a partnership. Members of the newer professions on the other hand, though they may have latitude for varying degrees of independence, are nevertheless professional employees, who can like other kinds of labour be hired and fired. But most are involved in work in which they are relatively unsupervised. Moreover, the work done may involve people's lives, just as much as the work of a doctor or barrister.

The professional person is less likely to be bored by his work for he undertakes jobs for which he has to rely on his own judgement; to do this he must have an independent mind, be committed to his work and be capable of subordinating his own interests to those of his client or the job in hand.

So far as salaries are concerned, incomes of professional people have generally been maintained over the years, with some groups, particularly the professional employees in science and engineering, advancing dramatically.

Most middle class jobs are generally secure; the chance of losing one's job is low. There are differences here between the independent professional person, such as the doctor, and the professional employee. In the independent profession once a man has been accepted as a full professional person, then only outrageous personal or professional conduct is likely to debar him from practising his profession. Here the professions have their own methods of disciplining their members, as with the doctors. Professional employees, on the other hand, may be fired, or may for economic reasons, become redundant to the company they serve. Even here there are more guarantees of security through the payment of severance money, 'golden handshakes', or guaranteed income for a period until the person has found another suitable post.

Lastly, the status situation of the professions reflects the different values placed on them by society. The more society values a particular profession, the greater independence it can claim for itself and the case for greater financial rewards becomes more possible. This is not always the case; clergymen still have high prestige, much independence but relatively poor salaries. It would seem that the doctors and the lawyers have set a model to the rest of the professions in that they have staked out a claim for their independence, recognising only those whom they wish to as members of the profession, and serving as the agent both for deciding on who qualifies and for disciplining those who are members.

JOHN RAYNOR, *The Middle Class*

1 What are the main differences between the older and the newer professions according to Raynor?
2 Give three examples each of older and new professions not mentioned in the extract.
3 What characteristics do the older and newer professions have in common, according to Raynor?
4 Find out what is meant by a 'professional code of conduct' and how it works.
5 How far do you agree with Raynor that a professional person is 'capable of subordinating his own interests to those of his client or the job in hand'? Give examples to support your answer.
6 What is the only way in which a member of the older professions can be prevented from practising his or her profession? Give examples to illustrate your answer.
7 Suggest reasons why the number of women members of the older professions is quite small.

8 Suggest reasons why it is easier for the sons and daughters of members of the older professions to be accepted into the profession than the children of non-professional parents.

Social class: upbringing and opportunity

Study the three personal accounts below very carefully, making notes about social class, background, early life, income, education and employment. Using your notes, write an essay to compare the ways in which their social class has affected the life, work and behaviour of each of the three people.

Christopher Gotch, architect

The youngest of three, I was born at Kettering, Northamptonshire, in 1923. Until the age of five I played hide and seek, much as I have been doing since, in the ample grounds of the family house before being dispatched, presumably because I had become an embarrassment to my parents, to boarding school. There I remained in seclusion until a road accident and the outbreak of the Second World War forced my father to economize.

Freed from the hell that was Marlborough College, at sixteen my father forced me into the LDV (forerunner of the Home Guard); that and the early blitz and a year at home were sufficient to induce me to falsify my age to join the RAF in 1941. After a year's training mostly in Canada, I joined a fighter squadron as a tenderfoot commissioned pilot, only to be wounded at Dieppe a few months later. In 1943 I was posted to the India and Burma theatre; a squadron leader at twenty-one, flight commander of a Mosquito squadron, I was wounded again.

I qualified as an architect in 1953; my first private commission came two years before and more followed until by 1958 it was clear that I had to decide between remaining a salaried architect or developing my own business. Since 1960 I have practised alone.

During this period I became involved in the community life of Hampstead, where I have lived since 1947, believing that it provides the most nearly perfect urban environment of anywhere in Britain and one especially suitable for children in their early years. Realizing that architects cannot work in a vacuum, I have over the years been instrumental in forming the New Hampstead (Civic) Society, the Camden Society of Architects and, rather of a different nature, a professional Opera Company, Group Eight. As a consequence of these activities I am now an itinerant, persuasive lecturer on architecture, a pontificator on the environment in a local weekly paper, and have been an RIBA award and Civic Trust award juror.

Author of five books, only one of which has been published, it's clear that I am an arch-dabbler, for I also paint and sculpture in wood, and when disgusted with all these pursuits turn to rug making. These are of inordinate size and occupy me for years – a sort of permanent labour of Hercules. Opera is an obsession and keeps my wayward emotions at bay, while photography panders to my frustrated creativity.

Through studying Robert Mylne, an obscure eighteenth-century architect and engineer, on whom I have published several articles and am now considered an authority, I discovered the canals of Britain, a different section of which I explore each year by boat in an orgy of getting away from it all.

RONALD FRASER (ed.), *Work 2* ·

Bryan Slater, assembly line worker

I was born in 1933, in Nottingham. My father happened to be on the dole at the time, and wasn't able to get work until the war started. I didn't think it strange, having him at home all the time, but sometimes it was unpleasant if he was feeling particularly low.

I did my bit of schooling at a secondary modern, but spent more time playing truant than in the classroom. The schoolboard man came so many times to our house that one would have thought he lodged there. I used to write a note for the teacher saying I was sick, sign it with my mother's name, and go fishing or looking for birds' eggs or take some of my brother's books and sit by the Trent, reading. I learned more by myself than I could have at school where most of the time was spent in prayers, thanking God for the slice of bread and jam we'd had for breakfast. I never knew there had been a revolution in Russia, and didn't know the meaning of the word 'revolution' until I started work and joined a union.

My father, brothers and sisters worked in the Raleigh bicycle factory, and that was where I went. I worked in the three-speed shop, and now that money started coming in I often went to the pictures, sometimes with my father. He could never see enough gangster films, and when I asked him why he told me he'd been carted off by two buck policemen for getting too much into debt. He got six months in gaol, and said he'd have got off except that he told the judge what he thought of him and the whole idea of being pulled in because he'd only tried to get some food for his kids. His favourite scene in any film was when a policeman was shot.

At eighteen I was called up. The only good thing the army taught me was how to handle a rifle and fire a machine gun, which I think might come in useful one day.

I met my wife just after coming out of the army. She was a Shropshire girl, and that's where we live now. Our council flat overlooks the village cemetery, and sometimes from my window I can see the men digging holes and later, especially at weekends, they carry the bodies in.

I am a member of the AEU and the Labour party. I hope that my daughter gets a better education than I did; I don't want her starting work at fifteen. My main pastimes are cooking, fishing and reading. I have always wanted to know how to paint, to make pictures.

RONALD FRASER (ed.), *Work*

Richard Fry, accountant

I was born in Kilburn, London, in 1925, where I lived until I was nine. My family then moved to a housing estate in Southall where I stayed until I married.

My father was the son of a Welsh horse-and-cart greengrocer. Unwilling to return to Wales after the First World War, in which he was wounded, he went into domestic service for a year or two, where he met my mother, who was also in service. She was the daughter of a roadmender. Later my father got a job as a porter on the London Electric Railway. He was a staunch trade unionist, active in the 1926 strike; at sixty-five he retired with a pension of 13s. a week.

I left elementary school at Easter, 1939, and started accountancy a couple of years later at the age of sixteen. I qualified in 1949. Five years later, having built up a small connexion by working in the evenings, I was able to start my own practice. During that time and subsequently my illness deteriorated very considerably; today I need assistance to walk, but this has not limited my activities.

I am a director of a number of companies. I like poetry, the theatre, music, politics, good food and drink, and animals. I dislike racialists, nationalists, censorship, religions, ungenerosity. Politically I am on the left — a convinced nuclear disarmer for the UK and opposed to the present large defence spending. I would spend more on education, the social services etc. But I regard the biggest (and so far untackled) need is for a cash programme to increase national income substantially, not just by 2 per cent a year.

RONALD FRASER (ed.), *Work*

Social mobility?

John Beckworth came from a working-class family, went on to university and entered industry as a junior manager. But that was where the social mobility ended.

I took this two year training course for works manager. At first the men were a bit suspicious of me. They thought who was this youngster coming to tell them how to do their jobs. But by and by they saw that even though I had ideas, nothing ever came of them. I wasn't allowed to do anything by myself, all my ideas were passed to my superior, who passed them to his superior, who referred them to his - and that was the last you heard of them.

They took two kinds of graduates. There was me and my kind. But there were others that joined at the same time - right regiment, background, right car, knew how to handle a pair of guns and a fishing rod. They got on like a house on fire. Up and up they went, just like that - they'll be on the board of managers by now. But I felt that I was left behind in a corner, just neglected. No matter what I did. No matter how good the ideas. Nothing happened. After two and a half years they offered me a job I could have done when I was sixteen. It was like starting at the bottom again. It was like playing at snakes and ladders, only my kind are the ones who always come down the snakes. I gave my notice in.

B. JACKSON and B. MARSDEN, *Education and the Working Class*

1 What does John Beckworth mean by 'my kind'?
2 Compare his experience with Ron Pack's comments on page 19. How far do you agree or disagree with their views about the class system? Give full reasons for your answer.

Rich and poor

The Royal Family are perhaps the best known members of the upper class. They have vast amounts of private wealth as well as the subsidies they get for state duties and expenses.

Under the immediate liking and respect which most people have for the Royal Family, lie two qualifications which are quick to come out in the bus queue or at the bar. First, there are too many hangers-on: and secondly, they do get paid an awful lot of cash.

The visible sums, paid by the people and therefore decently and publicly accounted for, are considerable enough. The Queen's Civil List, before the pending rise, stands at £1,905,000. The Queen Mother gets £155,000, Prince Philip £85,000, Princess Margaret £55,000, Princess Anne £50,000 and Princess Alice, Duchess of Gloucester £25,000. Prince Andrew and Prince Edward will each have £20,000 at the age of 18 and another £30,000 after marriage.

The money is voted to help the Royals with their job and the impression that much of it goes on essentials connected with Royal visits and the like usually calms people down. But the heaviest burdens of the Royals' work do not come out of the Civil List and are not so public nor so scrutinised.

Since 1901, when repairs at Buckingham Palace, Windsor Castle and Holyrood House were transferred to a public fund of their own, the Government has gradually taken on the most expensive accounts. The Royal yacht, which costs nearly as much again as the Queen's Civil List to keep afloat, is paid for by the Ministry of Defence. The Royal train (£201,000 in 1975) comes under the Ministry of Transport. State visits with all those processions and special flagstaffs in The Mall are debited to the Government's Hospitality Fund.

These expenses stretch to almost every part of the Royals' life, from their phone calls to their stables (where horse fodder, much increased in price, has recently upped the bills). As well as outright grants, they come in rebate and exemption forms. On her private lands, for instance, including the 80,000 plus acres at Balmoral, the Queen pays no tax on produce or profit but only the local council's rates.

Public subsidies are common to most of the world's heads of state (though few escape tax on their private possessions). But the unusual thing about Britain's arrangements is the way the funds are scattered about and not publicly drawn up. As Willie Hamilton MP will tell anyone who cares to ask, and in vigorous language, the tabulating of all the public monies paid on behalf of the Royals is a taxing business and not one in which officials energetically rush to help.

Beyond this lies the second cause of resentment, the mysterious coffers of the Royals' private wealth. Because they are mysterious, they are also assumed to be bottomless and the family's hedgy attitude to them only encourages this belief. The most blatant example was in 1974 when the Morning Star discovered that the Companies Act had been amended under Royal influence to disguise the whereabouts of the Queen's shares. But on hundreds of humdrum occasions, the Palace is not to be drawn on the private side of Royal cash.

For the Royals' critics, privacy over the source (rather than the spending) of any Palace money is not justifiable. Privacy is the main sacrifice the family accepts for its lavish privileges and stately surroundings. And the origin of the personal fortune (which in turn accounts for its undoubted size) is not quite the same as any other millionaire's.

George V argued cogently in 1931 that he would have to sell his carriage horses and disband the Beefeaters if his civil funds were cut as the government wanted. Equally, the Palace argues today - and senior ministers have accepted - that the probable 10 per cent rise to be announced on April 7 covers essential wage rises for the Queen's 370 staff and increased pensions for their predecessors. But as long as the 'personal' fortune remains undetailed and the accounts of public subsidy scattered, the public is left with suspicions and not facts.

MARTIN WAINWRIGHT, *Guardian*, March 1978

1 What is meant by the Civil List? Where does the money come from and how is it spent?
2 Who pays for the upkeep of the royal palaces, the royal yacht, the royal train and the cost of state visits? Where does the money come from?
3 What are the two main criticisms made about the subsidies paid to the Queen and her relatives in this report? How far do you agree or disagree with them?

York is not a poor city. Compared with most northern cities it is positively affluent. Indeed its unemployment rate in 1977 was 5.4 per cent - much lower than most Midland cities of the same size. In the 1930s the famous social reformer Seebohm Rowntree, did a study of poverty in York.* About fifty years later a *Guardian* newspaper reporter, Melanie Phillips, still found evidence of depressing poverty among the working class as this account shows.

Tonight, in the city of York, a young woman will be carrying a pail up to her sons' bedroom to serve as a chamber-pot. There is no inside lavatory in the house, and she doesn't want them to use the privy in the yard at night.

Elsewhere, in a Victorian terraced house with no running water, let alone a bathroom or lavatory, a woman of 89 will be boiling water in a saucepan to wash herself at the stone kitchen sink, as she has done for the past eight years.

Over on a post-war council estate, a family of four adults, of whom three are out of work, will be dining off a piece of cheese, their last food until tomorrow lunch-time.

These are three faces of modern poverty in York, the city in which the social reformer Seebohm Rowntree conducted his classic study of poverty during the 1930s. Although scale and definition have changed, his three main categories of poverty - old age, unemployment and low pay - still cause some acute distress, despite the welfare state.

Rowntree found in the thirties that about six per cent of the population were

---

* Rowntree's earlier (1899) study of poverty in York is discussed on pages 119 and 126.

desperately poor, and about 30 per cent could not manage to live at a minimum level of subsistence. Although most of the nineteenth-century slums had gone, he found about 3,000 houses that needed to be either modernised or demolished.

Today, the city is not an obvious example of the evils of economic crisis. Unemployment at 5.4 per cent is lower than the national average, mainly because of the stable, dominating industries of confectionery and the railways. Tourists flood into York almost all year to admire the historical monuments, the half-timbered buildings and the quaint Victorian terraces that still remain.

But despite the absence of any estimate of the extent of poverty in the city, it is clear that all is not quite so cosy behind the charming facade. Shelter estimates that in this city of 101,000 inhabitants, about 2,300 houses lack basic amenities such as running water, bathrooms and lavatories.

Living standards among the elderly in York - there are about 19,000 pensioners in the city - give Age Concern, at least, cause for alarm.

In one pre-war council house, a woman in her 70s was sitting in a cold, dingy living room, clothed in a food-spattered cardigan and fur-lined boots.

She said she could not afford to heat the room as coal was so dear. Age Concern recently found her scratching around outside the house to find fuel to burn. Out of a pension of about £17 per week, she said £7 went on fuel bills.

After other bills were paid, she had about £5 left for food. She seemed depressed and defeated by her poor health, isolation and constant struggle to make ends meet. She fitted Rowntree's description of the old: 'pinching, scraping, often cold, often ailing - just waiting for the end'.

Not far away, in a dilapidated, Victorian terraced house, an 89-year-old woman was making tea. The milk was kept cool in the stone sink under the cold water tap, the only tap in the house. Two ancient, rusty irons sat on the stove, the only other feature of the 'kitchen'.

The living room was squalid. A clothes horse was squashed behind the sofa, which was disgorging springs and stuffing; a quarter of a lace curtain hung at the grimy window; the room was cluttered with a mangle, tables piled with cardboard boxes and by the budgerigar's cage, five packets of birdseed.

'Of course I haven't got enough to live on,' said the woman, 'I do a little cleaning job which brings in £2 a week on top of my pension. I save pennies and halfpennies in the cupboard to pay for the TV licence.

'I manage with food. I used to have a fish and chip dinner when I got my pension but I can't now, it's so expensive. I like a bit of stew, but I can't afford the meat. It's a game, isn't it? If I had more money, I'd buy myself a winter coat, or little luxuries now and again like a cake, something I'd fancy.'

Yet some old people's lives were so harsh at the time Rowntree was making his study that they now consider themselves well off. In another terraced house in spotless condition, an 83-year-old woman said she was better off on her pension of under £19 a week than she had ever been. True, the house had no bathroom or lavatory; but, she said, she was used to bathing in a tub in front of the living room fire.

'The electricity bills are big, but in winter I just go to bed,' she said. 'I spin my pension out. Usually I buy biscuits, maybe bread; sometimes two ounces of cooked ham, or maybe a quarter of polony from the butcher's. Meals on Wheels come twice a week, and I have a nice dinner then.'

Rowntree hardly mentioned one-parent families, possibly because the stigma attached to them meant they were included under other categories. Now, however, they are known to suffer some of the most acute poverty in York.

Pauline, separated from her alcoholic husband, draws £20 a week in benefits for herself and three small boys. The Department of Health and Social Security pays her rent and electricity bills but after bills for the gas cooker, television rental, insurance and clothing club are paid, she says, she has only £12 left for food. Every week she has to borrow money from a neighbour to pay for food.

She said she could not afford to buy fresh fish or meat except mince, occasionally. She buys mainly bread, potatoes, eggs, baked beans; the children usually have egg and chips for their main meal and fill up on bread and jam the rest of the time. She herself seemed nervous and unhappy; the children were dirty and the house dingy and tattered, with no indoor lavatory.

'It really worries me that the children don't eat properly,' she said. 'Often I have to go without so that they can eat. They hardly ever get things like icecreams or toys; I put away a bit each week in the club for toys for them at Christmas. Most of our clothes come from jumble sales; social security once gave me a grant of £16, but that only bought four pairs of shoes.'

Today, the unemployed tend to draw the anger of others who are themselves not well off. 'You'll find no real poverty in York', said one elderly man. 'There's plenty of work around for them that wants it.'

Yet in a council house riddled with damp and with the furniture falling to pieces through age, a family of four adults were sitting, apparently totally demoralized watching television. The father, a man in his 50s, had been out of work for three years through ill health. The son, aged 23, had been unemployed for a year after being sacked, he said, because he was epileptic. The daughter, aged 17, had been unable to find a job since she left school. 'I go after jobs all the time,' she said. 'I was turned down for one as an assistant in a sweet shop because I didn't have any O levels.'

Only the mother worked, in a part-time job which brought in £16 a week to supplement an income made up of two invalid benefits and one unemployment benefit. After rent, fuel, insurance, television, hire purchase and other bills, she said, there was £20 a week left for food and clothes.

'We have no breakfast and only a bit of cheese for supper,' she said. 'Sometimes we split ten fish fingers between three for our dinner. Our clothes are falling off us.' Unlike supplementary benefit, which is accompanied by a range of discretionary grants, invalidity benefit provides no extras.

Three children, all under 10 seemed to be the chief sufferers in another family, where the father had been out of work for 18 months - losing his job as a van driver, he said, after he was off sick for 16 weeks.

The family was drawing about £35 a week in benefits and was paying off a large number of debts. Last winter, the electricity was cut off when the bill wasn't paid. From that time, said the mother, one child had been wetting the bed. Another, aged nine, had already been caught stealing a car. 'He's started to pinch things because we can't give him what he wants,' she said.

'When the social worker came round about the electricity, she said we should start selling things like the TV. I kicked her out for that; everything in this house was paid for when my husband was working. He earned it. We've got an alsatian dog which costs about £3 a week to feed. Why should we get rid of it? It's our only pleasure in life.'

She said they spent about £20 a week on food. The rest went on fuel, HP, clothing club and their debts; social security paid their mortgage. 'We never go out, even for a drink,' said her husband.

He said that the jobs he had been offered only paid about £25 a week - £10 less than he drew on benefit. Low pay is certainly a feature of life in York, according to the city's Job Centre. The railway and confectionery industries, which employ about 21,000 people between them, set the standard. Rowntree-Mackintosh, for example, pay an average £53 for a 40 hour week, compared with a national average of £64.80.

In other industries, particularly the large hotel trade, pay is correspondingly low. Advertisements in the Job Centre offer a launderer £30.52 a week, a process worker £36.82, a cook £28.88.

MELANIE PHILLIPS, *Guardian,* October 1977

1   Who was Seebohm Rowntree?
2   When and where did he carry out his study of poverty?
3   According to Rowntree what sort of people were most likely to be poor?
4   What kind of evidence made Melanie Phillips think that poverty is still very evident in York?
5   Suggest reasons why the wages offered by local industries are so low in York.

3 Questions and answers

Test your class-consciousness

In the left-hand column, in no particular order, is a list of occupations. In the right-hand column are the seven categories used by sociologists to decide a person's social class.

Occupations	*Categories*
Chartered accountant	*Upper class:* Aristocracy and large property owners
Shop assistant	
Secondary school Head Teacher	*Upper middle class:* Professional
Police Inspector	*Middle class:* Managerial and technical
Chef	
General Practitioner	*Lower middle class:* Non-manual, white collar and clerical
Newsagent and tobacconist	*Upper working class:* Skilled manual
Dock labourer	*Working class:* Semi-skilled manual
Personnel manager	*Lower working class:* Unskilled manual
Primary school teacher	

Occupations
Company director
Waiter
Solicitor
Railway porter
Electrician
Road sweeper
Gentleman farmer
Farm labourer
Pop star
Commercial traveller
Newspaper reporter
Medical officer of health
University lecturer
Insurance agent
Methodist minister
Miner
Costing clerk
Police constable
Fitter
Social worker

1 Which of the seven categories listed above do you think each occupation should fit into?
2 Compare your answers with those of other students in the class. Which occupations cause most disagreement? Suggest why.
3 What are the main problems involved in deciding people's social class by reference to occupation?

Consider the following characteristics:

Attends the Church of England regularly
Reads *The Times*
Keeps pigeons in the back garden
Plays polo
Drives a Mini
Owns a semi-detached house in the suburbs
Wears hand-tailored clothes
Reads the *Daily Mirror*
Has been educated at university
Drives a Rolls-Royce
Drinks a pint of mild
Takes holidays in the south of France
Lives in rented accommodation

Plays bingo
Sends children to public school
Takes holidays in Blackpool
Gambles
Watches BBC-2 regularly
Votes Labour
Is likely to have a police record
Enjoys classical music
Owns two or more houses
Watches rugby union
Drinks scotch on the rocks

1   Which of these characteristics do you think are most typical of upper-
    class people?
2   Which are most typical of middle-class people?
3   Which are most typical of working-class people?
4   Which could be equally true of any class?
5   Compare your answers with those of other students in the class.
    Which characteristics did you agree and disagree about most? Suggest
    reasons why there should be so much agreement over some character-
    istics and so much disagreement over others.

Children and social class

Wealth can be inherited and, despite death duties, some inequality of income
perpetuated. A high income enables parents to give their children the advantages
that money can buy. It is a great help to a child to live in pleasant surroundings, to
be provided with educational toys, to go to a private school with a low staffing
ratio, to receive stimulating experiences such as foreign travel and to have the
entry into 'the right circles'. In the words of the German sociologist, Max Weber,
such children are receiving better life chances than the children of poorer parents.
The family not only transmits these material benefits to its offspring but it also
passes on some of the more indefinable and immaterial aspects of social class.
The child undergoes social experiences of power and prestige upon which his
ideas of class are built. The ways in which his parents treat others and are treated
by them give him the cues as to how he must later deal with his superiors and
inferiors in class position.
      Children of primary school age seem to mix very freely with children who to
adults appear to be oviously of another social class. But an interesting experiment
was carried out with 179 children between 6 and 10 years of age in Glasgow.
Drawings were prepared that showed adults of obviously different social classes
in incongruous circumstances. The children usually spotted this. For instance,
when a picture of a workman wearing overalls and shaking hands with a man in a
suit carrying a briefcase was shown to a child he commented that men dressed in
that way do not shake each other's hands.
      A study has also been made of the views of British adolescents on social class.

The survey was carried out among boys and when asked if they knew what social class meant, 60% said they did not know. But it was found that they had already acquired a thorough understanding of our social class system. Their views were very like those of adults and had been picked up unconsciously in their day-to-day-life. Amongst those who understood the term 'social class' the usual frame of reference was wealth or possessions, unlike adults who more often refer to occupation. A third of these boys were aware of status symbols and appreciated that a person can be judged by dress and accent. They also had an understanding of the idea of social mobility; 60% considered that upward mobility was associated with achievement, intelligence and personality though some laid stress on manners, dress and speech. Adults of all classes stress education much more and manners hardly at all. Boys of below average intelligence spoke just as easily about social class. It would seem that knowledge of class is gained through the process of socialization and is a further indication of the important social role played by the family.

P. W. MUSGRAVE, *The Sociology of Education*

1 In what ways does social class membership advantage some children and disadvantage others?
2 Explain in your own words - with examples if possible - how children's 'social experiences of power and prestige' give them information about their own social class.
3 What evidence does Musgrave quote to show that children do learn what social class means in practice, even if they can't define it in words. Can you give any other illustrations from your own experience to support his argument?
4 Do you think that changes in society since the research Musgrave refers to was carried out (the 1950s) have made children less class-conscious or more class conscious? Give as much evidence as you can to support your answer.

Checkpoints

1 Which categories of occupation have most job security on the whole?
2 Why is the class system in Britain 'like a pyramid'?
3 What is the difference between income and wealth?
4 What percentage of the population owns one-half of the wealth in Britain?
5 Who is the Registrar General?
6 How many categories are there in the Registrar General's scale?
7 What are the three main ways of achieving social mobility?
8 What is meant by the term 'capitalist'?
9 What are the main differences between the older professions and the new professions?
10 Who was Seebohm Rowntree?

O-level questions

1 'It is, for instance, far less easy to assign people to their appropriate
   social category on the basis of the clothes they wear when not at work
   or how lavishly their houses are equipped with durable consumer
   goods such as television receivers or washing machines. The milkman
   is almost as likely to have a car and go on a continental holiday as the
   bank clerk.' (J. Newson and F. Newson, *Patterns of Infant Care in an
   Urban Community*)
      Does this mean that we are all becoming middle class?

2 The classification of occupations used in the census of Great Britain
   gives over 35,000 different occupations which are then grouped into
   the Registrar General's five social classes. Discuss the connection
   between occupation and social class.

3 Is Britain a classless society?

4 Take two of the following terms and show that you understand their
   meaning by giving examples of their appropriate use in a sociological
   context: social class, social mobility, wealth, social status, capitalist,
   profession.

5 What do sociologists mean by 'social class'? How useful do you find
   the term social class in studying society?

6 Look at Figures 1, 2, 3 and 4 on page 22. Discuss the argument that
   Britain is now a classless society, making some use in your answer of
   the figures mentioned in the tables.

7 How far do you agree that because of social mobility and higher wages
   we are all becoming middle class?

8 Income may be important in deciding a person's social class but there
   are other factors which are also important. What are the other important considerations?

3 The family

1 Background information

The relationship between society and the family is a very important one and provides countless questions for sociologists about the social influences on human behaviour.

Universal but different

The first thing to notice is that families - in one form or other - seem to be universal. In every society known to us people have chosen to live, not as individuals independent from each other, but in some kind of close social relationship with others who are related to them by blood, birth or marriage.

The organization and characteristics of family life vary enormously. In some cases a man and woman will live together with their children. In others, a husband may have several wives or, more rarely, the wife may have several husbands. In some families elderly parents, married relatives and their children all live and work together in a communal way. In some societies people choose who they will marry. In others the choice is made for them and marriages are arranged by parents or village leaders. In some societies divorce is easily available and quite acceptable. In others it is impossible.

Relationships within the family also vary between different societies. In some the elderly have a great deal of power and influence. In others the men are most dominant. In others family life seems to revolve around the needs and demands of the children.

Studies of family life in different societies, in different parts of the world, or at different periods of time, reveal fascinating differences in behaviour and values, but something they all have in common is that they are all closely related to the economic and social characteristics of the society in which they operate. Put simply, the family is one of the main ways in which society organizes the production of its new recruits and makes sure they are brought up and looked after until they are old enough to fend for themselves. Within the family they begin to learn what is expected of them by the society they live in and begin the preparation for their future roles as adults, workers and parents.

The family in Britain

The family is the unit in British society, as in many others, in which resources like housing, furniture, food and consumer goods are pooled and living is shared. It is the unit in which people share with each other the tasks of earning wages and making the domestic arrangements necessary for its members to be fed, clothed, cleaned and generally looked after. Family members are expected to be close, mutually affectionate and caring in an otherwise competitive society and to recognize their responsibilities to each other as fathers and husbands, wives and mothers, parents and children.

As in other societies it is the duty of the family to give birth to and bring up the next generation of adults and workers to ensure that society survives. Obviously society has a vested interest, therefore, in making sure the family does its job well - to see that not too many or too few recruits are born, that family adults perform roles which will make the business of earning wages and doing domestic tasks as efficient as possible, to give enough professional help and financial assistance to ensure that family members are healthy, happy and content to live more or less the same kind of life as everyone else.

There are two ways in which society could achieve its ends - by force and by persuasion. Force is seldom used in Britain, although the criminal courts can be involved in preventing husbands beating their wives or parents grossly mistreating their children. Persuasion is far more effective, and by this sociologists mean the whole complex business of conditioning people to behave, react and think in approved ways, by socialization, education, legal and bureaucratic administration, mass communication, religion and morality.

Of course, society is not always right and is frequently resisted by individuals who do not want to be conditioned to behave in a certain way. Neither is society always successful. Individuals do not always do what is expected of them. Some couples, for example, choose to have lots of children, others decide to have none. Some couples find that life together is not happy or rewarding, so they separate. Some children are brought up by single parents, others live with a group of adults who are neither married nor related, in a kind of communal arrangement. Society has to tolerate a lot of individual differences in family and living arrangements but it is always careful to ensure that not too many people 'rock the boat' by trying to be different. Divorced people, for example, are persuaded by the difficulties of living on their own, the romantic view of love and marriage encouraged by mass communications, and the social assumption that most 'normal' people are happily married, to remarry again as soon as they can.

Some types of 'different behaviour' are actually defined by society as a problem, for example, drunkenness, violence or low income, and social workers, marriage guidance counsellors and welfare state officials of various kinds are employed to try to solve the problems and help individuals or families to behave in a way which is thought to be 'more normal'.

Of course, ideas of what is normal change as society changes, and while there are characteristics of family life which have stayed much the same over the years, many other characteristics have changed. Families these days tend to be smaller than they were a hundred or even fifty years ago. People marry younger and get divorced more often. Relationships between husbands and wives are changing as more women go out to work, have fewer children and more access to wider educational and job opportunities. The old idea of man as breadwinner and woman as housewife is no longer so clear cut. Families are much more mobile these days too and are more likely to move away from elderly parents and close relatives in search of work and a new place to live. And distance obviously affects the amount of contact and closeness that is maintained.

Changes like these have led some sociologists to predict the death of the family. But it is interesting to note that sociologists who believe this usually ask, 'Why do more divorces occur these days and what will be the effects on family life?' rather than, 'Why should couples want to stay married?' They ask what the effects of the increasing emancipation of women from the role of housewife and mother will be on the domestic arrangements in the home and the care of children rather than why women should be still assumed to have the major responsibility for child-minding and house cleaning. They more often ask whether increasing industrialization and geographic mobility is breaking up the kinship system rather than why individuals should be committed to relationships with kin anyway.

The sort of questions some sociologists ask should remind you that people's views about the family are always very emotional. In society generally the family is thought to be a 'good thing' that should be protected and supported at all costs. Family life, marriage and the closeness of relationships are often romanticized and it is often overlooked that a good deal of family life is not happy, many marriages do not work and feelings of duty and guilt can often place terrible pressures on family members.

As you read through the information and resources which follow keep asking yourself why a study of family life is so important in revealing why people behave as they do and how society tries to influence them.

Family organization

Sociologists usually make a distinction between 'extended families' and 'nuclear families'. The term nuclear family refers to a unit made up of husband, wife and their dependent children. An extended family, on the other hand, refers to a residential unit made up of husband, wife, dependent children, married sons and daughters and their spouses and offspring.

Sometimes the terms are used inaccurately, however. We are told that all pre-industrial communities that existed in the past, or live on in tribal societies today, do so in extended family arrangements. The nuclear family is usually depicted as a modern phenomenon that has come about because industrialization and the factory system, geographic mobility by people in search of work, birth control and the emancipation of women from the home have all encouraged smaller families who are not dependent on social relationships and support from their other relatives. This type of family arrangement is thought to be typical of middle class families today. The exception is said to be the extended family arrangements of working-class people in traditional working-class communities. Here two or three generations of the same family may live close together in neighbouring streets, see each other regularly every day, help each other out in times of need, work in the same industries and spend leisure time in each other's company.

There is an element of truth in all these descriptions. But it is important to remember that they do not provide hard and fast rules. In many pre-industrial societies only some, and not all, of the offspring live with their parents and relatives. Investigations by historians into town records and parish registers have shown that nuclear families existed in sixteenth- and seventeenth-century Britain long before the industrial revolution. The classic studies of working-class extended family life in Bethnal Green in London and Nottingham were all carried out in the 1950s and early 1960s and since then slum clearance, redevelopment and increasing affluence among the working-class has meant that, more and more, life is lived in nuclear family units very similar in size to middle-class families and sharing the same isolation from daily dependence on relatives and kin.

The terms are useful, however, to describe different kinds of family arrangements which do exist in different societies and have existed in the past. And as long as you remember that there are always exceptions to the rule, it is of interest to find out how the characteristics of the two types of family organization differ, where and in what conditions they are most common, and how each of them is related to the changing social and economic needs of society and the people who live in it.

Family breakdown

In societies like ours people often react to divorce as a tragedy or a problem and point to rising divorce rates (something like one in five of all marriages in Britain today) as evidence that the family system is breaking down. This attitude is partly to do with our religious heritage in which both protestant and catholic churches were influential enough and powerful enough to condemn divorce and make it a rare event. Also, our notion that marriage is based on love leads to the conclusion that divorce must mean failure.

But increasingly in our society people tend to have a high expectation that marriage will fit in with romantic ideals of love and mutual harmony which the story-books, magazines, adverts and popular music tell about. Thus when strains appear divorce is used as a way of ending something that does not live up to expectations. In some other societies divorce is less easy, and ways are found of encouraging people to lower their expectations of what to expect from marriage, so that strains seem less of a reason for splitting up. In some pre-industrial societies, for example, relationships with kin are more important than those between husband and wife.

Until quite recently divorce was still disapproved of and seen as something to feel guilty and ashamed about in Britain. Largely, as I have said, because the churches disapproved and the law was used to make divorces both difficult and only available on grounds which demonstrated 'immoral' or 'intolerable' behaviour. During the last ten years or so society has taken a much more enlightened and understanding attitude. Although many people do need to be able to get a divorce because the behaviour of their spouse is quite intolerable, there are many less extreme reasons why people might want to split up. New legislation which came into effect in 1971 made it possible for couples who had been married for more than three years to get a divorce if their marriage was 'irretrievably broken down'. And instead of having to prove marital crimes like adultery, cruelty or desertion against their partner, as in the old days, they could instead claim 'irretrievable breakdown' by proving that both wanted a divorce and had been living apart for two years. The new legislation made other improvements in the old laws, too, especially in favour of people living separately, but where one person refused to give the other a divorce, perhaps to prevent him or her marrying again.

Although when it was introduced it was heralded as the 'Cassanova's Charter', which would encourage irresponsible and promiscuous behaviour especially among men, the new legislation has, in fact, taken a lot of the misery, shame and guilt out of divorce. It has enabled many people who were living in unsatisfactory marriages, or with partners who refused to give them a divorce, to have new grounds to free themselves. In practice this has meant an incredible rise in the divorce rate since 1971. This can partly be explained by changing attitudes to marriage, especially among the young, and the increasing emancipation of women from social and economic dependency on unsatisfactory husbands, but it is also because divorces which were impossible to obtain before 1971 are now legally possible.

It would be wrong to assume that divorce is now mainly an automatic and painless operation, however. When most people get married they do so expecting the marriage to last and few breakups occur without a good deal of unhappiness on the part of the people involved. Also society has a vested interest in preserving and protecting the family unit as I suggested earlier. Great care is taken in the courts to look after the legal and financial protection of children especially, and complicated custody and maintenance arrangements have still to be made between divorced couples to ensure the best possible protection for their dependent offspring. And far from being 'an end to the family', most information proves that divorced people marry again relatively quickly in the hopes of achieving the kind of marriage which high expectations of romantic love and economic security have encouraged them to believe in.

The family and socialization

Strange as it may seem, infants have to learn how to behave in a human way. It does not just happen instinctively. They are born with a certain amount of innate ability and various physical characteristics which differ between them and which considerably affect their later development in life. But they are also born with a vast amount of potential for learning and this is common to all children. The way in which this potential is used and the extent to which it is developed depends to a large extent on the different life experiences of the children. In this sense their social environments are vitally important.

Social environments are made up of many influences. Obviously the most immediate, and probably most important, to a young child is his or her family and home. The type of area and society in which that home is situated is important, as is the social class or status of the parents. Friends, neighbours and relatives may also be influential, as may the general behaviour and attitudes of other people round about. Whether the society is rich or poor, industrialized or rural, relatively democratic or relatively authoritarian all affects the environment of the child and the ways in which he or she learns to behave.

It is from their environment that, using their abilities and potential, they learn the language, behaviour, customs, attitudes and mannerisms of their particular society. A child brought up in an igloo by an Eskimo family in Alaska will learn a totally diferent way of life from a child raised in a floating reed boat by marsh Arabs in Iraq. Similarly a child who learns the middle-class lifestyle of a well-to-do suburban family in Kent or Essex will have had a very different social environment from a child brought up in a coal miner's family in the Welsh valleys or in a small fishing community in the outer Hebrides, and will be different because of it. The different environments of these children will have played an enormous part in moulding the potential they all share for learning and in affecting the ways in which they have learned to behave. This process of learning which begins in the family is called socialization.

Heredity or environment?

In the past sociologists were unable to agree which factor in children's make-up was most important in their later development. There were those who argued that their nature, their innate ability, the biological characteristics which they inherited and were born with were of absolute importance in deciding their future lives. And there were others who replied that the environment which nurtured them, their early experiences in the family and the influence of others were the most important factors in deciding what kind of people they would turn out to be. This argument came to be known as the nature-nurture controversy and there were many supporters on both sides. Today, however, it is usually thought to be a combination of the two factors working together that affects learning. Sociologists are most interested in the effects of the environment, however, and are swift to point out how inadequate the purely biological mechanisms of a child are when they act in isolation (see 'Anna and Isabelle', page 71).

2 Looking at the evidence

Family and marriage in pre-industrial societies

The Kgatla tribe lives in parts of what is now Botswana in southern Africa. Although life has changed there over the last fifty years or so the people traditionally lived in extended family groups. Isaac Schapera describes what it was like in the 1930s when he did his research.

The household consists typically of a man with his wife or wives and dependent children, but often includes other people as well. It may be a simple biological family, or comprise two or more which are very closely related. Members of the same household associate together more intimately than the members of any other group in the tribe. They live, eat, work and play together, consult and help one another in all personal difficulties, and share in one another's good fortune. They produce the great bulk of their own food and other material wants; they form a distinct legal and administrative unit under their own head; they are the group within which children are born, reared and trained in conduct and methods of work; and they perform the ceremonies connected with birth, marriage, death and other ritual occasions. The self-contained character of the household appears most strongly perhaps at the fields, where for part of the year it lives as an isolated unit. In structure it tends to be of the *patriarchal type*, in that a wife normally lives with her husband among his paternal relatives, and, with her children, is legally under his authority, while succession, descent and inheritance of property, are all *patrilineal.* . . .

Each household normally produces the great bulk of its domestic requirements. It gets its food by cultivating Kafir corn and other crops, breeding livestock, hunting, and collecting wild edible plants. Deficits are made good by gifts or loans from relatives or friends, or by exchange for some other commodity, but nobody ever obtains all or even most of his food in this way. Each household also builds its own huts and granaries, and does its own housework. In all these activities everybody except the infants take part, men, women and children, having specified occupations according to sex and age. The women and girls till the fields, build and repair the walls of the huts, granaries and courtyard, prepare food and make beer, look after the fowls, fetch water, wood and earth, collect wild plants and do all the other housework. The men and boys herd the cattle and small stock, hunt, and do all the timber-work in building. Tasks that a household is too small to carry out for itself, or wishes to complete more rapidly than is possible working alone, are generally done either with the aid of relatives, or by organizing a work-party and paying with meat, beer or some similar commodity, the neighbours coming to help. Poor people have no other means of getting sufficient labour for such big undertakings as clearing or weeding a field, threshing corn, or building a hut; and since they are accordingly all dependent upon one another, it is good policy to help others when invited. The only specialist doing work for which most households are not equipped is the magician, whose services have to be hired for the protective and beneficient doctoring of compounds, fields and cattle-posts.

ISAAC SCHAPERA, *Married Life in an African Tribe*

1 What are the main social and economic tasks shared by the Kgatla extended family?
2 Explain in your own words what is meant by the terms 'patriarchal' and 'patrilineal'.
3 Make a list of the men's jobs and the women's jobs in the Kgatla household.
4 In this division of labour, who is responsible for doing the most work?
5 What is the only specialist task in which the members of the household are not self-sufficient?

6   Summarize in your own words the main characteristics of an extended
    family in Kgatla society.

Margaret Mead spent a lot of time with Manus people in New Guinea in
the 1920s before the impact of modernized societies like America and
Australia had much influence on their way of life. In Manus societies
marriages were arranged and the relatives lived together in extended
family groups.

The relationship between husband and wife is usually strained and cold. The
blood-ties with their parents are stronger than their relationship to each other,
and there are more factors to pull them apart than to draw them together.

The bridegroom has no attitude of tenderness or affection for the girl whom he
has never seen before the wedding. She fears her first sex experience as all the
women of her people have feared and hated it. No foundation is laid for happiness
on the wedding night, only one for shame and hostility. The next day the bride
goes about the village with her mother-in-law to fetch wood, and water. She has
not yet said one word to her husband.

This sense that husband and wife belong to different groups persists
throughout the marriage, weakening after the marriage has endured for many
years, never vanishing entirely. The father, mother, and children do not form a
warm intimate unit, facing the world. In most cases the man lives in his own
village, in his own part of the village, near his brothers and uncles. Near by will
live some of his sisters and aunts. These are the people with whom all his ties are
closest, from whom he has learned to expect all his rewards since childhood.
These are the people who fed him when he was hungry, nursed him when he was
sick, paid his fines when he was sinful, and bore his debts for him. Their spirits are
his spirits, their taboos his taboos. To them he has a strong sense of belonging.

But his wife is a stranger. He did not choose her; he never thought of her before
marriage without a sense of shame. Before he married her he was free in his own
village at least. He could spend hours in the men's house, strumming and singing.
Now that he is married, he cannot call his soul his own. All day long he must work
for those who paid for his wedding. He must walk shame-facedly in their presence,
for he has discovered how little he knows of the obligations into which he is
plunged. He has every reason to hate his shy, embarrassed wife, who shrinks with
loathing from his rough, unschooled embrace and has never a good word to say to
him. They are ashamed to eat in each other's presence. Officially they sleep on
opposite sides of the house. For the first couple of years of marriage, they never go
about together.

The girl's resentment of her position does not lessen with the weeks. These
people are strangers to her. To them her husband is bound by the closest ties their
society recognizes. If she is away from her people, in another village, she tries
harder than does her husband to make something of her marriage. If the bride has
married in her own village, she goes home frequently to her relatives and makes
even less effort at the hopeless task of getting along well with her husband. For
her marriage her face was tattooed, her short curly hair was dyed red. But now her

head is clean shaven and she is forbidden to ornament herself. If she does, the spirits of her husband will suspect her of wishing to be attractive to men and will send sickness upon the house. She may not even gossip, softly, to a female relative about her husband's relatives. The spirits who live in the skull-bowls will hear her and punish. She is a stranger among strange spirits, spirits who nevertheless exercise a rigid espionage over her behaviour.

When she conceives, she is drawn closer, not to the father of the child, but to her own kin. She may not tell her husband that she is pregnant. Such intimacy would shame them both. Instead, she tells her mother and her father, her sisters and her brothers, her aunts and her cross-cousins. Her relatives set to work to prepare the necessary food for the pregnancy feasts. Still nothing is said to the husband. Then some chance word reaches his ears, some rumour of the economic preparations his brothers-in-law are making. Still he cannot mention the point to his wife, but he waits for the first feast when canoes laden with sago come to his door. The months wear on, marked by periodic feasts for which he must make repayment. His relatives help him, but he is expected to do most of it himself. He must go to his sisters' houses and beg them for beadwork. His aunts and mother must be asked to help. He is constantly worried for fear his repayments will not be enough, will not be correctly arranged. Meanwhile his pregnant wife sits at home making yards of beadwork for her brothers, working for her brothers while he must beg and cajole his sisters.

A few days before the birth of the child the brother or cousin or uncle of the expectant mother divines for the place of birth. The divination declares whether the child shall be born in the house of its father or of its maternal uncle. If the former is the verdict, the husband must leave his house and go to his sister's. His brother-in-law and his wife and children move into his house. Or else his wife is taken away sometimes to another village. From the moment her labour begins he may not see her. The nearest approach he can make to the house is to bring fish to the landing-platform. For a whole month he wanders aimlessly about, sleeping now at one sister's, now at another's. Only after his brother-in-law has worked or collected enough sago, one or two tons at least, to make the return feast, can his wife return to him, can he see his child.

Now begins a new life. The father takes a violent proprietary interest in the new baby. It is his child, belongs to his kin, is under the protection of his spirits. He watches his wife with jealous attention, scolds her if she stirs from the house, shouts at her if the baby cries. He can be rougher with her now. The chances are that she will not run away, but will stay where her child will be well cared for. For a year mother and baby are shut up together in the house. For that year the child still belongs to its mother. The father only holds it occasionally, is afraid to take it from the house. But as soon as the child's legs are strong enough to stand upon and its small arms adept at clutching, the father begins to take the child from the mother. Now that the child is in no need of such frequent suckling, he expects his wife to get to work, to go to the mangrove swamp to work sago, to make long trips to the reef for shell-fish. She has been idle long enough, for, say the men, 'a woman with a new baby is no use to her husband, she cannot work'. The plea that her child needs her would not avail. The father is delighted to play with the child, to toss it in the air, tickle it beneath its armpits, softly blow on its bare smooth skin. He has risen at three in the morning to fish, he has fished all through the cold dawn, punted the weary way to market, sold some of his fish for good bargains in taro, in betel nut, in taro leaves. Now he is free for the better part of the day, drowsy, just in the mood to play with the baby.

Father is obviously the most important person in the home; he orders mother about, and hits her if she doesn't 'hear his talk'. Father is even more indulgent than mother. It is a frequent picture to see a little minx of three leave her father's arms, quench her thirst at her mother's breast, and then swagger back to her father's arms, grinning overbearingly at her mother. The mother sees the child drawn further and further away from her. At night the child sleeps with the father, by day she rides on his back. He takes her to the shady island which serves as a sort of men's club house where all the canoes are built and large fish-traps made. Her mother can't come on this island except to feed the pigs when no men are there. Her mother is ashamed to come there, but she can rollick gaily among the half-completed canoes. When there is a big feast, her mother must hide in the back of the house behind a hanging mat. But she can run away to father in front of the house when the soup and betel nut are being given out. Father is always at the centre of interest, he is never too busy to play. Mother is often busy. She must stay in the smoky interior of the house. She is forbidden the canoe islands. It is small wonder the father always wins the competition: the dice are loaded from the start.

On the eve of the birth of a new baby, the child's transfer of dependence to its father is almost complete. While the mother is occupied with her new baby, the older child stays with its father. He feeds it, bathes it, plays with it all day. He has little work or responsibility during this period and so more time to strengthen his position. This repeats itself for the birth of each new child. The mother welcomes birth; again she will have a baby which is her own, if only for a few months. And at the end of the early months the father again takes over the younger child. Occasionally he may keep a predominant interest in the older child, especially if the older is a boy, the younger a girl, but usually there is room in his canoe for two or three little ones. And the elder ones of five and six are not pushed out of the canoe, they leave it in the tiny canoes which father has hewn for them. At first upset, the first rebuff, they can come swimming back into the sympathetic circle of the father's indulgent love for his children.

MARGARET MEAD, *Growing Up in New Guinea*

1 Write a description of the type of society in which Manus people live, using the headings; geographical features, the work of the people, religious beliefs, food and clothing.
2 The young man has not chosen a girl whom he loves to marry. Explain how and why the marriage has come about.
3 How does the husband's relationship with his wife compare with his relationship with his family?
4 What duties does the husband owe to those who paid for his wedding?
5 Describe in your own words the wife's relationship to her husband and to his family.
6 Why must she be careful of the 'spirits who live in the skull bowls'?
7 What happens when the wife finds out she is going to have a child?

8 Explain what happens to the relationship between husband and wife
   when the child is born.
9 Explain what kind of relationship exists between (*a*) the child and its
   mother (*b*) the child and its father.
10 From what you have learned about Manus family life, write an essay
   to explain the main ways in which it differs from our own.

Family life in traditional working-class England

In Bethnal Green in London in the 1950s working-class people usually
lived in extended family relationships as this account by Michael Young
and Peter Willmott shows.

The overwhelming majority of Bethnal Green men are manual workers, with a
particularly high proportion of unskilled people. It is worth noting, too, that the
professional classes are not like those elsewhere. The local government officers,
teachers, doctors, welfare workers, and managers of the borough do not, on the
whole, live within its borders. They travel in to their work every morning from the
outside. More than half of the 'white-collar' people in our general sample actually
living in Bethnal Green were shopkeepers and publicans, in many ways more
akin to the working-class people they serve than to the professional men and
administrators with whom they are classified. The tone of the district is set by the
working class.

Since they have similar jobs, the people also have much in common. They have
the same formal education. They usually reach their maximum earnings at the
age of twenty-one and stay at that level, unless all wages advance, for the rest of
their lives. Though wages may vary from £8 to £20 a week, they are nearly all paid
by the hour. They are no more secure than other hour-paid employees, liable to be
dismissed without notice and deprived of pay during sickness, and, to counter
insecurity, they have built the same trade union and political organizations.

Since relatives often have the same kind of work, they can sometimes help each
other to get jobs. They do this in the same way as they get houses for each other -
by putting in a good word in the right quarter - and reputation counts for one as
much as for the other. A mother with a record of always being prompt with the
rent has a good chance of getting a house for a daughter; a father with a record of
being a good workman has a good chance of getting a job for his son, or indeed for
any other relative he may recommend.

People get news all the time from their relatives about the jobs with better pay,
better conditions, or more overtime, and their comparisons may induce men to
change. 'I got my present job as a lorry driver through my brother-in-law,' said Mr
Little. 'At that time I used to work for Blundells and he came down there and saw
me. I was shifting big sacks about and he said, "Blimey, do you have to move these
sacks by hand? You don't have to do that. Why don't you come over to us? There's
none of that lark down there." So I went down to see them and got a job with them.'

In the docks, the markets, and in printing the right to family succession has
been formally acknowledged. There are plenty of other examples in the district

too, especially where there was heritable property - of shops where 'Brown & Son' meant what it said, of newspaper sellers who had inherited their 'pitches', of costermongers who had worked with their families because, in a business where confidence is essential, they did not have enough faith in anyone else.

Wherever father works with son and brother with brother, family and workplace are intertwined. When there is a quarrel at work, it spreads over into the family.

'My husband went to work for his brother Jim. Jim was a foreman scaffolder. Once when I was in hospital with a burnt hand, he came to see me and was late for work. Jimmy told him off and they had a tiff over it. My husband left and branched off on his own and we never see Jimmy any more.'

And where there is harmony at work it also spreads over into the family. Men who work with fathers or with brothers naturally see them every weekday, and often see a good deal of them when off work as well. Mr. Aves, for instance, not content to work alongside two brothers and a brother-in-law in the same small building firm, sees them continuously at week-ends too.

'I see one of my brothers every Saturday at football, and then every Sunday the whole family comes down for a drink on Sunday morning. They've always done it. The men, my brothers and brothers-in-law, go round to the pub and then the women get the dinner cooked and come round for the last half hour for a chat and a drink. Oh, it's a regular thing in our family.'

M. YOUNG and P. WILLMOTT, *Family and Kinship in East London*

In Ashton in Nottingham in the early 1950s miners and their wives lived almost separate lives.

In adolescence the young man starts work, and the pattern of manliness which is so important in this community takes on its adult form. The strong inter-dependence of the men at work is reflected in their out-of-work and social relations. If the woman's place is in the home, the man's place is as definitely outside it. After work, the men go home for a wash and a meal, and then go out again to meet their friends at the club, the pub, the corner, the sports-ground. It is here that the men experience most fully the emotional satisfactions which social life affords; it is with other men that they are at their most relaxed, at ease and emotionally expansive. A man's centre of activity is outside the home. He works and plays and makes contact with others outside his home. It is outside his home that the criteria of success and social acceptance are located.

The male group, over the years, develops a set of attitudes and ideas which very deliberately exclude women, children and strangers. One of the exclusive mechanisms which define the limits of the group is the use of swear-words; these are directed familiarly to members of the group and offensively to those outside. Women are not supposed to hear these words from men, though they may use them in their own women's circle. Thus for instance the bookie's office is part of the men's world, where women have no place. A woman going into the office is subjected to jokes and language which in a more neutral locality would lead to a fight. The pub is somewhat less a male preserve than it was. A man in a pub swore in the hearing of a girl, was stopped and apologized. A minute or so later he repeated the offence. Her escort bristled. 'I'm sorry, old lad, but she must expect to hear what comes out if she comes into the place at all.' Nevertheless, the offender had to leave. This swearing is known as 'pit-talk', characteristically used in the pit and left behind there except in so far as the conditions are reproduced in other typically male assemblies.

The distinction between men's conversation and women's conversation is determined not only by 'pit-talk'. Just as the men in the clubs talk mainly about their work and secondly about sport and *never* about their homes and families, so do their wives talk first of all about *their* work, i.e. their homes and families, and secondly within the range of things with which they are all immediately familiar. The men discourage any transgressions over the line of this division of interst. When a woman does express any interest in politics or other general topic, she speaks rather apologetically, and can be prepared for her husband to tell her not to interrupt intelligent conversation: 'What the hell do you know about it?'

Except at the weekend, when the men's clubs and the Miners' Welfare Institute allow women in, the women keep together much as the men do. For women as for men, the enjoyment of the company of others is a major source of leisure-time satisfaction. (The other leisure interests of the women are also as few and uncreative as those of the men.) At one or other house in the street, the women will be 'callin', taking a cup of tea, with family, neighbours or both, spending some time in the morning or the afternoon regularly in this way. At these women's gatherings there is endless gossip about the neighbours, about their own husbands and children, about the past. . . .

Just as industrial conflict is endemic, so is conflict in the home. Many disagreements between husband and wife are essentially concerned with the question: in which sector of the community shall the money be spent - in the family and the home, or in the club? A girl of eighteen, who had been married two months, replied, when surprise had been expressed at her having a row with her husband: 'Oh, that's nowt. We have a row regularly every Saturday when I ask him for my wage and he doesn't want to take me out with him.' It is not an exaggeration to say that the row is an institution for the present-day family in Ashton. It is the conventional way of expressing the conflict. At the same time it is a release.

The wife's role is defined in terms of the husband's convenience much as the husband's role of employee is defined in terms of management's convenience. (The children, similarly, are firmly kept in their place and from an early age made conscious of the social differences between the sexes.) The husband pays his wife an agreed weekly sum, called 'her wages'. She may not know how much he earns or what proportion of his earnings is given her. Indeed, one woman, when asked whether her husband worked in town or nearer home, had to call a neighbour to ask if she knew. With her wage, the woman rules the household and makes all expenditure decisions, except for big items, such as a new cooker, for which her husband will pay out a further share from his wages. This practice is a great help to the wife, for ordinary hire-purchase items are paid out of her wages.

The pattern is established before marriage. The young single men are earning well and very generous in buying each other drinks. Once married, who is going to get the free money? The men's custom of paying the wife a regular wage ensures fairness at home (fairness here referring to the men's feeling that they have fulfilled their contractual obligations) and yet enables them to pay their proper share when drinking with the boys. The club, the pub, the bookie, have first claim on the free money. Leisure may also be bought with it, and the wife is conventionally prevented from putting pressure on the man to go to work. If money is plentiful, why not knock off work for a day? It isn't as though the work were so attractive.

The increased prosperity of the miner has not added in fair proportion to the wife's wages. Rather, because his pleasures are centred in the male group outside the home, it has added to the free spending money. By spending his money with his friends in the way which is conventional in Ashton, the Ashton way of life is perpetuated: the miner maintains his own standing while that of the women is as low as ever.

Unlike the husband, the wives spend little on themselves without the approval of their spouse. The husband will query expenditure on items outside the normal household budget. This budget includes little for her clothes, less for her leisure, nothing for self-improvement. In this way the wife's life is restricted to her family and her neighbours.

Restricted to the home as they are, wives do not appear actively to resent it. When pressed they will acknowledge jealousy of their husband's freedom, but many of them say that they find satisfaction in the care of their children. (Indeed the confinement of the wife to the internal affairs of the family brings her much closer to her children than the father.) The husband having fulfilled his obligations when he has paid over the wife's wage, it is part of the women's side of the bargain that the home must be a comfortable place to come back to after work, with a meal prepared, a room tidy and warm, and a wife ready to wait upon him. There must be no cold meals, late meals, washing lying about, or ironing to do while he is at home. These duties should be performed while he is at work; when he is at home, the wife should concentrate on his comfort. The wife agrees with these stipulations; both acknowledge that a miner's work is hard and that it is a 'poor do' if the wife cannot fulfil her part of the contract as long as the husband fulfils his. In one instance, a wife had gone to the pictures after asking her sister to prepare a meal and serve it when the husband came home. The husband so confronted threw the dinner 'to t'back of t'fire'. It was his wife's duty to look after him. He would accept no substitute.

In fairness, it must be said that the contractual relation shows in a better light when one considers what happens when the man is unable to fulfil his part of the bargain. If the man is out of work or paid very low wages, he may agree that the wife should go out to work. Then the bargain changes, a new contract is made: he may cook or make the beds if he comes home before she does. That this is a deviant pattern is shown by the embarrassment of the man in acknowledging that he does this. That it is a socially permitted alternative is shown later in the history of this very man who had thrown the food away. Because of deafness he was forced to change to a job with much lower pay. His wife now goes out to work at 7 a.m. and returns at 5.30 p.m. He helps her in all manner of ways in the house and has a meal ready for *her* when she returns home.

Marriages in Ashton are a matter of 'carrying on' pure and simple. So long as the man works and gives his wife and family sufficient, and the woman uses the family's 'wage' wisely and gives her husband the few things he demands, the marriage will carry on.

Because of the division in activity and ideas between men and women, husband and wife tend to have little to talk about or do together. Here, in Ashton, the family is a system of relationships torn by a major contradiction at its heart; husband and wife live separate and in a sense secret lives. Many married couples seem to have no intimate understanding of one another; the only occasions on which they really approach each other is in bed, and sexual relations are apparently rarely satisfactory to both partners. The stress on manliness defined as absence of tenderness, and the connexion of sexual matters with pit-talk, are obvious components for an explanation of this. In addition, the lack of give-and-take, the contractual view of all relationships, and the unusually rigid division of labour must be taken into consideration.

J. KLEIN, *Samples from English Culture*

1 Suggest reasons why the term 'extended family' is applied to people living in traditional working-class communities.
2 Give examples from the description of life in Bethnal Green to show the ways in which members of an extended family help each other out.
3 Why do the people in Bethnal Green have a great deal in common?
4 Explain in your own words the part played by relatives in Bethnal Green in helping to get jobs.
5 Suggest reasons why coal mining as an occupation makes the men of Ashton particularly close.
6 Describe the typical relationships in Ashton between (*a*) the men; (*b*) the women, (*c*) husbands and wives.
7 How does the 'men's talk' and the 'women's talk' differ in Ashton?
8 From your own knowledge or experience, discuss how accurate the accounts of working-class family life are today. Have things changed at all? Give as much evidence as you can to support your answer.

Nuclear families

As the people of Bethnal Green were rehoused on Greenleigh estate twenty miles out of London their extended family living arrangements began to change.

That busy, sociable life is now a memory. Shopping in the mornings amidst the chromium and the tiles of the Parade is a lonely business compared with the familiar faces and sights of the old street market. The evenings are quieter too: 'It's the television most nights and the garden in the summer.' Mrs Harper knew no one when she arrived at Greenleigh, and her efforts to make friends have not been very successful. 'I tried getting friendly with the woman next door but one,' she explained, 'but it didn't work.' It is the loneliness she dislikes most – and the 'quietness' which she thinks will in time 'send people off their heads'. . . .

Mrs Harper seldom sees her relatives any more. She goes to Bethnal Green only five or six times a year, when one of her elder sisters organizes a family party 'for Dad'. 'It costs so much to travel up there,' she said, 'that I don't recognise some of the children, they're growing up so fast.' Tired of mooching around an empty house all day, waiting for her husband and children to return, with no one to talk to and with the neighbours 'snobbish' and 'spiteful', Mrs Harper has taken a part-time job. 'If I didn't go to work, I'd get melancholic.' Her verdict on Greenleigh – 'It's like being in a box to die out here.'

Mrs Harper's story shows how great can be the change for a woman who moves from a place where the family is linked to relatives, neighbours, and friends in a web of intimate relationships to a place where she may talk to no one, apart from the children, from the moment her husband leaves for work in the morning until he comes home again, tired out by the journey, at seven or eight at night. It is not just that she sees less of relatives than before: as a day-to-day affair, as something around which her domestic economy is organized, her life arranged, the extended family has ceased to exist. . . .

In Bethnal Green, people with relatives close by seldom go short of money in a crisis. If they do not belong to a family club from which they can borrow a loan, some relatives will lend them money. Borrowing from relatives is often more difficult at Greenleigh. 'You notice the difference out here', said Mr Tonks, 'when you fall on hard times. Up there you were where you were born. You could always get helped by your family. You didn't even have to ask them - they'd help you out of trouble straight away. Down here you've had it. . . .'

The question about help at childbirth showed the same decline in dependence on relatives. The kindred of Bethnel Green were no longer predominant. Out of the 29 wives in Bethnal Green helped by relatives at their confinement, 18 were helped by their mothers: out of 19 at Greenleigh only one wife was - the Mrs Chortle whose mother lives with her. Of the remaining three relatives, two were living at Greenleigh, and one came out to stay. Of the other 15 families, neighbours helped only 5; one family turned to a Home Help; 7 husbands stayed off work; and in 2 families the children looked after themselves.

In day-to-day affairs, too, the neighbours rather rarely took the place of kin. A few wives said they went to the shops with another woman, or that they got errands for each other, or that they took turns at fetching the children from school. The most usual reaction was like that of Mrs Todd, who complained, 'When the baby was ill, not a soul knocked at my door to get me an errand.' Even where neighbours were willing to assist, people were apparently reluctant to depend on them too much or confide in them too freely. . . .

Husbands not only do more to aid their wives in emergencies; they also spend less on themselves and more on their families. When they watch the television instead of drinking beer in the pub, and weed the garden instead of going to a football match, the husbands of Greenleigh have taken a stage further the partnership characteristic of modern families. The 'home' and the family of marriage becomes the focus of a man's life, as of his wife's, far more completely than in the East End. 'You lose contact with parents and relations when you move out here,' said Mr Curtis. 'You seem to centre yourself more on the home. Everybody lives in a little world of their own.'

M. YOUNG and P. WILLMOTT, *Family and Kinship in East London*

1 What is meant by the term 'nuclear family'?
2 Describe the life of a nuclear family recorded by Young and Willmott in Greenleigh.
3 What are the main differences between family life in Greenleigh and Bethnal Green?
4 Mr Curtis says, 'You seem to centre yourself more on the home. Everybody lives in a little world of their own.' Suggest ways in which the mass media, and especially advertising men, play upon this 'home-centredness' as a means of influencing behaviour and attitudes and of selling products.
5 From your own knowledge or experience discuss how accurate this description of nuclear family life is today. Give as much evidence as you can to support your answer.

In industrialized societies like America the trend to younger marriages and the pressures of a consumer society make nuclear families a lucrative source of income for businessmen.

With the revolutionary discovery of the teenage market, teenagers and young marrieds began to figure prominently in the surveys. It was discovered that young wives, who had only been to high school and had never worked, were more 'insecure', less independent, easier to sell. These young people could be told that, by buying the right things, they could achieve middle-class status, without work or study. The keep-up-with-the-Joneses sell would work again; the individuality and independence which American women had been getting from education and work outside the home was not such a problem with the teenage brides. In fact, the surveys said, if the pattern of 'happiness through things' could be established when these women were young enough, they could be safely encouraged to go out and get a part-time job to help their husbands pay for all the things they buy. The main point now was to convince the teenagers that 'happiness through things' is no longer the prerogative of the rich or the talented; it can be enjoyed by all, if they learn 'the right way' the way the others do it, if they learn the embarrassment of being different.

In the words of one of these reports:
49% of these new brides were teenagers, and more girls marry at the age of 18 than at any other age. This early family formation yields a larger number of young people who are on the threshold of their own responsibilites and decision making in purchases. . . .

But the most important fact is of a psychological nature: marriage today is not only the culmination of a romantic attachment; more consciously and more clearheadedly than in the past, it is also a decision to create a partnership in establishing a comfortable house, equipped with a great number of desirable products.

In talking to scores of young couples and brides-to-be, we found that, as a rule, their conversations and dreams centred to a very large degree around their future homes and their furnishings, around shopping 'to get an idea', around discussing the advantages and disadvantages of various products. . . .

The modern bride is deeply convinced of the unique value of married love, of the possibilities of finding real happiness in marriage and of fulfilling her personal destiny in it and through it.

But the engagement period today is a romantic, dreamy and heady period only to a limited extent. It is probably safe to say that the period of engagement tends to be a rehearsal of the material duties and responsibilities of marriage. While waiting for the nuptials, couples work hard, put aside money for definite purchases, or even begin buying on an instalment plan.

What is the deeper meaning of this new combination of an almost religious belief in the importance and beauty of married life on the one hand, and the product-centred outlook, on the other? . . .

The modern bride seeks as a conscious goal that which in many cases her grandmother saw as a blind fate and her mother as slavery: to belong to a man, to have a home and children of her own, to choose among all possible careers the career of wife-mother-homemaker.

BETTY FRIEDAN, *The Feminine Mystique*

1 Why do American businessmen concentrate a lot of marketing attention on teenage brides?
2 Suggest reasons why the modern American bride actively 'seeks' what her grandmother regarded as 'fate' and her mother regarded as 'slavery'?
3 How far do you agree with this as an accurate description of the behaviour and attitudes of young brides in Britain? Give as much evidence as you can to support your answer.

Lee Comer describes how the organization of wage labour and domestic labour in the British nuclear family is exactly the kind of arrangement which benefits a capitalist society.

One of the first requirements of a capitalist economy is a mobile, docile workforce. Men and women who are 'free' to acquire the skills that the economy needs and who are prepared to move wherever their skills are in most demand. And this they cannot do if they are tied, either emotionally or by obligation, to the larger family network. Even in such a highly industrialized country as Britain, there are still many pockets of extended close-knit families and communities, whose members are reluctant to uproot themselves. Significantly, they are in areas of greatest despression and unemployment - Glasgow, South Wales, Devon and Cornwall. Grudgingly the State pays them dole but urges them to move, leaving their families and community, to go and live in strange and unwelcoming towns where they might find work.

Not only are people expected to be geographically mobile, they are also expected to be 'socially mobile'. That is, through hard work, extended education and a willingess to move frequently, people can hope to rise out of their class and enjoy the dubious trappings of more money and status. But to do it they must break links with their background, reject their families and class in order to identify with the class they are aspiring to.

For the purpose of a capitalist economy then, the very best arrangement a man can make, regardless of everything else is to:

1 Take a wife who will care for him and see to all his needs and bear his children.
2 Live with them in a small isolated group and preferably away from his first family with whom his links must be only nominal (aged parents are a liability).
3 Be intent on improving his standard of living, thereby committing himself to overtime or professional ladder climbing, both of which require long hours away from home and a patient uncomplaining wife.
4 Be prepared to move house and town from time to time but not to strike.
5 Support a wife and growing family.

For the purposes of capitalism, the best arrangements a woman can make go parallel to a man's. Her goals must mirror her husband's. She must be prepared to work long, unpaid hours in the home while he improves his lifestyle. But as well as applying herself wholeheartedly to her husband's and her children's needs, she must also be prepared to work outside the home for 'pin money' (i.e. low pay), but not to get too attached to her work role. She must only see her job as important in so far as it adds to the family spending power and gives her something to do when the children grow up. Her work must never give her independence. Where her husband goes, so must she. So that if she is laid off at work, or subjected to bad working conditions, it will not matter too much.

Thus two basic needs of capitalism are met by the behaviour of nuclear families - a motivated, mobile male workforce supported by a secondary, female domestic labour force and source of cheap, casual labour.

LEE COMER, *Wedlocked Women*

1 Explain what Comer means by a 'capitalist economy'.
2 Why does capitalism need nuclear families according to Comer?
3 What kind of general standard of living is typical of these working-class people who still live in extended family units?
4 How does modern capitalist society encourage the breaking-up of extended families and traditional communities?
5 What kind of relationship between husband and wife best suits the needs of a capitalist economy, according to Comer?
6 Do you think Comer is sympathetic to or critical of the influences of capitalism on family life? Give examples from the passage to support your answer. How far do you agree or disagree with her analysis?

The changing roles of husbands and wives

Many studies of marriage published during the last twenty years or so stress the increasingly equal relationships of husbands and wives compared with the nineteenth and early twentieth centuries (see, for example Ronald Fletcher, *The Family and Marriage;* Robert Blood and Donald Woolfe, *Husbands and Wives;* and Peter Willmott, *The Symmetrical Family*). They attach a good deal of importance to the legal emancipation of women and to the increase in the number of married women working outside the home. They also agree that husbands participate in housework and bringing up children much more than they used to. Ann Oakley wanted to find out just how true this is. So she interviewed forty housewives – twenty working-class and twenty middle-class. Her findings, outlined below, were published in *The Sociology of Housework.*

Division of labour in the home

Husbands were graded 'high', 'medium', or 'low' depending on their participation in both housework and child-care (see Tables 1 and 2).

Table 1 *Husband's participation in housework by social class*

Social class	High no. (%)	Medium no. (%)	Low no. (%)	Total no. (%)
Working class	2(10)	1(5)	17(85)	20(100)
Middle class	4(20)	9(45)	7(35)	20(100)
Total	6(15)	10(25)	24(60)	40(100)

Table 2 *Husband's participation in child-care by social class*

Social class	High no. (%)	Medium no. (%)	Low no. (%)	Total no. (%)
Working class	2(10)	8(40)	10(50)	20(100)
Middle class	8(40)	4(20)	8(40)	20(100)
Total	10(25)	12(30)	18(45)	40(100)

Three main conclusions can be drawn from these tables:
1   Only a minority of husbands gives the kind of help which could be called 'shared' or 'equal' responsibility in the home (15 per cent have a high level of participation in housework and 25 per cent in child-care).
2   There is a difference between the behaviour of working-class and middle-class husbands.
3   Husbands are more likely to help with child-care than housework.

Marriage generally

Oakley also asked questions about how far decision-making, financial arrangements and leisure activities were shared. She found that decision-making and leisure activities were more likely to be shared in middle-class homes than in working-class homes. She described a good deal of sharing as a 'joint' marriage, and one in which the husband and wife had very different decision-making, financial and leisure activities as a 'segregated' marriage (see Table 3).

Table 3 *Social class and segregation/jointness of marital role-relationship*

| | Social class | | |
Marital role-relationship	Working class no. (%)	Middle class no. (%)	Total no. (%)
Segregated	15(75)	2(10)	17(43)
Joint	5(25)	18(90)	23(58)
Total	20(100)	20(100)	40(100)

But 'jointness' in leisure activities and decision-making did not necessarily mean that husbands rated high in housework and child-care. In fact, many 'joint' marraiges that appeared to be egalitarian concealed a good deal of traditional role-playing by the husbands and wives.

In general, the women in 'joint' marriages were more satisfied with their marriages, however, and more content with their lives generally. Oakley found that thirteen out of seventeen (75 per cent) of the women with segregated marriages were dissatisfied generally, while seven out of twenty-three (30 per cent) of the women with joint marriages were dissatisfied generally. She concluded that,

For women whose marriages are characterized by shared interests and activities - the emotional rewards do a lot to compensate for the dissatisfactions of housewifery. Women in segregated marriages lack these compensations and are much more dependent on relationships with others. In traditional working class communities other women and the female members of the family (mothers, daughters, sisters and sisters-in-law) provide a strong support group. But where old patterns of community life are broken up this prop is removed.

'Joint' marriages are still frequently those in which the husband's domesticity is low and the wife's high. If a husband is employed and a wife is not (i.e. outside the home) - then a high level of female domesticity may seem logical. Particularly so if the husband's job is especially time-consuming or demanding. If a wife fails to play a supportive domestic role in middle class homes, the man may be handicapped in his efforts to establish his career. The very presures which affect a husband pursuing a career are also pressures serving to confine his wife to domestic concerns at the expense of job or career ambitions for herself. This connection is also true of working class marriages in which aspects of the husbands' jobs (e.g. long hours) are similarly demanding. Here too, women's job and career prospects outside the home are likely to be seen as of secondary importance to those of their husbands.

Beliefs and attitudes

Oakley wanted to know whether women's attitudes were changing about whether husbands should become more domesticated in the home. She asked two questions, 'Does (or did) your husband change the baby's nappy?', and 'What would you think of a marriage in which the wife went out to work and the husband stayed at home to look after the children?'

So far as nappy-changing went neither class of husband was very keen (see Table 4).

Table 4 *Answers to question, 'Does (did) your husband change the baby's dirty nappy?', by social class*

Social class	Answer to question		
	No/occasionally /under protest no. (%)	Yes no. (%)	Total no. (%)
Working class	17(85)	3(15)	20(100)
Middle class	13(65)	7(35)	20(100)
Total	30(75)	10(25)	40(100)

In general, child-rearing, so far as the husband was concerned, meant playing with the children. Things like changing nappies, washing and cleaning up after children were still usually thought to be a mother's responsibility.

When asked about women going out to work and men staying at home, the answers showed a firm belief that it is 'natural' for women and 'unnatural' for men to be domesticated. Thirty out of forty women rejected the idea of a reversed-roles marriage. None of the others really approved of the idea but said that it depended on the couple or their circumstances. Asked why men could not take over the housewives' role, most replied that women were better at domestic chores than men and could not earn as much as men outside the home. No one suggested that men are bad at domestic chores because, unlike women, they have never had to learn how to do them, or that women's equal pay and better job opportunities can and are being won by legal and political changes. Oakley concluded from her research that men and women's roles in the family, their attitudes to marriage and their beliefs about equality are not changing as quickly as is often suggested. None of the women she interviewed questioned the assumption that a woman's first and most important duty is to be a wife and mother.

1 Compare the different participation of middle-class and working-class husbands in housework, according to Oakley's sample.
2 Compare the different participation of middle-class and working-class husbands in child-care, according to Oakley's sample.
3 What were her conclusions about husbands' involvement in housework and child-care?
4 Suggest reasons why there should be a difference between working-class and middle-class behaviour. Give any evidence you can to support your answer.
5 What does Oakley mean by 'joint' marriages and 'segregated' marriages?
6 How do women in joint and segregated marriages compensate for housewifery, according to Oakley?
7 How does a husband's job effect a wife's opportunities according to Oakley?
8 What conclusions does Oakley draw about the state of men and women's attitudes to marriage and family life generally these days?

Has the family a future?

Family-centred society
Because the family is deemed the only organization in which to live, all those who live outside it are thought to be either odd, abnormal or, in the worst cases, social

outcasts. Our self-image depends, to a large extent, on where we are in the family cycle - daughter/wife/mother/widow. The young who are growing out of their first family, and are plainly on their way to their second, are the only large body of people whose existence outside the family structure is tolerated. But we have categories for the rest - those who, whether or not they chose to, find they have missed the boat - spinsters, divorced people, single parents, lesbians and homosexuals, childless couples, middle aged bachelors and ageing widows and widowers. Whatever their personal circumstances, these people are daily reminded, with everything from ideal happy family type advertisements to banter from their workmates, that they don't fit into society's straight jacket. ('Waiting for Mr Right are you?', 'We'd prefer a family man for this job', 'This one'll get you to the altar. You can't hold out much longer.') They are the curiosities and casualties of a family-centred society.

Single and divorced people are supposed to be lonely and bitter and if they're not then there must be something wrong with them. Homosexuals and lesbians' only usefulness is as a subject for dirty jokes and ridicule. Not only are they outside the family, but because they threaten it, they were until recently outside the law. Childless couples are pitied or badgered with questions, and suffer endless innuendoes about the 'patter of tiny feet'. One-child families are always considered incomplete ('Don't you think it's cruel/selfish/niggardly to have an only child?').

It's because the family is the only socially acceptable unit for living in that everything which threatens it takes on the proportions of a serious social problem. Judging from the publicity accorded to them, and the way in which people get steamed up, the issues of the day are illegitimacy, abortion, permissiveness, homosexuality, pornography and promiscuity, all of which must be 'stamped out', 'cured', 'labelled obscene' or 'made illegal'. Even contraception and divorce, despite apparent increases in tolerance, make people lower their voices and are still regarded as regrettable. And just why are unmarried mothers considered such a serious problem? And why should children born out of wedlock have to hide the fact? And why do homosexual people have to resort to such furtive secrecy? And why are promiscuity and broken homes dirty words? And why shouldn't women have free and easy access to contraception and abortion? The thread which connects all these things is the fact that each one poses a threat which, if allowed free rein and social acceptability, would seriously erode the inflexibility of family life.

LEE COMER, *Wedlocked Women*

1   Give as many examples as you can to either support or reject Comer's argument that we are a family-centred society in which everyone who isn't part of a nuclear family is treated like a social misfit.
2   Why does Comer suggest that people who do not fit into conventional family roles are considered to be social problems?
3   Make out a case to either support or refute the argument that family life is under threat from the permissive society.

Family breakdown

In the last few years, violence within the family - wife or baby battering - has aroused widespread concern. In so doing, it has possibly also focused attention upon the family unit. The changing role of women and the soaring divorce rate have further provoked some alarm about whether the family has a future at all. In 1951, the divorce rate stood at 2.6 per 1,000 married people; in 1975, it was 9.6 per 1,000, or 40 per cent of the number of first marriages. At the centre of the pressure on the family, however, stands the change in women's expectations and the reluctance of society to acknowledge that change. The advent of the contraceptive pill, the Abortion Act, 1967, and the free family planning service from 1974, gave women unprecedented control over their bodies. With such freedom - plus economic necessity and a deeper questioning of traditional roles - came an increase in the number of women at work.

Lady Howe, deputy chairman of the Equal Opportunities Commission, said last month: 'The traditional single-role family, where the wife stayed at home and the husband went to work, is disappearing. As a society, we are right to worry about what is now happening to women as they struggle to carry the double burden of their traditional duties and their role as workers. And it isn't only women who are feeling the strains. There are, for example, some 100,000 single parent families headed by men, and involving about 158,000 children, who also face the same dilemma.'

Yet, while the number of working women has increased, the number of local authority day care places for the under fives has dropped - from 72,000 day nursery places in 1944 to 25,000 in 1975. A recent survey showed that 32 per cent of the under fives received day care and it was wanted for a further 33 per cent. Such paucity of provision may not simply be due to a reluctance to spend the necessary money. A TUC working party report on under fives says: 'The related questions of women's employment and child care facilities raise strong emotions and it is clear that while social attitudes are changing, there is still widespread disagreement in society at large and an ambivalence in government circles as to whether it is desirable for the mothers of young children to work outside the home. . . . It is the working party's view that as things stand at present both our very young children and their parents are being grossly and inexcusably exploited.'

MELANIE PHILLIPS, *New Society*, 8 June 1978

1 What evidence is used by some commentators to suggest that the family may have no future at all?
2 What is the most significant change to affect family life, according to Melanie Phillips.
3 What evidence is quoted by Phillips to suggest that the state is doing little to help working women and their families?
4 How does she explain the state's reluctance?
5 Using Comer's arguments on pages 68-9 describe how she would explain the state's reluctance to help.

Socialization

Anna and Isabelle

Anna was an illegitimate child whose grandfather strongly disapproved of the mother's indiscretion and who therefore caused the child to be kept in an upstairs room. As a result the infant received only enough care to keep her barely alive. She was seldom moved from one position to another. Her clothing and bedding were filthy. She apparently had no instruction, no friendly attention.

When finally found and removed from the room at the age of nearly six years Anna could not talk, walk, or do anything that showed intelligence. She was in an extremely emaciated and undernourished condition, with skeleton-like legs and bloated abdomen. She was completely apathetic, lying in a limp supine position and remaining immobile, expressionless, and indifferent to everything. She was believed to be deaf and possibly blind. She of course could not feed herself or make any move on her own behalf. Here, then, was a human organism which had missed nearly six years of socialization. Her condition shows how little her purely biological resources, when acting alone, could contribute to making her a complete person.

By the time Anna died of haemorrhagic jaundice, approximately four and a half years later, she had made considerable progress as compared with her condition when found. She could follow directions, string beads, identify a few colours, build with blocks, and differentiate between attractive and unattractive pictures. She had a good sense of rhythm and loved a doll. She talked mainly in phrases but would repeat words and try to carry on a conversation. She was clean about clothing. She habitually washed her hands and brushed her teeth. She would try to help other children. She walked well and could run fairly well, though clumsily. Although easily excited, she had a pleasant disposition. Her improvement showed that socialization, even when started at the late age of six, could still do a great deal towards making her a person. Even though her development was no more than that of a normal child of two to three years, she had made noteworthy progress.

Isabelle was found at about the same time as Anna under strikingly similar circumstances when approximately six and a half years old. Like Anna, she was illegitimate and had been kept in seclusion for that reason. Her mother was a deaf mute and it appears that she and Isabelle spent most of their time together in a dark room. As a result Isabelle had no chance to develop speech; when she communicated with her mother it was by means of gestures. Lack of sunshine and inadequacy of diet had caused her to become rachitic. Her legs in particular were affected; they were 'so bowed that as she stood erect the soles of her shoes came nearly flat together, and she got about with a skittering gait'. Her behaviour towards strangers, especially men, was almost that of a wild animal, manifesting much fear and hostility. In lieu of speech she made only a strange croaking sound. In many ways she acted like an infant. 'She was apparently utterly unaware of relationships of any kind. When presented with a ball for the first time, she held it in the palm of her hand, then reached out and stroked [the donor's] face with it. Such behaviour is comparable to that of a child of six months.' At first it was even hard to tell whether or not she could hear, so unused were her senses. Many of her actions resembled those of deaf children.

Once it was established that she could hear, specialists who worked with her pronounced her feeble-minded. Even on non-verbal tests her performance was so low as to promise little for the future. 'The general impression was that she was wholly uneducable and that any attempt to teach her to speak, after so long a period of silence, would meet with failure.' Yet the individuals in charge of her launched a systematic and skilful programme of training. The task seemed hopeless at first, but gradually she began to respond. After the first few hurdles had at last been overcome, a curious thing happened. She went through the usual stages of learning characteristics of the years from one to six not only in proper succession but far more rapidly than normal. In a little over two months after her first focalization she was putting sentences together. Nine months after that she could identify words and sentences on the printed page, could write well, could add to ten and could retell a story after hearing it. Seven months beyond this point she had a vocabulary of 1500-2000 words and was asking complicated questions. Starting from an educational level of between one and three years, she had reached a normal level by the time she was eight and a half years old. In short, she covered in two years the stages of learning that ordinarily requires six. She eventually entered school where she participated in all school activities as normally as other children.

KINSLEY DAVIS, *Human Society*

1   Anna 'received only enough to keep her barely alive'. Which early learning experiences did she miss?
2   What effects did this have on Anna by the age of six?
3   Which particular human characteristics were missing from the child?
4   Anna was taken away and given a normal upbringing. What changes did this bring about in the child?
5   Which three human characteristics were particularly undeveloped in the behaviour of Isabelle?
6   What conclusions did the first experts who contacted Isabelle come to about her behaviour?
7   What was the real trouble with Isabelle?
8   Describe in your own words the progress she made once a systematic programme of socialization was begun.
9   What important conclusions about socialization can be drawn from these two case studies?

Learning sex roles in British society

In most respects, the human infant is everywhere the same - helpless, capable only of reflex actions and totally dependent on adult care for several years. From these same beginnings human beings grow up to be anything from an Australian Aborigine to an Eskimo, from an assembly line worker to an aristocrat.

The fact that we are all human with the same needs and desires should go without saying. We wear clothes, make love, speak to each other, build houses, grow food, work and provide for our young and old. But the differences between us appear so marked that many people in the industrialized societies believe that those who are not like us are, for that reason, not quite human. Both the assembly line worker and the aristocrat regard the other as being of a different breed. So it is worthwhile us reminding them that if either of them had been taken at birth and placed in an Eskimo society, they too would *be* Eskimos.

The process by which the human infant is moulded to fit the society into which he or she is born is called socialization. The term is defined by William Goode as the way in which a member of a given society 'acquires the values and knowledge of his group and learns the social roles appropriate to his position in it.' It is no accident in our society, therefore, that the characteristics assigned to men and women are precisely those required to maintain the present structure of society both in social class terms and sex terms.

The picture which emerges from the studies of girls' and boys' upbringing shows clearly that far from things getting more equal the division between the sexes is growing deeper. The influence of the toy market, television and education confirm and increase the pressure on boys and girls to pursue their separate ways at an even earlier age.

The groundwork is begun in the family. Although parents claim to treat their boy and girl children alike, deeper examination reveals great differences. All the studies undertaken in the West on child rearing patterns show that the qualities encouraged in girls are precisely those they will need in their adult role - dependence, obedience, domesticity and conformity whilst boys are encouraged to be self reliant, active, dominant and outward-looking. How exactly is it done? In the first place by trial and error. The young child learns that approval from parents, friends and teachers depends upon behaving in ways which are acceptable. Take dirt for example. A TV advert for washing powder shows a young mother standing guard over her washing machine when her small son enters from the garden where other boys can be seen playing war games; mother smiles lovingly to herself thinking 'Just like a boy' but Persil will solve her problems. And we know that he will continue to behave 'just like a boy' and she is doomed to send him out in a clean shirt only to wash it again the next day. A girl could never be used in such an advert because girls are not supposed to get dirty. Rather, the girl would be scolded for playing in the mud. Girls are shown much more frequently and to much greater effect in adverts for washing up liquid where they can be shown rehearsing their adult trade. Activities which are approved of in a girl, but discouraged in a boy, are not so far away from the world of adverts. The stereo-type and the reality meet when the little girl spends her time playing nurse to her brother's doctor, or demanding a toy sewing machine for Christmas, pushing a toy pram, trying on mother's make-up, weighing the flour for a cake or singing lullabies to her doll and refusing to join in the rough games of the boys. For a while she may climb trees, play football, get into scrapes and generally copy acceptable male behaviour but only on the condition that she grows out of it. No such tolerance is extended to the boy. The boy who goes around exclusively with girls, plays girls' games and rejects his male friends would probably be referred to Child Guidance.

Toys which mirror the lifestyle of the grown ups are now big business. For small boys this is manifested in toy guns, rockets, cars, aeroplanes and hovercrafts. The situation is very different for the girls. Here, the toys are exact replicas of the everyday tools of their mother's trade. Rehearsing their adult role is a much more serious business for girls than it is for boys. Girls may not dream of a life of excitement, adventure and travel away from home, husband and family. But they can dream of the kind of home they will have and who they will marry. To this end the market is flooded with every conceivable kind of domestic toy, from dolls to miniature baking tins. Even neutral playthings are not immune. On the cover of a pack of interlocking bricks the girl is shown how to assemble a sewing machine while the boy is shown a gun. A reporter from the Sunday Times was told at the British and International Toy Fair held in 1972 that 'painstaking research has revealed that the new target for toy makers is the mother-to-be of the mid-eighties'. The exploitation of little girls with their 'demand' for expensive toy prams, pushchairs, dolls and cradles, cookers, washing machines and even washing lines and pegs, toy hoovers, dustpans and tea sets has brought every manufacturer in the business to her immediate service.

By the time children are old enough to go to school they have learnt a good deal about the division of labour, activity and power between the sexes. They have a very good idea of what women are for and what men are for. They see their mothers working in the house but know that what their mother does is not work because it's their father who goes out to work. Work means being out of the house and earning money.

LEE COMER, *Wedlocked Women*

1   Why is it that people from different societies and different social classes often regard each other as being 'of a different breed'?
2   How does Comer define socialization?
3   How does William Goode, a sociologist interested in studying family life, define socialization?
4   What other factors besides the behaviour of parents in families affect a young child's socialization in the West?
5   What kind of different characteristics do boys and girls learn during their socialization? Can you give any examples, besides those used in the extract, to illustrate other ways in which boys and girls in Britain learn their sex roles?
6   Explain in your own words what Comer means by the phrase, 'the stereo-type and the reality meet'.
7   Suggest reasons why tom-boyish behaviour is tolerated in a girl but effeminate behaviour is not tolerated in a boy. Do you have any evidence to support your answer?
8   What are the main differences between boys and girls' toys? What effects could the toys they play with have on their later lives?
9   Suggest reasons why people like Comer are critical of the socialization of young children into very different behaviour according to whether they're boys or girls. How far do you agree or disagree with this criticism? Give as many reasons as you can to support your answer.

Young girls in Samoa

From birth until the age of four or five a child's education is exceedingly simple. They must be house-broken, a matter made more difficult by a habitual indifference to the activities of small children. They must learn to sit or crawl within the house and never to stand upright unless it is absolutely necessary; never to address an adult in a standing position; to stay out of the sun; not to tangle the strands of the weaver; not to scatter the cut-up coconut which is spread out to dry; to keep their scant loin cloths at least nominally fastened to their persons; to treat fire and knives with proper caution; not to touch the kava bowl or the kava cup; and if their father is a chief, not to crawl on his bed place when he is by. These are really simply a series of avoidances, enforced by occasional cuffings and a deal of exasperated shouting and ineffectual conversation.

The weight of the punishment usually falls upon the next oldest child, who learns to shout, 'Come out of the sun', before she has fully appreciated the necessity of doing so herself. By the time Samoan boys and girls have reached 16 or 17 years of age these perpetual warnings to the younger ones have become an inseparable part of their conversation - a monotonous, irritated undercurrent to all their comments. I have known them to interrupt their remarks every two or three minutes with 'Keep still', 'Sit still', 'Keep your mouths shut', 'Stop that noise', uttered quite mechanically although all the little ones present may have been behaving as a row of intimidated mice. On the whole, this last requirement of silence is continually mentioned and never enforced. The little nurses are more interested in peace than in forming the character of their small charges, and when a child begins to howl it is simply dragged out of earshot of its elders. No mother will ever exert herself to discipline a younger child if an older one can be made responsible. Thus each child is being disciplined and socialized through responsibility for a still younger one.

By the time a child is six or seven she has all the essential avoidances well enough by heart to be trusted with the care of a younger child. And she also develops a number of simple techniques. She learns to weave firm square balls from palm leaves, to make pin wheels of palm leaves or frangipangi blossom, to climb a coconut tree by walking up the trunk on flexible little feet, to break open a coconut with one firm well-directed blow of a knife as long as she is tall, to play a number of group games and sing songs which go with them, to tidy the house by picking up the litter on the stony floor, to bring water from the sea, to spread out the copra to dry and to help gather it when rain threatens, to roll the pandanus leaves for weaving, to go to a neighbouring house and bring back a lighted faggot for the chief's pipe or the cookhouse fire, and to exercise tact in begging slight favours from relatives.

But in the case of the little girls all these tasks are secondary to the main business of baby tending. Very small boys also have some care of the younger children, but at eight or nine years of age they are usually relieved of it.

All the irritating routine of housekeeping, which in our civilization is accused of warping the souls and souring the tempers of grown women, is here performed by children under 14 years of age. A fire or a pipe to be kindled, a call for a drink, a lamp to be lit, the baby's cry, any trifling errand of a thoughtless adult - these haunt them from morning until night. With the introduction of several months a year of Government School these children are being taken out of the home for most of the day. This brings about a complete disorganization of the native households, which have no precedents for a manner of life where mothers have to stay at home and take care of their children and adults have to perform small routine tasks and run errands.

MARGARET MEAD, *Coming of Age in Samoa*

1   Find out the whereabouts of Samoa.
2   What type of society is it?
3   What are the main things a child in Samoa has to learn not to do from the time of birth to the age of 4 or 5?
4   Make a list from your own experience of at least six things a British child of the same age must learn not to do.
5   Who is responsible in Samoan society for making sure that the children behave themselves properly?
6   Write a piece to explain how much influence older brothers and sisters have in bringing up children in this country.
7   What other skills besides baby-minding has a Samoan girl learned by the age of 6 or 7?
8   Why do Samoan girls take on the main responsibility for minding the house do you think?
9   What effects has 'progress' had on the Samoan girls' responsibilities at home?
10 Write a piece to compare and contrast the life of a Samoan girl of 14 years old with that of a British girl of the same age.

Manus children

The children are taught neither obedience nor deference to their parents' wishes. A two-year-old child is permitted to flout its mother's humble request that it come home with her. At night the children are supposed to be at home at dark, but this does not mean that they go home when called. Unless hunger drives them there the parents have to go about collecting them, often by force. A prohibition against going to the other end of the village to play lasts just as long as the vigilance of the prohibitor, who has only to turn the back for the child to be off, swimming under water until out of reach.

   Manus cooking is arduous and exacting. The sago is cooked dry in a shallow pot stirred over a fire. It requires continuous stirring and is good only for about twenty minutes after being cooked. Yet the children are not expected to come home at meal-time. They run away in the morning before breakfast and come back an hour or so after, clamouring for food. Ten-year-olds will stand in the middle of the house floor and shriek monotonously until someone stops work to cook for them. A woman who has gone to the house of a relative to help with some task or to lay plans for a feast will be assaulted by her six-year-old child, who will scream, pull at her, claw at her arms, kick and scratch, until she goes home to feed him.

   The parents who were so firm in teaching the children their first steps have become wax in the young rebels' hands when it comes to any matter of social discipline. They eat when they like, play when they like, sleep when they see fit. They use no respectful language to their parents, and indeed are allowed more licence in the use of obscenity than are their elders. The veriest urchin can shout defiance and contempt at the oldest man in the village. Children are never required to give up anything to parents; the choicest morsels of food are theirs by divine right. They can rally the devoted adults by a cry, bend and twist their parents to their will. They do no work. Girls after they are eleven or twelve, perform some household tasks, boys hardly any until they are married. The community demands nothing from them except respect for property and the avoidance due to shame.

The child in Manus is lord of the universe, undisciplined, unchecked by any reverence or respect for his elders, free except for the narrow thread of shame which runs through his daily life. No other habits of self-control or of self-sacrifice have been laid. It is the typical psychology of the spoiled child. Manus children demand, never give.

MARGARET MEAD, *Growing Up in New Guinea*

1 Where do the Manus people live?
2 You have already learned something about Manus family life. Explain clearly what is special in Manus society about (*a*) marriage, (*b*) relationships between husbands and wives, (*c*) relationships between parents and children.
3 Give as many examples from the passage as you can to illustrate how the Manus child displays all the characteristics of a 'spoiled child'.
4 Why do you think the children are allowed so much freedom to roam around the village as they please?
5 Explain in your own words what are the only two demands the community makes on Manus children.
6 Why do you think the parents are so 'free and easy' with their children?
7 What important conclusions about socialization can be made from studying children's behaviour in different societies?

3 Questions and answers

Group project: The changing roles of men and women in British society

Make a study of the ways in which the roles of men and women have changed in British society over the last 100 years. Work in small groups on different aspects of the theme so that together you can produce as much information and evidence as possible. Here are some suggestions to help you. You can of course add any other relevant aspects which interest you and you should include pictures and photographs to illustrate your investigations.

1 *Pre-industrial societies compared* - marriage and courtship, men's jobs and women's jobs, cultural traditions and ceremonies
2 *Victorian Britain* - relations between husbands and wives in working-class families and middle-class families, Victorian morality, women in factories, mines and agricultural gangs
3 *Annie Besant's birth control movement* - the beginnings and gradual acceptance of family planning, reasons for the reduction of family size over the last hundred years
4 *The suffragettes* - votes for women
5 *Legal changes* - in divorce, property, care of children, legal aid, abortion, marital violence, equal pay and sex discrimination
6 *Working wives* - expansion of educational and training opportunities working conditions, pay and discrimination, women and the trade unions, child-care provisions
7 *The nuclear family* - 'home-centredness', equality in marriage, reversed-roles in marriage, men and women as consumers
8 *Questionnaire to wives* - do they feel emancipated, inferior, content bored?
9 *Questionnaire to husbands* - do they want their wives to work? To what extent do they share in the housework and upbringing of the children?
10 *Sex indoctrination* - how are children trained to accept the sexual characteristics of their society?
11 *The permissive society* - are divorce, pre-marital sex, illegitimacy and abortion seriously affecting relationships between men and women?
12 *Men and women in other industrialized societies* - how does the behaviour of men and women in Russia, America and Sweden compare with ours?

Checkpoints

1 'The family is an economic and social unit.' Explain what this statement means.
2 Why are families in modern Britain more geographically mobile than they were 100 years ago?
3 What is a 'nuclear family' and in what circumstances is it most common?
4 What is an 'extended family' and in what circumstances is it most common?
5 What new grounds for divorce were introduced by legislation in 1971?
6 What percentage of first marriages now end in divorce in Britain?

7 What is meant by the 'nature-nurture controversy' among sociologists?
8 What do sociologists mean by 'socialization'?
9 What do sociologists mean by 'pre-industrial' societies?
10 What is meant by the term 'sex-role conditioning'?

O-level questions

1 Select two of the following statements and show why they might be considered misleading.
a Bigamy is always a crime and morally wrong everywhere.
b The more available divorce becomes the more broken families are created.
c The extended family is simply a family with many children.
2 'All societies have ways of emphasizing the physical differences between men and women by the 'roles' they play in society, especially as regards sexual behaviour, reproduction and the upbringing of children. All societies have some kind of institution called 'marriage' which is really a collection of rules about permanent sexual relations and the duties and obligations of the people involved.' (Denis Lawton, *Investigating Society*)
  Choose any society and compare it with modern Britain in the areas discussed in the passage.
3 How and why has the relationship between husband and wife gradually changed in Britain during this century?
4 In what ways have relationships within the family changed during the last 100 years? What kind of evidence is there to support your views?
5 'It is because man is a cultural being that sociologists have attached great importance to the notion of socialization. By this is meant the transmission of culture: the process by which men learn the rules and practices of social groups.'
a What is meant by 'cultural being'?
b Give two examples of cultures transmitted from one generation to the next.
c Give two examples of rules men learn in social groups.
d If socialization takes place in all societies why do societies change?
6 'In early life a great deal of children's development is determined by their learning at home. This is not to overlook the importance of heredity, particularly in relation to physical growth and also for in-

tellectual development; nor to deny the influence of the wider environment of the neighbourhood and of the community. For the young child, however, the home and the family play the major part in drawing out and structuring his abilities, moulding his personality and behaviour, giving direction to his interests and shaping his attitudes'. (A. Davie *et al., Birth to Seven*)

a   Explain carefully the differences between heredity and environment.
b   What kind of evidence is there to support the views expressed in this passage?
7   What is the difference between an extended and a nuclear family? Which is the most typical in Britain today?
8   In what ways has studying sociology helped you to understand the family in Britain today?
9   'There has been a fall in the age at which people get divorced. This is reflected in the increase in the proportion of divorcing wives under 35 years from 50 per cent in 1961 to 58 per cent in 1969. The Registrar General has shown in his commentary for England and Wales: 1964, that the time between divorce and a second marriage for wives aged between 25 and 29 is well under two years. For some three-quarters of divorcing couples, divorce is a temporary condition between the dissolution of an unhappy first marriage and the beginning of a more hopeful second marriage. Such a high rate of remarriage, when linked to the rising divorce numbers, shows modern morality opposes the idea of continuing a defunct marriage, but does not reject the actual institution of marriage.' (C. Gibson, 'Social trends in divorce', *New Society,* 5 July 1973)
    Comment on the stability of the family in modern Britain using the above information and other evidence with which you are familiar.
10 'Some [social scientists] have cited facts such as the very high rates of divorce, the changes in the older sex morality, and until fairly recently the decline in birth rates, as evidence of a trend to disorganization (of the family) in an absolute sense.' (T. Parsons and R. F. Bales, *Family, Socialization and the Interaction Process*)
    Comment on the above passage using other evidence to support your comments where possible.
11 'Because man is a cultural being the concept of socialization is important in sociology.'
    Explain what is meant by socialization and cultural being and show how this may account for different behaviour in different societies.
12 What explanations have been offered for the increase in the divorce rate in the United Kingdom during the present century?
13 'Why should husbands not think of cooking as a normal and very pleasant part of their job in life? And why should we think of wives as

less capable of doing an intelligent job of work than men?'
(*Guardian*)

Answer one of the following questions:

a How does the concept of socialization help us to answer this question?

b What changes in the family in modern Britain have prompted these questions to be raised?

14 Imagine a country in which living in families was officially prohibited. Describe the differences this might make to that society.

4 Education and adolescence

1 Background information

Formal and informal education

Most of the things which people learn, from the second they are born, and in the many circumstances in which they find themselves during their life, happen outside the formal education system, from people not usually regarded as teachers and through experiences not always considered to be 'educational'. It is thought that young children learn more in their first five years of life, for example, than at any other period in the future. From the very moment of birth, they begin to learn and develop the behaviour, values and attitudes which are thought to be most acceptable by the society in which they live. Their family is the first setting in which learning occurs and parents and other relations act as their first 'teachers'. As a child grows older, friends and neighbours become more influential, as do adult contacts and work mates in later life. All of these provide 'informal' learning opportunities which continue throughout life. There are other influences, too, which affect learning - things like the mass media, traditions and customs and the whole range of legal, social and welfare arrangements which control and organize peoples lives.

But however important or influential these 'informal' agencies might be, they are not usually the ones which are considered when 'education' is being discussed. For most people education is what happens in schools and colleges and all the other easily identifiable institutions which are part and parcel of the education system.

So far as sociologists are concerned, most of their attention has been focused on schools since this is the part of the system which attracts most people and is both compulsory and universal. In this chapter we shall consider some of their main findings. We shall also look at some of the factors which influence young people's behaviour out of school.

The education system in Britain

In some poor countries of the world large sections of the population receive very little or no schooling at all. Many look with envy to societies like ours in which education is both compulsory and free. For eleven years of their life, for 200 days every year, children in Britain have to receive an 'efficient' and 'full-time' education. But the law says nothing about spending that time in school. There is nothing to stop parents educating their sons and daughters at home, so long as the education they provide is as good as that given in schools. But in the majority of cases parents prefer to let the schools do the job for them.

Although it may seem hard to believe, compulsory education for all children is a relatively recent development in our society. Of course some of the old grammar schools and public schools have existed for centuries and there has been a long tradition of children being taught in their own homes by governesses and private tutors. But these opportunities were always reserved for a tiny majority of the population - the children of the most wealthy and aristocratic classes in society.

Before 1870 education for the vast majority of people in Britain was virtually non-existent. Some elementary education was provided by religious bodies of various kinds and by 'dame schools' and 'Sunday Schools' but since most of them charged fees the only opportunities for really poor children were in 'ragged schools'. In all of these schools classes were large, teachers were badly paid and frequently unqualified. It is hardly surprising that in Victorian Britain only about 40 per cent of the population could read - and most of them with difficulty.

But in 1870 the state began to take its first real interest in education, and set in motion the legislation which by 1891 had made elementary education in Britain both free and more or less compulsory. Why did the state get involved? Well, for several reasons. Partly because high-principled philanthropists in the nineteenth century were claiming that the state had a 'moral responsibility' to make the 'benefits of education' available to all people, not just the wealthy. And partly because other legislation was being introduced to give the vote to new sections of the population and it was felt that they should be educated to use it properly.

The main reasons, however, were to do with the social and economic changes that were taking place in nineteenth-century Britain. During the nineteenth century Britain changed from a largely agricultural society, in which most people lived in villages and rural communities, into a society based on industry, factory production, new forms of communication and international trade, and with workers increasingly concentrated into towns near to their places of work. Many of the early arguments about providing education were concerned to produce better, more educated employees with sufficient ability to learn the basic skills they needed for their work. The education that was provided for the masses was intended principally to teach them 'respect for their betters', 'duty to their employers' and to divert them from the kind of 'revolutionary ideas' which were encouraging workers all over Europe to 'take to the streets' in open rebellion against their rulers. The beginning of state intervention in education in the nineteenth century is often referred to as a way of 'gentling the masses'. But whatever the early motivations might have been, once begun, the drive towards universal free and compulsory education could not be checked. During the last 100 years the struggle in education has been to extend educational opportunities and to modify a system which was used to provide one kind of education for the rich and another kind, which was not so good, for the majority. There are still important differences existing today, as we shall see, but a good many changes have taken place over the years, usually as a result of changes in legislation (see Figure 5).

Figure 5 *Development of the education system*

1870 Forster's Education Act set up locally elected school boards to build elementary schools. When he introduced the legislation in Parliament he said, 'Our purpose is to bring elementary education within the reach of every English home, aye, and within reach of those children who have no homes.' At this stage elementary education was neither free nor compulsory.

1880 Elementary education was made compulsory for all children although the law was not always enforced. Parents still had to pay between two and eight old pennies a week in fees.

1891 The Free Education Act allowed most children to receive a free elementary education.

1893 The half-time system was introduced to allow children of 10 or 11 to work half-time at school and half-time in employment.

1899 The minimum school leaving age was raised to 12.

1902 Balfour's Education Act replaced the school boards by local authorities who were also allowed to build secondary schools. The Act did not provide secondary education for all children as many hoped it would. Elementary schools still kept the majority of children from 5 until they could legally leave. Their buildings and facilities were inferior to those of the secondary schools. Their teachers taught larger classes, were paid less, and were less qualified than those in secondary schools. Only a minority of children went on to secondary school and in most cases their parents had to pay fees.

1906 All secondary schools supported by public funds had to provide one-quarter of their places free to children who won scholarships. The rest had to pay fees.

1918 The school-leaving age was raised to 14 and the half-time system was abolished.

1926   The Hadow Report encouraged the idea of transferring children at eleven from one type of school to another, and began the reorganization of all-age elementary schools into junior and secondary schools.

1944   The Butler Education Act raised the school-leaving age to 15 and made secondary education free. Secondary schools were divided into grammar schools, secondary modern schools and technical schools.

1965   The Labour government asked local authorities to submit schemes for reorganization of their different secondary schools into comprehensive schools and the big changeover to comprehensive schooling began.

1967   The Plowden Report on 'Children and their primary schools' recommended 'positive discrimination' (extra financial resources) for schools in poor areas.

1972   The school-leaving age was raised to 16.

1976   70% of secondary school pupils were in comprehensive schools.

The organization of secondary schooling in Britain today

The organization of state schooling in Britain today was largely decided by the Butler Education Act, although it has been modified and added to by some twenty or so Acts since 1944.

The tripartite system

At the time, the 1944 Act was welcomed as a new beginning. Although the Act recognized the principle of 'equality of educational opportunity' it assumed that there were different types of children, with different types of ability, who could be best catered for in different types of schools. It was thought that this ability could be measured by special intelligence tests which should be taken at eleven years old. On the basis of children's results in this '11-plus examination' they were allowed to one of three types of schools. The number of places varied in different areas, but in general the top 15-20 per cent of children passing the 11-plus went to *grammar schools* to follow a highly academic curriculum in preparation for GCE, O-levels and A-levels. The 'less academic' 11-plus passes were sent to *technical schools*, to follow a more practically biased curriculum, based on technical and vocational subjects. The large majority which remained, between 60 and 70 per cent of the school population who failed their 11-plus was sent to *secondary modern schools*, to follow a watered-down version of the grammar-school curriculum, geared to the needs of so-called 'less able' and 'non-academic' children, destined for unskilled and menial employment.

These schools, which together made up the tripartite system, were supposed to offer 'equality of opportunity' to all children, irrespective of their background, to enjoy the type of education most suited to their abilities. Although different, the schools were supposed to have equal status in the minds of the public. In practice, however, the tripartite system came in for a lot of criticism. The grammar schools always enjoyed a higher status than the others and attracted the best teachers, provided the best facilities and offered the best educational opportunities. Technical schools never really got off the ground in many places and, for most children, the only alternative to grammar schools was the local secondary modern. Some secondary moderns were extremely good, and when after 1952 their pupils were allowed to take GCEs for the first time, many of them did very well. But in general, they were seen as 'second-rate' schools with less qualified staff, poorer facilities and limited opportunities for their pupils. In working-class neighbourhoods and poorer areas they were particularly bad in comparison to the local grammar schools.

Another criticism of the tripartite system was the way in which the selection of children for different schools operated in practice. Sociological evidence gathered in the 1950s and 1960s demonstrated again and again that intelligence tests, the 11-plus, streaming and the existence of grammar schools all gave unfair advantages to middle-class children. Working-class children, far from enjoying 'equality of educational opportunity', were much more likely to find themselves in low streams, failing their 11-plus, and consigned to secondary modern schools which tossed them into the labour market at 15 with no qualifications.

Comprehensive reorganization
For all of these reasons, the organization of secondary education in Britain has been modified over the last ten to fifteen years. *Comprehensive schools*, which take in all the children of a given neighbourhood irrespective of their ability and social class background have become the most usual type of school arrangement. Labour governments have always been more sympathetic to the idea of comprehensive schooling than conservative governments. Conservatives represent middle-class voters whose children always did well out of the grammar school system and who could see no advantage for them in replacing grammar schools by comprehensive schools.

Private education
One of the side-effects of comprehensive reorganization has been the increasing tendency of wealthy and middle-class parents to avoid state

education by paying for private education for their children in *public* and *independent schools*. Public and independent schools, unlike state schools, are run without direct government financial assistance or interference. Independent schools have to apply to the Department of Education and Science for registration and are subject to inspection by Her Majesty's Inspectors. They can be refused registration and closed down in certain rare circumstances.

Public schools are even more outside the control of the state. They are run by a governing body created by some deed or trust or religious order, registered as charities and considered to be non-profit making. Entrance to public schools usually takes place at 13 and is decided by an interview and a Common Entrance Examination. In theory, there is nothing to prevent anyone from taking this exam, but since it usually requires a knowledge of Latin and Greek and a recommendation from a private, fee-paying preparatory school, most state-school-educated youngsters would not be eligible. Competition for places is severe and parents have to pay a considerable amount in fees if their children are successful. Many parents plan early and it is well known that boys are enlisted at birth for the top public schools like Eton, Harrow and Rugby. Moreover, sons of former pupils have a decided edge on the others. The schools are not required to publish examination marks or to justify the acceptance of some youngsters rather than others. Some are rejected. Others can secure a place if their parents are prepared to make 'additional donations' to the school funds. Generally speaking, the selection criteria are flexible enough to find room for anyone the schools want to accept. Tyrell Burgess, in his *Guide to English Schools*, estimates that one-fifth or more would never have passed 11-plus scholarships. This has led to the claim that public schools are the *real* comprehensives. In ability, maybe - but in no other way. Public school pupils are, with few exceptions, the children of the wealthy middle class. By being able to pay for education, their parents can ensure that their children are educated with others of the same social class, and are assured of future opportunities and careers which will bring them power, prestige and good salaries.

In 1965 the Labour government set up the Public Schools Commission, under the chairmanship of Sir John Newsom, to advise on the best way of integrating the public schools into the state system of education. The Commission's first report was published in 1968. To the relief of some and the disgust of others, it made no attempt to curtail private education. The position of the independent and public school is even more secure today as competition for places increases. Their continued protection seems to be the compromise that successive Labour governments have been prepared to make with the middle class in exchange for comprehensive reorganization in the state system.

Public school influence

The first report of the Public Schools Commission in 1968 showed that the products of private schools still dominated the important positions in business, the law and the professions, just as securely as they had done in the 1920s and at the end of the nineteenth century, as Table 5 shows.

Table 5 *Public school students*

Category	Date	Percentage (whose school is known) who attend(ed) public schools
14-year olds at school in England and and Wales	1967	2.6
17-year olds at school in England and Wales	1967	9.3
School-leavers (England and Wales) going on to all universities	1965-6	15.6
School-leavers (England and Wales) going to Oxford and Cambridge	1965-6	35.1
Vice-chancellors, heads of colleges, professors at English and Welsh Universities	1967	32.5
Heads of colleges, professors at Oxford and Cambridge	1967	49.3
Labour Cabinet	1967	42.0
Conservative Cabinet	1967	90.9
Labour MPs	1966	19.5
Conservative MPs	1966	76.6
Admirals, generals, air marshals	1967	55.0
Physicians and surgeons at London teaching hospitals and on General Medical Council	1967	68.0
Directors of prominent firms	1967	70.8
Church of England bishops	1967	75.0
Judges and QCs	1967	79.2
Fellows of Royal Society elected	1962-6	24.6
Governors and directors of the Bank of England	1967	76.5

And there is no evidence to suggest that this situation has significantly changed since these figures were collected. Today, as in the nineteenth century and throughout most of the twentieth century, schools are part of a parallel system of education. Now the majority of the nation's children are in comprehensive schools of varying quality run by the state, but a socially significant minority of wealthy children is still enjoying a separate, and many would say a superior, education in the private sector.

The roles that schools are expected to play

If you asked most people what schools are supposed to do in our society, they would probably say, 'teach children subjects like maths, English and geography'. And this is partly true. But schools also do a number of other things which help society to 'socialize' and 'train' the new generation of future adult workers and citizens. These are some of the most important roles which schools are expected to play.

To teach knowledge
In pre-industrial societies the education of children takes place within the family and the village, but as societies modernize and become more complicated the family is no longer capable of educating the children without the help of trained specialists. Schools are therefore set up to teach the information and ways of learning knowledge necessary in a complex industrial society.

To grade intelligence
Schools prepare pupils for a number of examinations which grade them according to how well they do, and provide them with the qualifications necessary for more education and different jobs in the future.

To meet the needs of employment
What goes on in schools is very much affected by the employment needs of the wider society. Indeed, some sociologists believe that the main purpose of schools is to produce the future labour force for our society - not just with the necessary qualifications and skills but also with the kind of attitudes which will allow a capitalist economy to continue. This means providing different sorts of workers for different levels of employment. A few show initiative and leadership and can take up managerial responsibilities or professional occupations. Some can work with intelligence and skill in non-manual and white-collar occupations and will not always need to be supervised. The majority will need to work according to rules and regulations, time-clocks and assembly lines, in unskilled and semi-skilled factory production, or in shops and service industries. If they are to come into contact with the public, their way of relating to other people will be important, but if most of their time is to be spent with machines, tools or in labouring, the most important qualities they will need will be a commitment to hard work and reliability. There

also needs to be a ready source of unskilled labour who can be set to work in bad conditions for low wages and do many of the jobs in industry, public transport, catering and domestic services that others are not prepared to do. In adult life this 'pool of cheap labour' is often made up of women, poor whites and black workers who are set to work or laid off as and when the economy needs them. In times of economic boom more people are needed. In times of economic crisis, unemployment increases.

Explained like this the schools role in producing employees for different levels of production seems rather tough on those destined for lower-status jobs. And though many teachers would argue that, by the use of examinations, these decisions are made purely on merit and intelligence, all the sociological evidence seems to confirm that social-class factors have a great deal of influence in deciding which pupils will be channelled into high-status and low-status jobs.

Although education provides the opportunity for some working-class youngsters to pass examinations, stay on at school and get good jobs in the future, most find themselves doing the same kind of unskilled and semi-skilled jobs that their parents did before them. The increase in white-collar jobs and service-industry employment since the Second World War gives the impression that working-class youngsters who go into these areas of work are 'moving up' in the occupational and class structure. But really, this is more a consequence of a change in the types of jobs they do rather than a significant improvement in their class position.

On the other hand, youngsters from middle class backgrounds in grammar schools, the top streams of comprehensive schools and in private schools will, with few exceptions, find themselves in middle-class occupations and with considerably better long-term prospects than their working-class neighbours.

To help achieve political ends

Schools are often used by the state to put into practice particular social policies. Comprehensive reorganization was certainly intended to remedy some of the failings of the tripartite system but it was also a result of a Labour government's wish to create more equal opportunities in society. The school system in America was used to help bring about racial integration and, at a time when health and welfare was a particular problem in Britain, free school milk, food and medical services were provided in the schools to improve the general health of the nation's children. Some schools in particularly deprived, run-down areas are given more teachers and more money to spend on their pupils than most other schools in the state system. This 'positive discrimination' in favour of poor areas may not do very much to reduce poverty, but it provides another illustration of schools being used by the state to enforce social policies and in this case to relieve social and economic deprivation.

To provide social control

Schools carry on the business begun in the family of teaching children the behaviour, beliefs, attitudes and traditions which are most valued by our society generally. In this sense it is possible to describe schools as exercising social control over children and trying to ensure that they learn the kind of behaviour which society expects of them.

Of course, schools do not 'teach' moral attitudes and social control in quite the same way as they would teach geography or physics, for example. This kind of 'teaching' is part of what sociologists often call the 'hidden curriculum' and is communicated to pupils most subtly through the kind of 'atmosphere' that exists in the school; the rules and regulations which operate; the house points, badges, cups and honours which are given to encourage behaviour that is officially approved of; and the sanctions used against those who do not conform. By learning to abide by school rules and to respect the authority of teachers, pupils are learning the discipline, respect for law and for their superiors that society expects of them in later life.

Again, you may think that this sounds tough, and smacks too much of 'duty and obedience' rather than independence. I am sure most teachers would also argue that they are encouraging their pupils to become independent and thoughtful citizens - prepared to criticize society when it needs criticizing but ready to support society when it needs defending. The privileges and responsibilities given to older pupils, the organization of extracurricular clubs and activities and the chance to 'work on their own' are all part of the 'hidden curriculum' intended to encourage independence and responsibility in pupils. But if it is true that society needs citizens equipped to be justly critical of some of its misdemeanours, schools do not always seem to be the best places to practise these skills. Pupils who do not conform to the rules, and those who question the authority of the teachers, often find themselves in a lot of trouble. And, of course, those who misbehave and present schools with discipline problems are usually treated with little sympathy!

Education and social class

The opportunity for working-class children to receive a full and rewarding education is less likely than for middle-class children, and the key to their very noticeable disadvantage lies in the class structure of society and the kind of role education plays in preserving it.

As we have seen, schools are responsible for preparing people for different levels of employment, thus helping to reproduce the occupational structure of society and in turn the class system. They also teach pupils the accepted values of society. Since most of the powerful people in society are middle class, this process tends to reflect a middle-class point of view. Although individual teachers, and a good many schools, are 'on the side' of working-class children, and try to make their teaching and the school curriculum relevant to the needs and interests of their pupils, schools are by and large middle-class institutions. They are staffed by teachers who may have come from working-class backgrounds originally, but who, because of their education and training, have often adopted middle-class values and attitudes.

Faced with middle-class values, working-class children can be at a disadvantage because their upbringing and their family's view of things is often quite different. It is not that their values and behaviour are worse than middle-class ones, merely different. But since most teachers and schools represent the middle-class point of view, working-class children and their families can be seen as 'inferior'.

There are other factors which affect a child's success at school besides the attitudes of the teachers and the influence of upringing. Take environment, for example. Many working-class children are likely to live on large estates or in poor housing in the older parts of town, where the environment is bleak, depressing, noisy and cramped. Play maybe restricted to bomb sites, occasional playgrounds, dusty roads, terraces and back yards. Middle-class children, on the other hand, are more likely to live in the suburbs where the air is fresh, space is plentiful, and where the roads are often wide and tree-lined. Their houses will be bigger and there will be more gardens, parks and play provision. Educationalists believe that pleasant environments are a real advantage to children when it comes to education. And, of course, schools built in these environments tend to take on the characteristics of the area around them, whereas schools built in poorer areas are likely to reflect the general poverty and drabness of their surroundings.

The waste of ability
A good deal of sociological research in the 1950s and 1960s showed that the potential and ability of many working-class children compared to middle-class children was being wasted in the school system. Middle-class children were more likely to stay on at school longer than working-class children. In the sample shown in Table 6, taken when the school-leaving age was 15, only 16 per cent of upper-middle-class children left school early whereas 77 per cent of lower-working-class children left at 15. And the difference had little to do with their intelligence.

Streaming
Streaming or banding is a system which is still widely used in our schools to separate children into different classes according to their supposed ability. In practice, decisions about streaming are made for a variety of reasons. Sociologists have found that children who speak and dress well, arrive at school punctually and who are well behaved are likely to impress

the teachers and be considered 'top stream material'. Children who do not conform to middle-class standards of dress and speech and whose behaviour is regarded as troublesome are often considered to be inferior in intelligence. In fact, sociological evidence has done a good deal to discredit the view of streaming as being an accurate way of assessing a child's ability, and has shown how it can be very unfair, biased and positively harmful to children who are placed in low streams. Children labelled 'C' or 'D' at an early age are often made to feel inferior to other children. Their reaction is either to give up trying and so become worse and worse, or to rebel against the system which appears to be rejecting them and so become difficult to teach and to control.

Table 6 *Percentage of children leaving school at 15*

Eleven-year test score	Middle class		Manual working class	
	Upper (%)	Lower (%)	Upper (%)	Lower (%)
54 or less	35.6	72.6	80.0	89.3
55-60	12.6	23.4	32.1	40.0
61 and over	0.6	3.4	2.6	12.8
All	16.5	46.4	62.3	77.4

SOURCE: J. W. B. Douglas, *The Home and the School*

Streaming is made worse by the fact that the best and most qualified teachers are usually kept for the best classes, in the same way as the best equipment and school facilities tend to be kept from low-stream pupils. Since streaming seems to reflect the class system in society, low-stream children are in most cases from lower-working-class homes and poorer families. A child who has fallen behind because of social class disadvantages is so often placed in the worst learning situation in school and thus has little chance to catch up.

The self-fulfilling prophecy
Once children are placed in a particular stream and labelled 'A', 'B', 'C', or 'D' they tend to take on the characteristics expected of them, so that the forecasts about their ability when they are put into those streams tend to be fulfilled. A-stream children achieve as A-stream pupils are expected to achieve by their teachers, and D-stream children achieve as Ds. Table 7 shows how children with the same measured ability at 8 years old improved in upper streams and deteriorated in lower streams.

Table 7 *Effects of streaming on children's measured ability*

Measured ability at 8 years	Change in score, 8-11 years *	
	Upper stream	Lower stream
41-5	+5.67	-0.95
46-8	+3.70	-0.62
49-51	+4.44	-1.60
52-4	+0.71	-1.46
55-7	+2.23	-1.94
58-60	+0.86	-6.34

* (+) = improvement; (-) = deterioration.
SOURCE: W. B. Douglas, *The Home and the School*

Comprehensive reorganization

One of the main reasons for introducing comprehensive schools has been to try to prevent some of the worst affects of streaming, the tripartite system and class bias limiting the opportunities of working-class children. Research figures suggest that some working-class youngsters are staying on at school these days and more pupils generally are getting GCE and other qualifications. But, on the other hand, some politicians, some employers and many parents feel that standards and discipline in schools are not as good as they used to be. In 1977 Shirley Williams, the Minister of Education in the Labour government, launched a series of national public debates for teachers, industrialists, parents and the trade unions to discuss the quality of educational provision in British schools. Some thought standards were improving and others thought they were getting worse. Perhaps it is still too soon to judge the success of comprehensive schools. Some have only been in operation for a few years and many suffer a number of disadvantages by being built on split-sites or in poor neighbourhoods with out-dated facilities. A steep rise in youth unemployment in recent years has been another problem for schools to deal with, and of course differences in wealth, occupational choice and social class still operate in the wider society. So there is still a long way to go before schools can hope to provide 'equality of educational opportunity' for all their pupils irrespective of their social-class backgrounds.

Out of school

How often do you hear older people looking back to their school days and regretting the fact that they did not 'work harder' or 'take more interest in the lessons'? But at the time, other distractions often seem more important and interesting to young people - the kind of things that happen to them out of school.

Adolescence

Adolescents have received a good deal of attention from sociologists and others. Adolescence is the time when young people reach physical maturity. Bodily changes make it possible for them to procreate and they begin in size and appearance to look more like adults than children. In some pre-industrial societies young people become adults 'almost over night' and a traditional ceremony is arranged to 'initiate' them into adulthood. In industrialized societies there is more of a time-lag between youngsters reaching 'physical maturity' and being regarded by others, the law and society generally as adults. Consider, for example, the discrepancy between the age when you reach puberty and the age of majority, the age when you can marry and when you can vote, when you can procreate and the age when you leave school. Table 8 shows some other 'age limits'.

Table 8   *Age limits*

Age	Permitted behaviour
13	Buy fireworks Be employed for certain hours of the week Buy a pet animal Be fingerprinted if in custody charged with an offence
14	Be convicted if you are male of a sexual or unnatural offence (also before this age in certain circumstances) Own an air rifle Take part in a public performance without a licence Be held fully responsible for a crime Pawn an article at a pawn shop Play cribbage or dominoes in a room in a pub which is not a bar
15	Possess an assembled shotgun if under the supervision of someone over 21
16	Invest in premium bonds Sell scrap metal Join a trade union Leave school

Age	Permitted behaviour
16	Choose your own doctor Apply for Social Security benefit Work full-time Consent to sexual intercourse (girls) Leave home, with parents' consent Enter, or live in, a brothel Marry, with parents' consent Hold a licence to drive certain tractors, ride a motorcycle and invalid carriage Enter a bar of a pub but not buy a drink unless you are also buying a meal in which case you can order beer or wine
17	Hold a licence to drive any vehicle except certain heavy vehicles Enter a betting shop Buy or hire firearms and hold a licence to possess a firearm Apply for a private pilot's licence Engage in street trading
18	Age of majority Leave home Marry Vote Bring and defend accusations, in court Act as executor or administrator of a deceased person's estate Make a will Change your name Apply for a passport on your own responsibility Buy and sell goods Enter into hire purchase agreements Apply for mortgage Be a full legal owner of house and land Sue and be sued in the courts Go abroad for the purpose of singing, playing, performing or being part of an exhibition without a licence Buy drinks in the bar of a pub Pay adult contributions to National Insurance schemes Sit on a jury Do almost anything an adult can do, *except:*
21	Be a candidate in a parliamentary or local election Hold a licence to drive any mechanically propelled vehicle Hold a licence to sell intoxicating liquor

SOURCE: Nan Berger, *Rights: A Handbook for People Under Age*

For many youngsters this is a period of confusion in which they are expected by some to behave like adults while at the same time others still regard them as children.

In a good deal of the sociological literature and the reports of psychologists, criminilogists and social workers, youths are portrayed as 'troublesome' and as a problem group in society. Many of these adult commentators seem to forget their own youth and exaggerate the significance of what young people do with reports of mass drug-taking, football hooliganism, mugging, punk destruction, sexual orgies, rock festivals, drop-outs, venereal disease, glue-sniffing, vandalism, crime, etc., etc. The sociologist Stanley Cohen calls all of these 'moral panics' and shows how they stress the 'bad' and the 'dramatic' behaviour of young people out of all proportion to their actual significance. They can even provoke trouble by encouraging the police, social workers and magistrates to overreact.

Let us look at some of the characteristics which are said to be typical of young people and their relationships with adult society in Britain today, noting the reservations that ought to be made about such generalizations:

Generalizations

Reservations about generalizations

Generation gap

The values and attitudes of the young are different to those of the older generation. Conflict can occur because neither generation really understands the other.

It is wrong to 'lump together' all young people as part of the same generation and assume that they are all the same as each other. For example, 'gentle hippies' objecting to the aggression and materialism of adult society are very different from punk rockers and boot boys.

Youth culture is classless

Youth culture centred around fashion, music, leisure activities attitudes and behaviour cuts across class barriers. Young people in different classes and different societies have more in common with each other than with other generations.

All young people are not the same even though they may dress similarly, listen to the same kind of music and talk the same language. The social class system in society affects what people learn, who their friends are, how they view things and what opportunities they have. Social class divides and creates differences among youngsters just as much as adults.

Generalizations	Reservations about generalizations
Rebellion and conflict The more traditional moral code by which parents were brought up is now confronted by the influence of the permissive society. Young people are less impressed by authority and likely to be more critical and rebellious than their parents were. They are victims of the mass media and encouraged by films, television and pop music to be irresponsible and permissive in their behaviour.	In fact the influences of parents, schooling and the environment in which youngsters grow up is very strong. Society has changed since their parents were young and new generations have to learn to adapt in new ways, but many share the same experiences and problems as their parents' generation. The majority carry on and develop the old traditions of family work and social behaviour and do not break away.

It is probably best to see the majority of youngsters as just younger versions of adults in our society. The rate of social change makes them open to many more influences than adolescents of fifty years ago and, of course, industry has discovered that teenagers are a lucrative market for the sale of fashions, music, sports and leisure activities. But all of these factors also apply to other generations. As society changes, all generations have new experiences and new adaptions to make. It would be inaccurate to describe these as only affecting adolescents. And so far as the 'moral panics' go - if it is the case that there is an increase in drug-taking, vandalism, crime, etc., we have to ask why this is and what factors occurring in society have led to the increase.

2 Looking at the evidence

The organization of education

Tripartite education

The 1944 Education Act set out to make secondary education universal; and formally it has done so. Yet opportunities for advancement are still not equal.

First, the intention was, since it was recognized that the grammar schools would retain their superior quality and hence their differential advantage as an avenue to the better occupations, to throw open this advantage, by abolishing fees and standardizing entry procedures, to all social classes on equal terms. This aim has not yet been fully realized. The class distribution of the grammar-school population is still markedly askew. An investigation in 1951 showed that the middle class was still heavily over-represented, the upper working class, with one-third of grammar-school places, now reasonably well represented: but the lower working class, with only 15 per cent of places, still heavily underrepresented.[1] And not only do proportionately more middle-class children enter the grammar schools, but once there they do much better. Children from professional and managerial families account for 15 per cent of the total population, 25 per cent of the grammar school population, and 44 per cent of the sixth-form population. 'From the children of [such] parents at one extreme to the children of unskilled workers at the other there is a steady and marked decline in performance at the grammar school, in the length of school life, and in academic promise at the time of leaving.[2]

These contrasts are much larger than can be explained on genetic grounds. No doubt the proportion of high IQ children is greater amongst the middle class than amongst the working class: but given the far higher absolute numbers of the latter, one would still expect them to show significantly better results than they do. The explanation must be looked for partly in social influences – the less educated parents, the more crowded (and noisy) homes, the smaller opportunities for extra-curricular learning, of working-class children: and partly in financial factors - a child continuing at school is still a heavy financial strain on working-class parents, and one which could at least be mitigated, and early leaving thus discouraged, by more generous maintenance payments and an extension of family allowances. But, for the present, equal opportunity is subject to definite limitations.

But the question of grammar school places is relevant only to the above-average child. Matters are much worse when we turn to the average child. The least we can ask for is that all ordinary children, irrespective of social background, should enjoy a good primary and secondary education in decent buildings, with classes of reasonable size, and up to a reasonable age. This the children of better-off parents enjoy in the independent schools. But many working-class children, owing to the appallingly low quality of parts of the state educational system are still enjoying nothing of the sort.

The handicap arises mainly from overcrowding and bad buildings. The deficiencies on these two counts are by now notorious. The Select Committee on Estimates wrote in 1953 that at every point they were confronted with overcrowding, lack of schools, a shortage of teachers, and often rapidly deteriorating and even dangerous school buildings. . . . The condition into which many of the older schools in the country have fallen is the worse feature. Some of them are no better than slums. No doubt matters are gradually - though very gradually - improving and the situation will be greatly eased when the population 'bulge' has finally left the schools in the early 1960s.

But one cannot speak of even an approach to equal opportunity until the average size of class in State schools has been substantially reduced: the 'all-age' schools, which still deny a proper secondary education to over 700,000 children have been reorganized: the black-listed slum schools have been closed down: the many structurally sound but grimly forbidding Victorian Gothic schools in industrial towns have been improved: the school-leaving age raised: and County Colleges opened as envisaged in the 1944 Act.

ANTHONY CROSLAND , *The Future of Socialism*

[1] A. H. Halsey and L. Gardner, 'Social mobility and achievement in four grammar schools', *British Journal of Sociology* (March 1953).
[2] *Early Leaving* (HMSO 1954).

1 What were the main provisions of the Butler Education Act of 1944?
2 Describe in your own words what is meant by the 'tripartite system' of education.
3 What criticisms did Anthony Crosland make about the tripartite system?

Public school education

It is not, in short, the quality of their education alone which first sends the products of the public schools to Oxford and Cambridge and then enables them to become prominent in the upper reaches of government, business and the professions. This owes even more to the fact that they come from a socio-economic elite and that their public school background gives them easy entry to a select world.

It goes almost without saying that the public schools are privileged in terms of staff, equipment and facilities. Whereas the London County Council aimed after the Second World War to provide schools of three and a half acres for up to 1,000 pupils in Inner London (and did not always achieve this ratio), many public schools have half an acre or more for *each child*. Stowe school has 600 boys and 750 acres. In 1967 about 100 independent schools had a teacher:pupil ratio more generous than 1:7.5. In 1968 the ratio in primary independent schools recognized by the Department of Education and Science as efficient was 1:13.0; in independent secondary schools, 1:11.0. This compares with the 1968 figures for council schools -1:27.9 in primary schools, 1:19.1 in secondary moderns, 1:17.9 in comprehensives and 1:16.6 in grammar schools.

It may be, as the Public Schools Commission asserts, that some of the more obnoxious features of public school life are on the way out. According to the Commission corporal punishment and fagging are on the decline, the importance of games has been reduced and 'school spirit' is no longer the thought-controlling influence of the past. The Commission may be right, though a reading of John Wakeford's *The Cloistered Elite* (1969) may leave some doubt on this point. In any case, it is rare for these features of public school life to have been abandoned completely. The public school ethos remains powerful, along with the evils of single-sexed education and the unquestioning assumption that boarding schools (starting at age eight in prep. schools) is the right form of upbringing for our future rulers. Such an education not only leaves the desired mark on those who experience it, but in various ways influences most state secondary schools to try to inculcate similar values in their pupils. For example, the prefect system and the insistence on ridiculous caps perching on the heads of six-foot sixth formers in a 'good' comprehensive school can hardly be seen except as the apeing of the public school tradition.

Education for democracy means that those who are in greatest need should receive the greatest advantages. Our present system, on the contrary, ensures that children - and, in particular, boys - of the wealthiest parents receive a privileged education, an open door to the best universities and professions, as well as an education which remains barbaric in certain respects. An undue proportion of financial and human resources are devoted to a tiny, privileged sector of the school population, while at the same time practices entirely unsuited to a democratic age are perpetuated. Most of these children, as the Public Schools Commission observes, 'would have been away to a good start whatever school they went to'. Our values, in short, are the reverse of what they should be. Without absorbing the independent, and particularly the public schools, into the state system, any talk of education for democracy remains a mockery.

DAVID RUBINSTEIN, 'The public schools', in *Education for Democracy*

Re-read the background information on pages 87–90 to help you with these questions.
1 What is the main difference between public and independent schools and state schools?
2 How are children selected for public schools?
3 Why is it difficult for children educated in state primary schools to be selected for public schools?
4 Suggest reasons why 'one of the side effects of comprehensive re-organization has been the increasing tendency of wealthy and middle-class parents to avoid state education by paying for private education in public and independent schools for their children'?
5 What advantages do they imagine public school education will give their children?
6 Look at Table 5 (page 89).
a What percentage of 14-year old children in the country attended public school in 1967?
b Do ex-public school pupils tend to go to an ordinary university or Oxford and Cambridge? Explain the significance of this.
c What is meany by a 'profession'? Make a list of the top professions in the country. What relationship exists between the public schools and the top professions?
d Suggest reasons why the Conservative party and cabinet have more ex-public school pupils than the Labour party and cabinet.
7 What does Rubinstein mean by the 'public school ethos'?
8 What are Rubinstein's main criticisms of the public school system of education? Give as many reasons as you can to explain whether or not you agree with him.

Comprehensive education
If one can speak at all of any general concept of education propounded by the frenzied campaign for the destruction of our present system and its substitution by a uniformly comprehensive structure, then it is this: the main purpose of education is not the acquisition of learning or skill but the implementation of social change. The advocates of comprehensivization make no secret of their aims: they have long ceased, in the face of irrefutable facts, to argue that a fully comprehensive system would be academically superior to our present arrangements. Their whole campaign is now concentrated on a single issue: the use of education as a means of breaking down the country's social structure and

creating 'equality of opportunity' - which is expected to lead inexorably to an egalitarian, possibly even 'classless' society.

The harmful consequences of comprehensivization for our country's educational standards, its civilization and well-being, have already been exposed. I shall therefore confine myself to an examination of the basic assumptions underlying the comprehensive movement. Is it true that our existing system of education strangthens and perpetuates class divisions and inequality? And would a fully comprehensive system bring about true 'equality of opportunity' for all children, and through it - the egalitarian millenium?

All progressive thinkers agree that our present wicked, inhuman and unjust differentiated system of secondary education is the root, if not of all evil, then certainly of the terrible class conflicts which are - in their inflamed imagination - tearing the country apart. It is 'class-ridden', it leads to the 'perpetuation of occupational and social privilege', it results in a 'waste of intellectual talent among working class children', in short, it is 'divisive'. (I have chosen these quotations at random - they could be multiplied a hundred-fold).

The evil thing must be destroyed. 'If you want equality of educational opportunity', thunders Dr A. H. Halsey, head of the Department of Social and Administrative Studies at Oxford University, 'you have got to abolish this system of privilege.' At times a distinct note of hysteria creeps in. The National Union of Teachers declared to the Commission on Public Schools that 'the social problem posed by the public school was so serious to the community at large that it could not be ignored'.

This simple thesis - that our educational system (a) offers unequal opportunities (b) is grossly unfair, (c) is socially divisive, and (d) should therefore be swept away in favour of a fully comprehensive structure before it is too late - has been repeated so often and at such length that by now it has become practically part of the accepted wisdom. What opposition it meets usually runs along the lines of defending the demands of quality against those of equality (an argument instantly labelled 'fascist').

Let us, however, clarify the term 'equality of opportunity'. It does *not* mean equality of education - rather the contrary, for equality of education would really mean the perpetuation of the social and economic inequality existing outside the school. Whatever the progressive ideologues may think, schools neither create nor preserve social and economic inequality: social divisions are a product of human society, and schools, as creations of the same society, merely reflect these divisions. Education is not and cannot be an instrument of 'social engineering': its purpose is not the establishment of social equality - but it can play an important part in offsetting the effects of existing social inequality. The object of the exercise is *not* to give every child an equal chance; it is to give every child the *best possible* chance to develop and make the most of his own special talents. This can be accomplished only by an *unequal*, differentiated educational system, which levels out the handicap created for the able pupil by the inadequacies of his family's social and economic position.

For generations the English grammar school - the finest institution of mass education in the world - has provided countless gifted working class children with the opportunity to break down the class barriers and achieve unrestricted scope for their talents. Sir Ernest Barker, the miner's son who became one of the most distinguished British scholars of his age, phrased it most movingly: 'Outside the cottage I had nothing but my school, but having my school I had everything.' *This* is true equality of opportunity - equality precisely because it compensates for a deficient background by giving the 'under-privileged' child of ability a privileged education. *This* is the instrument which has guaranteed our working class child an infinitely better opportunity in life, a far greater chance of social mobility, than any other West European country. And *this* is the institution which is now to be destroyed in the name of blind ideological prejudice. To be substituted by - what? Nobody really knows.

Inordinate claims are made for the comprehensive schools. They will rescue children otherwise misjudged at 11-plus from a fate worse than death; they will equalize and extend educational opportunity for all children; they will allow good students to move ahead and encourage the weaker ones to emulate them; they will develop every child's intellectual capacity to the utmost; they will make the best facilities and the finest teachers available to all, instead of a mere 'privileged elite' etc., etc. The fantastical nature of some of these claims is self-evident. But the basic fallacy of comprehensivism is contained in the very essence of the whole concept. A comprehensive school, because it is comprehensive, has to serve a particular catchment area and therefore becomes a neighbourhood school. Since our neighbourhoods are not, on the whole, very mixed socially, neighbourhood comprehensives would inevitably have a far narrower social intake than either grammar schools or direct grant schools. The comprehensive theorists have so far been unable to meet this argument. The notorious Circular 10/65, when laying down the policy for secondary school reorganization, expressed the pious hope that each comprehensive school would have a 'balanced social intake'. How this miraculous consummation was to be achieved remains a mystery to this day.

In plain truth, comprehensives will become one-class schools, with those situated in well-to-do areas creating an inbuilt advantage for their pupils, and the working-class district school offering no avenue for escape to a better education for its abler students. This system will well and truly reinforce and perpetuate class division and class-consciousness.

TIBOR SZAMUELY, in *Black Paper 2*

In June 1973 the NUT and the Campaign for Comprehensive Education carried out a survey of the effects on comprehensive schools when grammar schools still existed in their areas. A sample of one in ten of all comprehensive schools listed as existing in England and Wales was sent a survey questionnaire. 81% of the school heads responded to the questionnaire giving a total of 123 replies. These were some of the main findings.

Aims of the survey
This survey of comprehensive schools was undertaken to find out how many comprehensive schools had to operate in areas where grammar schools, and the 11-plus, were still retained; and of those which did, what their opinions were of the effects, if any, of grammar school coexistence on their ability to carry out their work as comprehensive schools. Just over half the existing comprehensive

schools surveyed (52% of the total) were found to be in coexistence with one or more types of grammar school. In England the figure was three out of five comprehensives operating with grammar schools in their immediate areas.

Loss of able pupils

These coexisting comprehensive schools in the survey were asked to estimate the percentage of pupils 'lost' in their immediate area by 11-plus grammar school selection. The average estimate from all coexisting schools was just over 10% of the local age group. Schools were asked to make a second estimate for the 'loss' of 6th form level. Here the estimated average percentage 'lost' was 24%. The detrimental effect of coexistence for comprehensives is usually thought of as existing at the age of 11-plus; these figures show that an even greater handicap could be at 6th form level.

Did coexistence handicap all comprehensive schools?

Twenty schools (16% of the survey total) claimed coexistence with selective schools did not affect their intakes or work adversely. They were younger schools than schools in the survey as a whole, their average date of first comprehensive intake being only 1969 (as against 1967 for all schools) which means the majority would not yet have experienced a complete five year comprehensive cycle, and fewer still comprehensive sixth forms. Also, more of these schools than of survey schools as a whole were without sixth forms in any case - e.g. were lower tier or short course comprehensive schools.

The handicapped majority

Sixty eight per cent of all coexisting comprehensive schools claimed that they were handicapped in some degree by the continuation of grammar schools in their areas. These 'handicapped' comprehensives were more likely than survey schools as a whole to be in eastern, southern or greater London regions, and much more likely to be in towns or cities than in rural areas. In fact, one out of every two comprehensive schools in a city or a town in England and Wales stated it was handicapped by having to coexist with grammar schools, compared to only one in six of comprehensive schools in rural areas or small county towns.

Two nations

The biggest difference between the 'handicapped' majority and the 'non-handicapped' minority of coexisting comprehensive schools was in the percentage 'lost' to grammar schools, however. The average which 'handicapped' comprehensives estimated they lost at 11-plus was just over 13% (compared to the 'non-handicapped's' 3%), while their average estimated 'loss' at 6th form level rose to the startling figure of 38% (compared to 'non-handicapped's' 4%). If comprehensive schools in areas with 13-plus selection were added (to those with 11-plus selection) the 6th form figure for 'handicapped' comprehensives would rise to 48%. Nearly one in every two sixth form pupils in grammar schools indicates a straight 'two nations' policy in these areas, and is particularly hard for a government to justify which has claimed to be so worried about the economic use of resources at this level.

Types of handicap experienced

The last part of the survey asked those coexisting comprehensives which stated they were handicapped by the retention of grammar schools to say how. A large majority (89%) said: coexistence deprived their schools of high ability pupils and increased their numbers of lower ability pupils: (80%) skewed their social intakes - e.g. deprived them of middle class pupils; (69%) increased the numbers of problem children above the numbers they would normally expect to have to take; (86%) lowered the level of esteem of the school in the community; and (86%) caused many parents of pupils in the comprehensive to think their children had been given a 'second choice' school. A majority (72%) also said 11-plus coexistence limited teacher applications to the school, particularly of specialists; and (72%) resulted in applications from teachers with lower qualifications and less experience than the comprehensive schools felt they would have had without competition from the grammar schools. Nearly three-quarters of the comprehensives (72%) also said coexistence for them resulted in uneconomic size teaching groups in the upper years, and nearly two-thirds (63%) said it lowered staff morale. A minority (47%) felt coexistence affected teacher turnover adversely; resulted in less expenditure (22%) on books and equipment than could have been expected otherwise; and (19%) limited the range of work comprehensive schools could offer.

Degree of effect

Since the survey showed that nearly one-third of all comprehensive schools state they are handicapped in some degree by grammar school coexistence, an application of this figure to the existing population of comprehensive schools (at September 1973 some 2,000 schools with 50% of the 11-year-olds) would mean well over 650 comprehensive schools could now be experiencing the effects of one or more of these handicaps in their efforts to educate the boys and girls in their intakes. This comes to well over 530,000 pupils (more than are at present in grammar schools) or 17% of the total secondary population.

CAROLINE BENN, speech given at 'Comprehensive – not Coexistence' symposium, London, 11 September 1973

1 Explain in your own words what is meant by a 'comprehensive school'.
2 Make a list of Szamuely's main criticisms of the arguments in favour of comprehensive education.
3 How far do you agree or disagree with Szamuely's arguments? Give as many reasons as you can to support your point of view.
4 *a* What were the aims of the survey carried out by the NUT and the Campaign for Comprehensive Education in 1973?
   b How did they gather their information?
   c What is meant by the term 'co-existence'?
   d Why is the 'loss of able pupils' thought to be bad for comprehensive schools?
   e What were the other main 'handicaps' reported by comprehensive schools co-existing with grammar schools?

f Suggest reasons why defenders of comprehensive schools are concerned about co-existence.

Education and opportunity

Social class and parents' attitudes

An eight year old child will greatly be influenced by the attitude of his parents to his school work. His own attitude to his work will be moulded by theirs and, if they are ambitious for his success, he will have the further advantage of home tuition in reading and probably other subjects. Even in the early years at the primary school his performance will show the effects of the support which, as he grows older and the 11+ examination aproaches, is likely to increase in intensity.

The middle class parents take more interest in their children's progress at school than the manual working class parents do, and they become relatively more interested as their children grow older. They visit the schools more frequently to find out how their children are getting on with their work, and when they do so are more likely to ask to see the Head as well as the class teacher, whereas the manual working class parents are usually content to see the class teacher only. But the most striking difference is that many middle class fathers visit the schools to discuss their children's progress whereas manual working class fathers seldom do so. The teachers' contacts with the working class families are largely through the mothers, and this may explain why they become relatively less frequent as the children get older, whereas with the middle classes they become more frequent. The working class mothers have a particular interest in seeing how their children settle in when they first go to school but may feel diffident about discussing their educational progress with the teachers at a later stage; and it seems either that their husbands are not prepared to take on this responsibility, or that they are unable to do so owing to the difficulty of taking time off work to visit the schools.

The parents who make frequent visits to the schools and are seen by the teachers as very interested in their children's education are also outstanding in the use they make of the available medical services. They seldom fail to bring their children to the child welfare centres or have them immunized against diphtheria and other diseases and they are regarded by the health visitors as giving a high standard of care to their children and homes. Their children benefit not only from the support and encouragement they get in their school work but also from the excellent personal and medical care they enjoy at home.

In contrast, the parents who seldom visit the schools and seem to be uninterested in their children's progress make little use of the available medical services, often fail to take their children to the welfare centres or to have them immunized and, according to the health visitors, often neglect their homes and give their children low standards of care. There is a greater amount of illness and school absence among their children, whose work suffers to some extent from this as well as from their parents' lack of interest in their educational progress.

J. W. B. DOUGLAS, *The Home and the School*

1 Explain in your own words the meaning of the '11-plus examination'.

2   What are the main differences described in Douglas between working-class and middle-class parents and the support and encouragement they give their children?
3   Do you agree with Douglas's comments about middle-class and working-class parents? Give as many reasons as you can to support your answer.
4   In what other ways do teachers' attitudes and the environment in which a child grows up affect his or her performance in school?
5   Do you agree that 'working-class children are at a disadvantage in the majority of schools compared to middle-class children'? Give as many reasons as you can to support your answer.

Poor environments

We have ourselves seen schools caught in such vicious circles and read accounts of many more. They are quite untypical of schools in the rest of the country. We noted the grim approaches - incessant traffic noise in narrow streets; parked vehicles hemming in the pavement; rubbish dumps on waste land nearby; the absence of green playing fields on or near the school sites; tiny play grounds; gaunt looking buildings; often poor decorative conditions inside; narrow passages; dark rooms; unheated and cramped cloakrooms; unroofed outside lavatories; tiny staff rooms; inadequate storage space with consequent restriction in teaching materials and therefore methods; inadequate space for movement and PE; meals in classrooms; art on desks; music only to the discomfort of others in an echoing building; non-soundproof partitions between classes; lack of smaller rooms for group work; lack of spare room for tuition of small groups; insufficient display space; attractive books kept unseen in cupboards for lack of space to lay them out; no privacy for parents waiting to see the head; sometimes the head and his secretary sharing the same room; and, sometimes all around, the ingrained grime of generations.

We heard from local education authorities of growing difficulty in replacing heads with successors of similar calibre. It is becoming particularly hard to find good heads of infant or deputy heads of junior schools. We are not surprised to hear of the rapid turnover of staff, of vacancies sometimes unfilled or filled with a succession of temporary and supply teachers of one kind or another. Probationary teachers are trained by heads to meet the needs of their schools but then pass on to others where strains are not so great. Many teachers able to do a decent job in an ordinary school are defeated by these conditions. Some become dispirited by long journeys to decaying buildings to see each morning children among whom some seem to have learned only how not to learn. Heads rely on the faithful, devoted and hard working regulars. There may be one or two in any school, or they may be as many as half the staff, who have so much to do in keeping the school running that they are sometimes too tired even to enjoy their own holidays.

We saw admission registers whose pages of new names with so many rapid crossings out told their own story of a migratory population. In one school 111 out of 150 pupils were recent newcomers. We heard heads explain, as they looked down the lines, that many of those who had gone were good pupils, while a high proportion of those who had been long in the school came from crowded, down-at-heel homes.

We ask for 'positive discrimination' in favour of such schools and the children in them, going well beyond an attempt to equalize resources. Schools in deprived areas should be given priority in many respects. The first step must be raise the schools with low standards to the national average; the second, quite deliberately to make them better. The justification is that the homes and neighbourhoods from which many of their children come provide little support and stimulus for learning. The schools must supply a compensating environment. The attempts so far made within the educational system to do this have not been sufficiently generous or sustained, because the handicaps imposed by the environment have not been explicitly and sufficiently allowed for. They should be.

The proposition that good schools should make up for a poor environment is far from new. It derives from the notion that there should be equality of opportunity, for all, but recognizes that children in some districts will only get the same opportunity as those who live elsewhere if they have unequally generous treatment. It was accepted before the First World War that some children could not be effectively taught until they had been properly fed. Hence free meals were provided. Today their need is for enriched intellectual nourishment. Planned and positive discrimination in favour of deprived areas could bring about an advance in the education of children in the 1970s as great as the advance in their nutrition to which school meals and milk contributed so much.

Children and their Primary Schools (Plowden Report 1967)

1 When was the Plowden Report published?
2 What did Plowden mean by 'positive discrimination'?
3 Why did Plowden recommend positive discrimination?

The effects of mixed-ability teaching compared to streaming

Mixed-ability teaching is the practice used in many comprehensive schools to avoid separating children into different streams or bands. Teaching all children together - clever and stupid - up to the age of 13 gives the slower ones a better chance of taking public exams at 16.

It makes no difference to the maths and reading of any of them when their performance at 16 is compared to that of children who were split into separate ability groups at 11.

Those are the main findings of a study of the effects of so-called 'mixed-ability' classes on children's progress. They appear at a time of heated debate about the merits of such classes. Mixed-ability groups have become increasingly common in secondary schools in the past few years.

When the first material for the study was collected,only one secondary school in 10 taught children in such broad ability classes. When the Schools Inspectorate carried out a survey two years later a quarter of all secondary schools did so.

Conservative Party education spokesmen have promised a ban on such classes in secondary schools except for a brief sorting-out period. They claim that clever children are held back by the slower ones.

The latest survey, a study of 6,000 children, does not support that claim. But nor does it support the claim that teaching all children together helps the slower ones.

The evidence comes from the National Children's Bureau's long-term study of all children born in one week in 1958, and is published in the latest edition of Educational Studies.

The National Child Development Study is one of the most important sources of hard facts about children's progress, since the sample covers children of all social groups and all abilities. They have been studied consistently since birth.

Reading, maths and general ability performances of the survey children at 11 years old were compared with their performance at 16.

No significant differences were found between those whose schools teach all abilities together in the first two secondary school years and those whose schools sort children out by ability into separate streams or separate classes as soon as possible.

Children in independent schools were left out of the survey and so were those who moved school between 11 and 16 or whose school did not produce any clear replies about its streaming policy. As a result the 6,000 are less than half the total sample.

The tests showed that it made no difference either in maths or reading whether the mixed-ability classes were in grammar schools - where by definition the range is much narrower - or in comprehensives.

Nor did it make any difference if the pupils were clever, average or stupid; if they were boys or girls; where they lived; or their social background.

Where mixed-ability classes up to 13 do seem to make a difference is in opening up to less clever children the opportunity to enter public exams. O-level entries were not much affected in England and Wales, because they are mainly confined to cleverer children.

But entry levels for the Certificate of Secondary Education (CSE) in England and Wales and for O-grade exams in Scotland (taken by a much wider range of children than O-levels) were higher from mixed-ability schools.

A further part of the present study which has not yet been published will look at the effects of mixed-ability classes, setting and streaming on behaviour, motivation, self-esteem and aspirations.

AURIOL STEVENS, *Observer,* 12 November 1978

1   What is meant by 'mixed-ability' teaching?
2   What are some of the main problems that can be caused by 'streaming' or 'banding'?
3   Suggest reasons why there is still a 'heated debate' about the merits of mixed-ability teaching compared to streaming.
4   What were the main findings of the study carried out by the National Children's Bureau on the effects of mixed-ability teaching?

Adolescence

The common psychological features of early adolescence include a sensitiveness about appearance, anxiety, a striving for approval and a lack of confidence. There is also an awakening interest in sex, a general restlessness, boredom and dis-inclination to work. But perhaps the most difficult problem of adolescence is the possibility of serious domestic friction within the family.

With the onset of puberty, girls, who only a few months previously showed no interest at all in the way they looked, commonly begin to show an interest in their clothes, hair, shoes, finger nails and general appearance. They become sensitive about what people think of their appearance and are particularly anxious not to appear foolish. They want to dress as their friends dress. They become interested in face powder, lipstick and other adornments.

Adolescents are commonly concerned not only with what people think about their appearance, but about their behaviour. They are anxious to conform with others and not to appear foolish.

It's also characteristic of adolescents that there should be a constant striving for approval. It can lead to some unfortunate consequences. It may lead to smoking, drinking or even drug taking, because the adolescent has not the maturity to realise that, even if it were true that the majority of people smoke, drink or take drugs, there is no need for him to do the same, for he has a perfect right to have a mind of his own. He does not have to follow the crowd. Some go further and in order to obtain the approval of others in a gang, they commit acts of delinquency and get involved with the police.

Restlessness, boredom and a disinclination to work are common features of the adolescent. He feels uncertain of himself. He is confused about the career which he wants to pursue. He may have to work hard for examinations at a time when he is thoroughly enjoying his social life. He tends to be easily bored by his work, his friends and his family. He is also easily tired and day dreaming is characteristic of the age. It is partly bound up with his boredom and with his thought of happier days or more interesting pursuits. All this may lead to premature leaving of school, with the resulting discarding of chances of higher education.

The young adolescent characteristically joins groups of one kind or another — religious groups, political groups, 'campaigns' or social groups. It is part of the desire to conform, but also part of the adolescent's intensity of feeling — about social issues, war and peace, sexual matters — perhaps because he sees so much that is wrong in the world of adults. He feels the burning urge to reform the world — and joins a group of young people who think the same way.

Some degree of awkwardness and clumsiness is common in teenage boys and girls. Mannerisms are common and lead to some embarrassment. For example, blushing with very little provocation is a common feature of this age period. Boys and girls of this age also have emotional ups and downs with rapid changes from laughter to tears; giggling is frequent. Adolescents are particularly sensitive to comments from parents and others and are easily offended, taking everything said as implying criticism. They are particularly likely to be infuriated by parental criticism of their clothes, appearance, hairstyle, or still more, of their friends. Failure of the parents to recognise the sensitiveness of the adolescent is one of the major causes of friction at home.

One obvious reason for friction is the transition from dependence to independence, and the more the parents try to keep control — the more they underestimate the maturity of the teenager — the more rebellious he becomes. Not unnaturally, parents find it difficult to relax discipline, to balance overprotection with unjustifiable carelessness. If they go too far one way, the adolescent rebels; if they go too far the other way, he may get into trouble.

Another source of friction is the difficult behaviour of adolescents. Moody, sulky, quarrelsome and obstinate behaviour are common features and lead to friction with their parents who cannot understand why they should act so. They are apt to be rude, to snarl and snap. They look for faults in their parents, they quarrel with their brothers and sisters. They become furious when teased in the gentlest of ways.

Adolescents want to think for themselves. Previously all decisions were made for them by their parents and now they rebel against this. They rebel against the ways and the thoughts of the older generation and hence adopt fantastic hairstyles and unconventional clothes as a token of rebellion against their elders. This rebellion against tradition may have more serious consequences — sexual licence, illegitimate pregnancy or venereal disease.

Adolecents are now no longer willing to accept all that their parents say as absolute truth. They want to know the reasons for everything. When they were younger they were forced to do as they were told. Now that they are becoming independent they want to think for themselves and they are no longer willing to accept the 'because I say so' approach.

Another source of friction is the choice of a career. Sometimes a boy (or girl) wants to leave school, whereas his parents know that he has the ability to train for some professional career. More often the parents try to force him to take up a career against his wishes or prevent him taking up the career of his choice. Sometimes the parents demand that the adolescent should leave school to earn money when the adolescent wants to stay on.

Who is the Adolescent?, Marshall Cavendish Learning System: Man and Medicine

1   Make a list of the characteristics that are said to be 'typical' of adolescents.
2   In each case explain fully whether you agree or disagree with the writer. Give as many illustrations as you can to support your point of view.

The pros and cons of teenage gangs

This is the age when boys, rather than girls, join 'gangs'. It is the gang which introduces its members to the use of tobacco, and later of alcohol, which will care for him if at first he's overcome by the effects of either. Since the psychology of a group is very different from that of a single individual, the gang may proceed to behaviour which would never be contemplated or tolerated by any single member on his own. The boys are rowdier, more impertinent, harder to control in class, rougher in the playground and tougher outside the school, than any one individual would be. This is because each, when he's with the group, wants to impress the others by his rejection of all rules. He also feels bolstered by the knowledge that he is acting for a number of like-minded friends, rather than for himself alone.

It surprised and shocked Mr and Mrs Pettifer, for instance, to learn that their fifteen-year-old Nick, who had never been any trouble at home, was one of a gang of youths in the neighbourhood which was obstreperous at school, called out dirty words after girls, tore round the country on motor-bikes at weekends, and frequented pubs just outside the immediate area. Nick's parents knew that he went out with friends at weekends, but it hadn't occurred to them that their quiet, shy boy was one of the crowd who weren't absolutely bad, but whose doings seemed quite out of keeping with what they knew of their son's personality. And they were right. The gang wasn't like the Nick they knew, but this was precisely why he needed them. He had to have the support of others who were more daring and more outgoing than he was, before he could venture on any of the things which he wanted to try out.

Although the authorities who have to deal with their exploits may find gangs tiresome, if no worse, they do represent a necessary feature in adolescent life. They provide the reassurance, which the fully fledged adult can't give, that other people are experiencing the same difficulties and can overcome them.

To impress themselves and others, the members of a gang may need to demonstrate their contempt, not only for convention, but also for the law. They will then experiment with soft drugs, possibly with others more harmful, the so-called 'hard' drugs. They will attempt some petty thieving, or help themselves to unguarded property. From this they may progress to robbery with menaces, which often imperceptibly becomes robbery with violence. They will first of all 'borrow' motor-bikes and cars, and later steal them. Their sexual adventures will probably still remain on the right side of the law, but they may be spurred on to more and more dangerous escapades, both in order to impress their girl-friends, and to obtain the cash which must pay for the display they want to put on.

This horrifying picture isn't true of more than perhaps one in every ten thousand 'gangs' of teenage boys. In gangs of girls, where such exist, it is more like one in ten million. Till now – though it is possible that as the roles of the two sexes are felt to be changing and becoming more nearly alike this won't remain true – it has been the adolescent boys who make up by far the greater number of delinquents. What we have to remember is that it is the disruptive, violent, sick gangs, which get into the news and it is from hearing of their activities that we form the picture of 'gangs' as always anti-social, often criminal in their scope. We sometimes forget the innumerable ordinary, relatively harmless gangs, consisting of a group of boys who prefer to spend their time together. There is no need for us to feel anxious about these friendships. The gang members may get up to more mischief together than separately, but basically they will remain law-abiding and responsible.

Often boys from stable homes may join up with a gang about which they don't know much and later discover the extent of its activities to be beyond what is legal or responsible. Most will, at this point, turn back from a mixture of prudence and fear. Others will stay on to get further and further involved. But their case is not hopeless. As long as they have contrived to avoid the dangers of serious addiction to either alcohol or drugs, and provided they have not come into grave conflict with the law, they can still free themselves from what has become a dangerous game. It is the young men and women who are never satisfied with what is offered to them within the conventions and rules of society, who continue to take their revenge by defiance. And most of these people have indeed been shabbily treated.

They come from homes where there has not been enough of anything – not enough love, not enough money, not enough education, good sense, care – to go round. The children have developed in an atmosphere of deprivation and indifference. It is not they, but the social conditions in which they have grown up which should be blamed, if their view of adult independence is that it provides an increased opportunity to pay society back in its own kind.

CATHERINE STORR, *Growing Up: A Practical Guide to Adolescence for Parents and Children*

1   Do you agree that boys are more likely to join gangs than girls? Give full reasons for your answer.
2   Why did 'quiet Nick' need his gang, according to Catherine Storr? From your own knowledge or experience comment upon whether or not you think her interpretation is correct.
3   Who does Catherine Storr blame for the delinquent behaviour of some gangs? How far do you agree or disagree with her? Give full reasons for your answer.

What happens to the girls?

What happens to the girls? At this age it's as if someone has knocked them on the head. At school they have scarcely considered careers other than the traditional nursing, secretarial, or hairdressing. Their apparent maturity has been bought at the high cost of absolute conformity. Among groups of girls of this age any oddness, any irregularity of dress, opinion, enthusiasm or behaviour casts you out of the group. The boys may have their own conventions, but they allow a far wider range of personality to be acceptable within the group.

The girls are so busy pretending to be little women that they haven't time for anything else. At 16 they can pass as adult, while boys are still boys. Because they can get themselves older boy-friends and lift themselves up into an adult world, they are prepared to sacrifice almost all of themselves in the effort. They mimic the outward signs of adulthood most successfully. Their lives are entirely given over to boys: going to discos to meet boys, pop music to fantasize about boys, make-up and hair styles to catch boys, preferably older boys. Interests outside these narrow fields are dangerous, might expose them to ridicule, or might link them perilously with school and childhood.

It isn't until later when they are older and secure in adulthood, that they can afford to allow more of their own individual personalities to grow, but by then it's often too late. By then they are entrenched in traditional female occupations, limited and without chance of promotion.

Whatever it is that happens to children in school between 14 and 16 it happens worse to girls, with the result that they try for and get the worst jobs with the least opportunities.

Plenty of 16-year-olds are late developers who don't show their abilities until later at work. With luck the boys will have gone into a job, however lowly, that could lead somewhere. The girls will almost certainly be stuck in a job with no prospects.

POLLY TOYNBEE, *Guardian*, 19 June 1978

Polly Toynbee argues that teenage girls, more than boys, practise absolute conformity as adolescents and are so busy trying to be 'little female adults' that they fail to develop their own individuality and potential. How far do you agree or disagree with her analysis? Give as many reasons as you can to support your point of view.

3 Questions and answers

Thinking about methods

Sociologists have long been concerned about the relationship between the home and the school in the education of young people. How would you go about finding out either,

a   how much support and encouragement a group of school or college students gets from their home backgrounds, *or*

b   how concerned a particular school or college is about involving parents in the activities that go on and the decisions that are made within it?

Choose either of these questions and, working in small groups of three or four, discuss together the main considerations you would have to take into account if you were trying to answer it. Here are some guidelines to help you:

1   Decide what kind of evidence you would need to answer the question.
2   How you would collect the evidence and what would be the most suitable method(s) of investigation.
3   Who you would approach to give you the evidence you need.
4   What kind of questions you would ask.
5   How you would analyse the evidence and present it as a response to the question you set out to answer.

Checkpoints

1   What was the importance of the Forster Education Act in 1870?
2   When did elementary education become *(a)* free, and *(b)* compulsory?
3   When was the tripartite system established?
4   What is a 'preparatory school'?
5   What was the Public Schools Commission?
6   What aspects of the education system were studied by the Plowden Report?
7   What is meant by the term 'co-existence'?
8   Why is the term 'adolescence' rather difficult to define?
9   At what age are youngsters considered by law to be 'fully responsible' for any crimes they might commit?
10 When is the age of majority?

O-level questions

1   'During the 19th century ... public concern with elementary education was ... the need to ensure discipline, and to obtain respect for private property and the social order, and that kind of instruction which was indispensable in an expanding industrial and commercial nation.' (D. Glass, *Education and Social Change in Modern England*)
    What are the functions of education in the United Kingdom today?
2   What is the difference between a tripartite system of secondary education and a comprehensive system? Outline the sociological evidence about the advantages and disadvantages of each system.
3   To what extent has your study of sociology helped you to understand secondary education in Britain?
4   'Innate ability is not always the most important factor in producing high achievement at secondary school.'
a What kind of evidence is there to support this statement?
b State what other factors are also important and discuss them briefly.
5   'All children can gain from nursery education but it is particularly valuable for children whose home and life are restricted, for whatever reason. While the government's aim is that nursery education should be widely available within ten years for children of 3 or 4, priority will be given to areas of disadvantage.' (*Education, a Framework for Expansion*, Government White Paper 1972)
a How has your study of sociology helped you to understand the meaning of 'whose home and life are restricted' and 'areas of disadvantage'?
b Comment on the proposals in the passage in the light of the available evidence concerned with the relationship between home and school.
6   'But if our investment in education is adequate to fulfill the purposes of education we get a long term return on our money that is second to no other investment.' (M. Hutchinson and C. Young, *Educating the Intelligent*)
    What are 'the purposes of education'?
7   A primary school situated in the 'twilight area on the fringe of the city' contains 300 children aged seven to eleven. The headmaster is quoted as saying, 'Only one in every hundred of my pupils stands any chance of going to university. . . . There are two nations when it comes to education. . . . That is not the school's fault or the fault of local education authorities.' (Adapted from the *Daily Mirror*, 12 April 1973)
a To what is the headmaster referring when he talks about the 'two nations'?
b What sociological explanations can you give for these apparent inequalities in the education system?
8   The importance of the relationship between home and school becomes

clearer as the child gets older.'
   What sociological evidence exists to support this statement?
9 Why do advanced industrial societies have schools and colleges?
10 Explain the meaning of any three of the following terms/ideas used in the sociological study of education:
a self-fulfilling prophecy
b parity of esteem
c positive discrimination
d equality of opportunity
e meritocracy
11 Why are youths so often portrayed as a 'problem category' in sociological literature and the press?
12 Sociological studies of youth culture often forget to mention social-class considerations. What effects does this have on such studies?

Unemployment Benefit Office

Open 9 To 4 Monday To Friday

New Claims And Enquiries – Entrance A
Signing Section – Entrance B

Department Of Employment

ENTRANCE
C →

RESERVED

5 The welfare state

1 Background information

A look at the past

A hundred years ago in Britain the general care and welfare of people in society was largely the responsibility of their families. If they were wealthy they had a better chance of being well fed, well clothed, living in a decent house and doing less arduous work than poorer members of society. They could expect to live longer, stay healthier and get medical help if they were ill. For the poor, however, life was short, hard and depressing. In 1899 Seebohm Rowntree made his first historic survey of working-class poverty in York. He found 20,302 people, or almost half the working-class population, living in a state of poverty without enough food, fuel and clothing to keep them in good health. About one-third of those living in poverty did not earn enough money each week to keep their families, the rest could only barely survive.

Ten years earlier Charles Booth, a Liverpool shipowner, had made a similar survey in London and found that roughly one third of its population earned less than £1 a week. These conditions were not confined to the towns. A few years later Rowntree discovered that farm labourers were in an even worse position. Needless to say, living conditions for these people were appalling. Many lived in dark, damp rooms without basic amenities. In the slums dustbins and lavatories were often to be found in the same brick-lined pit which Rowntree described as 'inches deep in liquid filth, or so full of refuse as to reach above the cemented portions of the walls'. And most of them were shared by several families.

In these conditions one child in four died before it was a year old. A meagre diet, shoddy clothing and no money for doctors' bills meant that those who lived were often deformed or decrepit at an early age.

The welfare state

Today the situation is much improved – although poverty still exists as we shall see later. The main difference, however, is that it is now considered to be everyone's responsibility through the provisions of the state, to make sure that essential services like education, housing, medical treatment and financial support for the old, the sick and the unemployed, are available for all citizens.

The money needed is collected in taxes and other financial contributions and used by the state to provide welfare facilities and financial benefits for everyone to use. The actual term 'welfare state' came into existence about thirty years ago and since then it has come to mean different things to different people. Its critics see it as a way of 'interfering in the lives' of ordinary men and women. Others blame it for taking money from the rich and redistributing it to the poor and the lazy. Those who support it, on the other hand, stress that it provides a measure of security for all and contributes to a more equal society.

In practice, however, the continued existence of the welfare state depends a great deal on Britain remaining a wealthy country. In recent years the economic crisis affecting Britain's prosperity, trade and industry has had important repercussions on the welfare state. Reductions in spending and the attempt to save money by cutting back on welfare state services has been a controversial policy and reminded people that however much they have come to expect welfare state benefits they cannot be entirely taken for granted.

The organization of the welfare state

The main responsibility for organizing the social and welfare services that make up the welfare state lies with central government. Different departments are responsible for different services, as Figure 6 shows.

Each department has overall responsibility for the services in its care. It does not administer all of them itself – some are administered nationally by central government departments, others are organized locally by local authorities (see Figure 7).

Local authorities are still responsible to and advised by national government, but they have a good deal of local independence from government control and this means that the standard of services often varies from one authority to another. Figure 8 shows the services they provide.

Charities and voluntary organizations

Charities and voluntary organizations are not part of the welfare state but exist as independent organizations with their own governing bodies and ways of raising money. Some voluntary organizations, like the NSPCC or Dr Barnardo's, complement the work of the welfare state and

Figure 6 *Government departments providing welfare services*

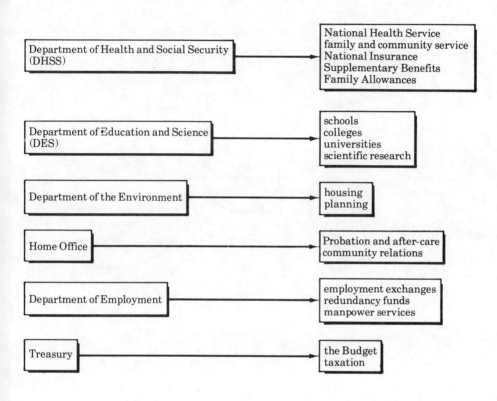

Figure 7 *Administration of government services*

Centrally administered services	Locally administered services
National Insurance	Education
National Health Service	Housing
Universities	Planning
Supplementary Benefits	Public health
Family Allowances	Family and welfare services
Probation service	
Employment services	

Figure 8 *Local authority services*

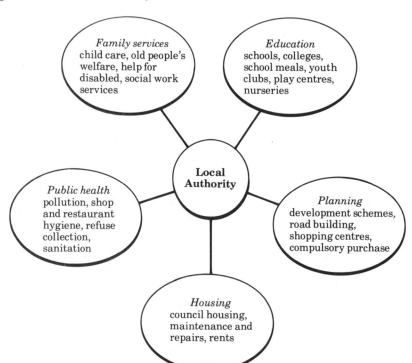

many people argue that a comprehensive system of welfare services would not exist without their contribution. Others, like the Child Poverty Action Group and Shelter (the campaign for the homeless) act as pressure groups (see page 240), pointing out the weaknesses and deficiencies of the welfare state and trying to persuade governments to do more for the particular disadvantaged groups they represent.

Where the money comes from

Each year the various services provided by the welfare state have to be paid for. The government collects the necessary money from three main sources – taxes on income (for example, income tax, surtax, capital gains tax, corporation taxes), taxes on expenditure (for example, customs and excise duties and VAT) and National Insurance contributions. At a local level rates (taxes paid by owners of houses, office blocks, shops, factories and warehouses) are paid to the local authority to meet the costs of local services.

Definitions of social welfare

Initially the definition of social welfare owed a great deal to the Victorians. It was mainly concerned to provide financial help and to ensure a 'basic standard of living' for everyone. Often stigma and shame were attached to those claiming state benefits. The 'undeserving poor' were depicted as feckless and lazy, while the 'deserving poor' were pitied and seen as being in need of charity. Today social welfare and its various institutions are a part and parcel of society and most people now believe that welfare services are the right of every citizen. In any one week over one-quarter of the population receives social service benefits and allowances of one kind or another – and this is without taking family allowances, employment benefits and pensions into account. In other words, most people at some point in their lives are likely to need help to meet the various crises and conditions which happen to them and with which they cannot cope entirely by themselves or within the family.

But although social welfare is now a much more accepted part of life than it was – it still carries a stigma in a few people's minds. Some people, especially the older generation, hark back to times when welfare benefits were a form of charity. And of course the mass media in recent years has done a great deal to exaggerate the irresponsible and work-shy behaviour of those they label 'welfare scroungers'.

The growth of the welfare state (Figure 9)

The foundations of the modern welfare state were laid by a Liberal government between 1906 and the outbreak of the First World War (see page 124). The principle of social benefits being provided for by graded taxes on incomes (in other words, the more you earn, the more you pay) and National Insurance contributions were established primarily by the Liberal Chancellor of the Exchequer, Lloyd George.

Between the world wars

This was the period of the Depression, during which time unemployment reached dramatic proportions and workers in the traditional industries of mining, iron and steel, shipbuilding and textile production found themselves out of work for months and years on end. Unemployment benefits were paltry and inadequate and were repeatedly cut back as economic conditions got worse. Apart from unemployment, housing was also a terrible problem. In 1918 Lloyd George had promised 'homes fit for heroes to live in' but for many people these were never to be. These and other bad conditions made both politicians and voters demand a new approach to social welfare provision.

Figure 9 *The early Liberal reforms*

Child welfare		By 1906 some local authorities had already set up child welfare centres and milk dispensaries for poor mothers.
1906		Local education committees were enabled to provide meals for needy schoolchildren.
1907		Local education committees were compelled to have schoolchildren medically inspected.
Young offenders 1908		The Borstal system was set up. Imprisonment was prohibited for children under 14 and limited for those between 14 and 16.
Old age pensions 1909	 5s	A non-contributory pension of 5 old shillings a week was given to people over 70 whose income was not more than 10 shillings a week. A married couple living together received only 7 shillings and 6 pence.
1909		Labour exchanges were set up throughout the country.
The National Insurance Act 1911 Part 1 Health	+7s	Workers earning less than £3 a week were provided with free medical attention, free medicine and sick pay of 7 old shillings a week. For this purpose they and their employers paid compulsory contributions which were added to by the state.
Part 2 Unemployment	+7s	Contributions collected from workers and their employers, and added to by the state, provided 7 shillings a week unemployment pay for fifteen weeks in any year. This at first applied to only a few industries.

The Beveridge Report

In June 1941 the government ordered a special committee, under the chairmanship of Sir William Beveridge, to make a thorough investigation of all 'the existing national schemes of social insurance . . . and to make recommendations' about how they might be improved. The committee's report, published in 1942, changed the whole way in which the state provided social welfare benefits and became the basis of the government's policy after the Second World War.

Beveridge proposed a comprehensive system of social insurance to which all citizens contributed. Everyone over school-leaving age and below the age of retirement, except students in full-time education, non-working wives, and self-employed people earning less than a specified minimum, had to pay a weekly contribution which was recorded by a stamp on a special card. Employers paid a part of their employees' stamp and men had to pay more than women. In return for these contributions, benefits were paid out to all citizens if their earnings were stopped by sickness, unemployment or retirement. The post-war Labour government put this scheme into operation with the National Insurance Act of 1946.

Legislation

In 1945 the Family Allowances Act was passed which gave an allowance of five shillings for each child after the first, up to the age of 16, or until he or she started work. The original amount, of course, has increased over the years. The cost of family allowances was not based on insurance contributions – the entire cost came out of taxation and any family could benefit regardless of its income.

In 1948 the National Assistance Act was passed to provide help for those who could not be expected to pay national insurance contributions because they were blind, deaf, crippled, insane, disabled, unemployed widows or the wives and children of criminals. The Act established a National Assistance Board which among other things had to provide Reception and Re-establishment Centres for the homeless and old people's homes. In 1953 one-quarter of the people living on retirement and widow's pensions could not manage without the additional help of the National Assistance Board. In 1966 the Board was merged with the Ministry of Pensions and National Insurance and is known today as the Department of Health and Social Security.

The National Health Service Act was passed in 1946. From now on the whole range of medical, dental, optical and hospital treatment was to be provided free to everyone. Those who wanted to continue paying for medical treatment could still go to doctors, dentists and opticians working in private practice but it was hoped that the state health service would be so good that everyone would want to make use of it.

All the teaching hospitals were nationalized and a national system of general practitioners was provided so that health service doctors could be available everywhere in the country. Local councils were to provide midwives and health visitors, ambulances and facilities for vaccination and immunization. As you can imagine, this was one of the government's most ambitious Acts and it was not passed without a good deal of opposition. Two months before it was due to come into effect, two out of every three doctors voted against joining the National Health Service. Some wanted to protect their private practices and others objected to state interference in their profession. The government refused to give way on any of the major points of the Act but they made one or two small compromises which proved enough for a few more of the doctors to change their minds.

Despite increases in government funding over the years the National Health Service has proved a costly service to maintain. The original idea of a completely free service has proved impossible to achieve in practice. Patients now pay varying charges for their prescriptions, glasses and dental treatment, although medical advice and hospital treatment is still free. Private medicine still flourishes for those who can afford it, but crowded surgeries, long waiting lists and hospital closures remind the rest of us of the serious economic problems faced by the Health Service today.

The appointed day

5 July 1948 was the 'appointed day' on which the welfare state in Britain was officially considered to be established. In explaining the new services to the nation, the prime minister, Clement Atlee, warned that the quality of the services would depend on the amount of money which the country could afford to spend on them. It was therefore important for everyone to work hard, he said, because the 'general level of production settles our standard of material well being'.

Definitions of poverty

In Rowntree's study of poverty in York in 1899 he divided people living in poverty into two groups: those who did not earn enough to meet their physical needs, and those who did earn enough to keep their families but who 'used' or 'wasted' some of their earnings on other things. For Rowntree the important thing was to be able to measure accurately which people were living in poverty and which were not. He thought we could do this by drawing a 'poverty line'. Those who fell below the line were poor, those who fell above the line were assumed to be all right.

Absolute poverty

He calculated where the absolute poverty line should be drawn by estimating the minimum amount of money a family of four would need each week to spend on food, fuel and clothing. In 1899 he decided that such a family in York would need 94½p plus rent to meet its basic requirements and keep it above the poverty line. But his calculations left no room for manoeuvre. Meat was thought to be a 'luxury' and so it was not taken into account. Other 'luxuries' like a cup of tea or a pint of beer or a ride on a bus were not taken into account either. If people wanted to 'use' or 'waste' their money on these things, they had to do it by going without food.

Rowntree's method of calculating the poverty line was adopted by Beveridge in his recommendations to the government in 1942. His calculations were based on figures for 1938 and on the strength of them he recommended that £1.60 was the basic amount necessary for a husband and wife to live on, with an average of 35p for every additional child. It has been this method of measuring people's 'minimum needs' that has been the official way of deciding on National Assistance and Supplementary Benefits ever since.

Many people are critical of this official and arbitrary way of deciding where the poverty line should be drawn, however, and of the assumption that it represents the point at which poverty begins. It seems unfair to expect the poor to live on a carefully controlled budget which takes no account of the extras like holidays, leisure activities and household emergencies which the rest of us take for granted. Current Supplementary Benefit rates are not very generous either, despite some press reports of 'welfare scroungers living in the lap of luxury'. Over the years they have stayed fairly constant at about 29 per cent of average earnings. Also the rates take very little account of real costs. Inflation (rapidly rising prices and a fall in the value of money) over the last few years has made any increases worthless in practice.

Relative poverty

The main problem with the poverty line, and its absolute definition of where poverty begins and ends, is that it is based solely on income, and takes no account of other features of life. In Britain today the richest in the population earn forty times as much as the poorest, those on Supplementary Benefits from the welfare state who receive less than one-third of the national average wage. Some families on low wages would be actually 'better off' on state benefits! Given this kind of situation, critics feel that an absolute poverty line disguises the many facets and the real extent of poverty in Britain and fails to recognize the kind of impoverished lifestyle which many people endure compared to more advantaged groups. For in reality, poverty is also the lack of good schools, being without a decent house to live in, a noisy and depressing environment, inadequate play space, the lack of the material possessions which other people take for granted and bad working conditions. Compared to the people who do not experience any of these things, those who do are poor. And so long as some individuals have very high incomes, vast amounts of wealth, countless possessions and a full range of opportunities in life, those who do not are relatively poorer by comparison. For these reasons many critics prefer to describe poverty in relative and comparative terms rather than attach much significance to the official poverty line.

Affluent Britain?

In 1959 a Conservative government was returned to power for the third time in succession with a large majority in Parliament. The election slogan chosen by the Conservatives was 'You've never had it so good'. The prime minister, Harold Macmillan, speaking in Manchester, confirmed that three million people a year were taking continental holidays, home ownership was rising and one family in three now had a motor car. So far as the politicians and many social commentators of the time were concerned, Britain was becoming an affluent middle-class country in which poverty was a thing of the past.

Housing

Despite claims to the contrary, the increases in home ownership only affected certain sections of society, however, for the majority of working-class people, council lettings provided by the state were still the main type of accommodation. The early philosophy of council housing was based on the notion that it was everyone's 'human right' to have a decent house to live in, and building homes 'fit for heroes' after the two world wars was claimed as a priority. But the supply of good housing has never been able to meet the needs of the people and this has been largely because financial considerations rather than housing needs have been the main influence on national and local government decisions.

During the thirteen years of Conservative rule between 1951 and 1964 the post-war vision of 'council housing for all' was replaced by a policy encouraging 'owner occupation' for those who could afford it and patching up old property or leaving the problem of housing the vast majority of working-class people to private landlords. The Labour government of 1964 also advocated 'owner occupation' as the goal of 'a long term social advance which should gradually pervade every region'. They returned to power committed to building half a million houses a year, at least half of which would be privately owned. So far as council housing went, the aim was to build fast and to build cheaply.

In practice this meant a vast increase in 'factory-built' houses and high-rise accommodation. Between 1964 and 1972 over half of local authority building was in the form of flats. Some were four storeys high which could be built without the added expense of lifts, but most were multi-storied. In addition, by 1968 the proportion of factory-built houses had doubled to 42 per cent. The large building firms benefited most and made huge profits out of contracts with various local authorities. Having developed methods of erecting houses in three or four days from pre-built sections, they sought contracts from local authorities committed to slum clearance and redevelopment for ongoing and massive building programmes.

Humanized planning, landscaping and adequate amenities were ignored in the 'overnight' construction of mammouth estates and high-rise 'concentration camps'. Not only were the socially bad effects of these soon to become apparent in the signs of depression, isolation and aggression displayed by the people consigned to them, but also the cheapness of the materials used and the shoddy ill-constructed buildings soon showed plenty evidence of damp, condensation, structural weaknesses and all the visible symptoms of newly created slums.

By 1968 the building boom was over. An economic crisis that year brought cuts in public spending which were soon to become very familiar and as in more recent times the housing programme was the first to suffer. Doctrinaire and fatal cuts were applied with special gusto by the Conservative councils returned to power in the 1967 local elections, who also capitalized on the familiar prejudice that 'council house tenants were enjoying the subsidy of hard-working ratepayers'.

When the Conservatives were returned to Government in 1970, private building was further encouraged while by 1973 local authority building had reached its lowest output since 1947. At the same time as the private property market was booming, largely to the advantage of the speculators, builders and estate agents, local councils were being encouraged to sell off their council houses to private buyers. No doubt this moved some more affluent workers into the category of 'owner occupiers', but it reduced the numbers of houses available for rent by the rest. The majority of working-class people still depend on renting and are in no position to contemplate buying their own house if insufficient council property is available.

As the economic problems of the 1970s got worse and public spending cuts increased, the provision of houses to satisfy housing needs were again subject to financial considerations. And as with other public spending cuts, those who were homeless or in the worst housing conditions had the most to lose from cuts and delays in building programmes.

Rediscovering poverty

During the early 1960s the government set up a series of commissions to investigate various aspects of life in Britain, for example, London housing (Milner-Holland), children and young people (Ingleby), primary education (Plowden), and the personal social services (Seebohm). One after the other, the reports emphasized 'areas of bad housing', 'deprived neighbourhoods' and 'families in special need'. The picture that emerged was a challenge to the complacency of Britain's affluent image of itself in the 1960s. Poverty obviously still existed and life for many families in Britain was a persistent struggle to make ends meet and a hopeless battle against appalling housing and terrible environments. And the figures suggested that the problems were much more widespread than the recent politicians had chosen to recognize.

In 1964 the Labour Party took over government and began a series of initiatives designed to reduce poverty. Its first move was to alter the rate support grant (money given by central government to add to the rates collected by local authorities and used to spend on local services). The change in policy meant that some local authorities with fewer resources were given more government aid than others. In 1968 the Urban Aid Programme was launched to give grants of money to voluntary and statutory organizations working to improve the education, housing, health and welfare of groups living in areas of special need.

Educational Priority Areas were recognized as a direct consequence of the Plowden Report and schools in these areas were given extra staffing and financial resources. In 1969 the Home Office set up the National Community Development Project and placed small teams of community workers and researchers in twelve deprived areas of Britain like Benwell in Newcastle, Saltley in Birmingham and Canning Town in East London. Their brief was to organize 'a neighbourhood-based experiment aimed at finding new ways of meeting the needs of people in areas of high social deprivation', and they were given the promise of more government spending and expansion once their recommendations had been reported.

In practice these and other government attempts to reduce poverty proved generally ineffective. In terms of government spending the positive financial discrimination available was always insufficient to meet the real extent of the problem. Taken together the various schemes never cost the government any more than £10 million a year after 1968. A lot of publicity was given to them and many people were led to expect great achievements. But some project workers, especially in the Community Development Projects, became very disillusioned by the extent of the task they were expected to undertake compared to the minimal resources they were given to do it with.

The economic crisis of the 1970s, together with inflation and the increase in unemployment, put paid to any notions of additional funding. In fact, public spending cuts became the order of the day and the welfare state had to face a new challenge.

Cutting the welfare state

The recent history of the 1970s has been one of serious economic difficulties for Britain. Unemployment has reached levels unheard of since the Depression and inflation has produced serious problems for successive governments to deal with. Understanding Britain's economic crisis is no simple matter. There are many national and international factors involved as well as the more obvious industrial ones. One of the main solutions the government has chosen to try, besides encouraging industry to expand and workers to restrict their demands for higher wages, has been spending less on social and welfare services.

The cuts began in 1973 under the Conservative government led by Edward Heath, but the same policies were continued when the Labour government came to power in 1974. In November 1973, for example, the Conservative government cut £111 million from the National Health Service budget. In 1976 the Labour government reduced it by a further £75 million and limited its future increases to 10 per cent a year. At a time when the yearly inflation rate was 25 per cent an increase of 10 per cent could not keep pace and proved, in real money terms, to be yet another cut in the money the Health Service has to spend.

In housing it was the same story. The cost of building and maintaining council houses rises every year with increases in the value of land, higher interest rates on the money borrowed by local authorities, and the cost of materials and building. The fact that councils have to compete with private developers adds to the problem. The consequence is that fewer new houses than are needed get built. Their quality is reduced and their rents are higher. Add to this local government's need to economize and cut public spending on, for example, repairs, maintenance and improvements, and you can see why council waiting lists grew in the mid 1970s and the quality of the housing they provided deteriorated considerably.

Money spent on education represents about 17 per cent of public spending each year. Some of it goes on capital expenditure (new schools, building improvements, furnishings, etc.) the rest on running costs (teachers' wages, heating and lighting, etc.). Between 1972 and 1975 capital spending on education fell by one-third, plans to build new schools or develop nursery facilities were cancelled and many old schools were denied their promised improvements. The next area to suffer was running costs. In 1975 the government issued a circular (no. 10/75) to all local authorities advising them about what had to be cut and where economies had to be made. Here were some of their instructions:

1   In large urban areas with falling populations teaching staff were to be reduced.
2   In higher education steps were to be taken to alter staffing ratios.
3   In primary education those local authorities which had recently allowed 4 year olds to be admitted full-time to ordinary infant classes had to review their policy in the interests of economy. Four year olds were not to be admitted unless they made no additional call on educational resources.
4   Maintenance was to be neglected. Standards of material provision and upkeep of premises had to remain below the level generally accepted as desirable in the recent past.

5 There was to be no scope for increased expenditure on the rest of the education service including the youth, recreation and community services or in the library and museum services.

It would be nice to explain away these cuts as merely a means of reducing unnecessary waste and making the services of the welfare state more economical and efficient. But all the evidence suggests that each year *more* money is required to maintain the *same* level of services, never mind improve upon them. When cuts are made the quality of the services suffer. This obviously affects to some extent, the quality of everyone's life, but more particularly those who are already poor, infirm, elderly or disadvantaged.

2 Looking at the evidence

Persisting poverty

From 1960 to about 1965 the British believed that something had happened which had never existed in all the world: there were no more poor. But even then there were a couple of million of them and their number was growing. Today conditions are normal again. There are a great many poor people, and we all recognize the fact. The fantasy is over.

When people talk about the poor, there is always a problem of definition to be got over at the start. What does 'poor' mean? Are we talking about people in 'absolute' poverty, like those who die in the streets of Calcutta, or are we talking about 'relative' poverty, in which the poor are rich by the standards of many countries, and only poor in relation to the rest of society in this country?

All poverty is relative. It's no use objecting that almost all the British poor would be rich in other countries. They don't live in them, they live here. And to reassure the sceptic, there are indeed some truly poor people too - like Rosie Bell who lived in a shack at Riverfields, Glen Faba, Essex, without heating, running water or sanitation. She died of starvation in 1970 and lay for days beside her husband who was too ill to move.

By what standard should we measure poverty? The simplest is the State's own - the level of Supplementary Benefit. By this standard there are some 5 to 7 million poor people in Britain, or between 1 in 10 and 1 in 7 of the population. What does it feel like to be poor? The money you get, either from earnings or from the government, is at best supposed to cover food, rent and a minimum of clothing. But the allowance is sparse. You live at least two to a room. Your kitchen is likely to be in your sitting room - which is also your bedroom. It will be dirty, ugly, small and dark, for you can't afford to decorate it and it is too crowded to clean properly. All the furniture you own is second-hand, scuffed and doesn't match. Nine months of the year your home is cold and damp. You wear lots of clothes, if you have them, and you heat it with paraffin heaters. These often tip over and set the house on fire, with considerable loss of life. You have no garden to grow flowers in, or to keep the neighbours at bay..There are no parks or open spaces in your part of town, so your children have to play in the street where they are not infrequently knocked down.

Because you have so little money, you have to buy food in small quantities. Since you can't afford to move about to search out shops, groceries in your area cost more than in middle class parts of town, and the quality isn't so good. If you want hot water you have to boil it by the pint on the stove, and it costs a good deal more than hot water out of a geyser, which again costs more than hot water out of a central heating system. It costs a lot of money to decorate your home because you can't – and the landlord won't – paint the walls, mend the gutters, repair the drains. So the walls run with damp, and the paper you painstakingly put up today – if you bothered – will be lying rotting on the floor in a couple of months time.

Because you live in a slum and cannot move anywhere else, and you're at the bottom of the council waiting list, the rent you pay is absurdly high. The money you pay in London for a couple of slimey basement rooms will buy a middle class secretary a share of a large airy flat a few blocks away. The landlord should take advantage of the government's renovation grant to make the place fit to live in. But since he already gets the maximum possible rent from you, any money he spends on improvements is money wasted. The only people who take up improvement grants are middle class people doing up slum houses for themselves.

You seldom leave this unpleasant environment because you haven't the money to take a bus or train. You have no holidays. You read few newspapers. You buy no books, you have no gramophone, you buy no records. You never go to the cinema or the theatre. Apart from the more popular television programmes, the cultural life of the twentieth century might never have been.

PETER LAURIE, *Meet Your Friendly Social System*

In an apparently affluent age why does poverty still exist?

One reason, of course, is that poverty is a relative concept. The poverty line has been pushed up as everybody's standard of living has improved. If, for example, supplementary benefits had only been tied to keep pace with price rises since the start of the welfare state in 1948, an unemployed married couple today would only be receiving £10.65 instead of £20.65. And unlike the 1930s, most welfare claimants today possess some consumer durable goods – a radio, television set, and usually an electric iron. But although today's poor may look well-off compared with yesterday's destitute, only the blinkered bigot can believe that the life of a welfare claimant today is a comfortable ride.

Surveys have shown that about two-fifths of sick and disabled claimants and three-fifths of unemployed claimants have stocks of clothing which fall below the strict guidelines the commission uses in deciding whether to make discretionary payments. In other words, about half the country's claimants have insufficient clothes. And contrary to popular myth, the money has not been thrown away on postwar luxuries. Fewer than one in 30 has a telephone and two out of three have neither vacuum cleaners, sewing machines, or record players. Far from cutting welfare expenditure we should – as the Supplementary Benefits Commission has urged – be increasing it. Recent statistics released by the European Commission put Britain second from the bottom – above only Ireland – of the nine member league on social spending (as a proportion of net national income).

The pattern of poverty remains similar to Rowntree's day with three of the biggest groups being the old, the unemployed, and the low-paid. This marks a reversal of the progress made in the immediate postwar period. In 1948, for example, at the start of the welfare state the unemployed represented only five per cent of all claimants. Today they represent 22 per cent. In a recent speech Professor David Donnison, the chairman of the Supplementary Benefits Commission, sensibly asked whether 'a scheme which grew up during the post-war years mainly to care for pensioners, with all the discretionary payments and the visiting that entailed, is now serving customers who are beginning to look more like those of 1934 than we had ever thought possible'.

Guardian, 10 October 1977

1   What is Peter Laurie referring to when he says, 'From 1950 to about 1965 the British believed that something had happened which had never existed in all the world: there were no more poor'?
2   Which definition of poverty does Laurie prefer?
3   Describe some of the conditions experienced by people living in poverty, according to Laurie. Do you think he presents an accurate picture of poverty? Give as many reasons as you can to support your answer.
4   Poverty is described as a 'relative concept' in the *Guardian* article. What is the difference between a 'relative' and an 'absolute' definition of poverty?
5   What evidence is presented by the *Guardian* to show that poverty still persists in Britain?
6   What evidence is presented by the *Guardian* to reject the view that the poor 'throw their money away on luxuries'?
7   In comparison to other countries in the European Economic Community, where does Britain stand in terms of public spending?
8   Which groups now make up the majority of poor people in Britain today?

Reorganization in the social services

Prior to 1970 (1968 in Scotland) the personal social services at a local authority level consisted of the Children's, Welfare and Mental Health Departments. They were considered as departments whose main concerns were social work, but it was also recognized that the Health, Education and Housing Departments also had aspects of social work within their responsibilities. Outside full local authority control (but closely associated with it), the Probation Department was also regarded as a social work service, while many hospitals, through their medical social workers, provided some social work help. The fact that in any one local authority eight social work agencies – more if voluntary bodies were included – could be encountered, gave rise to criticism concerning the fragmented and multiple nature of social work organization. Indeed some commentators believed that a crisis point had been reached.

In 1965 the Committee of Local Authority and Allied Personal Social Services was established under the chairmanship of Sir Frederick Seebohm. Its brief was 'to review the organization and responsibilities of the local authority personal social services in England and Wales and to consider what changes are desirable to secure an effective family service'. The committee's findings were published in 1968 and put into effect in the Local Authority Social Service Act (1970).

The Seebohm report outlined the weaknesses of the previously fragmented system which had led to difficulties of co-ordination. For instance, research by Dr Jean Packman had indicated that the services to prevent children going into public care – day nurseries, home helps, social casework – were spread amongst a number of departments. Frequently these departments could not co-ordinate their efforts in order to make all the services available to the children's families at the same time. Worse, evidence suggested that some departments attempted to off-load their responsibilities on to other departments.

If a lack of co-ordination was one disadvantage, a duplication of services was another. As the various needs of a single family could fall within the scope of a number of departments, opportunities existed for an overlapping of services. Indeed examples were found of families visited by a large number of different social workers, who served both to bewilder them, as well as to minimise the use of scarce social work skills.

Yet even with the twin evils of a lack of co-ordination and needless duplication, there were still gaps. The responsibility for certain groups like unmarried mothers, pre-school children and so called problem families were so ill defined as not to fall squarely within any department's orbit.

The solution proposed by the Seebohm Committee was to unite the personal social service departments into one family service – the Social Service Department. This recommendation was legalized by the Act of 1970 and put into effect on April 1, 1971.

However the pre-Seebohm Children's, Mental Health and Welfare departments did allow social workers to develop specialist skills in regard to particular needs. A major argument behind the reorganization of these departments was that one social worker should work with one family in order that its need should not be split into separate compartments. Following reorganization, many social workers found themselves dealing with a wider variety of cases than they had previously encountered. The demands were considerable. At the very least they were expected to understand a vast amount of new legislation. At most they were expected to possess the emotional capacity to tolerate frequent changes of roles and the intellectual ability to grasp wide ranging skills and knowledge. Not surprisingly the initial years of the new system gave rise to concern about declining standards. Few social administrators and social workers would support the idea of putting the clock back. Nonetheless a pressing problem for the new Social Services Departments is how to allow social workers to function in a general way without losing the specialized expertise which they had before.

Adapted from ERIC BUTTERWORTH and ROBERT HOLMAN (eds.), *Social Welfare in Modern Britain*

1   What was the main difference in the organization of the social services
    before 1971 and afterwards?
2   What was the Seebohm committee?
3   What were Seebohm's main criticisms of the social services in the
    report of 1968?
4   What did Seebohm recommend and how did the government respond?
5   What has been the main problem faced by the social services since
    reorganization?

State softness or state control?

Rhodes Boyson, MP, argues that the welfare state is a 'soft option' and
encourages people to be content to live on state handouts rather than their
own initiative. Compared to private enterprises, welfare state services, he
claims, are less attractive and less efficient.

In Britain the State now decides how half or more of a man's income shall be
spent, how his family should be educated, how their health care should be
organized, how they shall save for misfortunes and retirement, what library and
in many cases what cultural provision they should receive, and where and at what
cost they should be housed.

   The present Welfare State, with its costly universal benefits and heavy
taxation, is rapidly producing an economic and spiritual malaise among our
people. Planned, introduced and encouraged by good men who believed that State
intervention would bring both economic and spiritual returns, the end-product is
completely different.

   The National Health Service was introduced by men of compassion who wished
to improve the health of the poor and to remove the worry of medical bills. The
end-result has been a decline in medical standards below the level of other
advanced countries because people are not prepared to pay as much through
taxation on other people's health as they would pay directly on their own and
their families'. Long queues in surgeries, an endless waiting-list for hospital beds,
and the emigration of many newly trained doctors are among the unexpected
results. Small wonder that more and more people are looking to some form of
private insurance to give them wider choice in medicine and surgery.

   Unemployment schemes and other social security benefits have been
universalized and increased to their present level because people remembered the
millions of unemployed and the poverty and deprivation of the 1930s. But all they
do is to provide encouragement for the lower paid with large families to become
unemployed or to go sick. Similarly, millions of workers are encouraged to break
the monotony of factory routine by strikes when meagre strike pay can be
augmented by supplementary benefits to their families and tax rebates for
themselves. The reliable and industrious worker looks with irritation and
animosity at his idle fellows whom he helps to maintain and the general sense of
responsibility and personal pride declines. National economic strength and
personal moral fibre are both reduced.

State education, introduced 100 years ago by men and women concerned first to provide the benefits of universal literacy and later to develop leisure and cultural pursuits, is more and more coming under control of the trendy 'expert', who seeks to make his name at the children's expense while he gathers his money from the state. There is little choice of school either by type, discipline or area and the neighbourhood comprehensive school with a complete egalitarian ethic could have disastrous effects upon educational standards.

Housing subsidies and rent controls, also introduced by good if short-sighted middle men, have produced the appalling slums and homelessness of the present day. Many working-class families are virtually prisoners of their council houses since they would lose the subsidy – and perhaps a roof – if they moved elsewhere. The large tower blocks with their tragic effect upon young and old inmates would never have multiplied in a free market where the producer has to take careful account of the preferences of the sovereign consumer.

The result of all this extra State interference financed by taking over 50 per cent of the gross national product in taxation has been not the production of an economically viable society but what might be called rampant stagflation, that is to say stagnation in production and raging inflation which further destroys belief in the future. The moral fibre of our people has been weakened. A State which does for its citizens what they can do for themselves is an evil State; and a State which removes all choice and responsibility from its people and makes them like broiler hens will create the irresponsible society. In such an irresponsible society no one cares, no one saves, no one bothers – why should they when the State spends all its energies taking money from the energetic, successful and thrifty to give to the idle, the failures and the feckless?

RHODES BOYSON, *Down with the Poor*

Peter Laurie believes that the welfare state is used as a means of social control and of keeping people both helpless and dependent upon it while at the same time acting as a warning to others about what will happen to them if they allow themselves to fall on hard times.

Although we are proud of our Welfare State it does not do a great deal for the poor. Why does our system take pains to create these enclaves of the poor – prison camps in all but name and fence? The reason is to encourage the others, to create a place where life is noticeably *worse* than is normal in society, to act as a stimulus, to concentrate people's minds, to point to the virtues of cooperation.

So long as society is based on production and consumption, it will always be necessary for the State to keep a threat in reserve to make sure the majority play the game. If there were not the ultimate possibility of ending up in a slum, who – in the end – would bother to turn up at the factory gates at 8 a.m.? If the State exercises its major control of forcing people to work so they can earn enough money to stay respectable, to keep up with the Joneses, it cannot at the same time hand out equal amounts of money to those who do not work.

The need to have a really deplorable way of life waiting at the bottom of the pile for those who do not cooperate poses the State a pretty problem. A hundred years ago it was easy; there was a small cherished governing class, and as for the rest, those who would not or could not work, starved. That was an end of them. But the expansion of the middle classes, the creation of vast numbers of specialists, who each must be trusted and treated as responsible human beings, means that the State was forced to turn from government by privilege to government by equality. It invented the Welfare State with its central idea that every life is as valuable as every other life. The problem now in dealing with poverty is to appear to operate an equitable arrangement, while in practice working acute discrimination. It uses a number of techniques to achieve this. The first is obviously the device of low pay. The second way is by paying low welfare benefits and pensions. The third way in which the welfare services are effectively prevented from relieving poverty is by restricting public knowledge of their provisions, and by making it difficult or impossible to get the forms necessary for application. For instance, in 1970 the Child Poverty Action Group in Manchester surveyed post offices for three basic forms. They found that 1 in 5 did not have the form to claim for supplementary allowances on pensions, 2 in 5 had no form for free prescriptions, and 3 out of 5 had no form to obtain free milk. Two years later a similar survey showed worse results. Even when the forms are obtainable they are often so complicated and obscurely written that the system can expect, with some complacency, that few will make enough sense of them to apply.

For those who do, the benefits given by the welfare state to the poor – housing, medicine, money, advice – form in themselves a powerful means of social control. Their main function is to reduce desperation which might become rebellious. If people are given something to lose, however slight, they will think twice before they forfeit it. So the Welfare State owes its existence to the need to damp down the poor, to make their lives not totally intolerable, to create a situation in which it is possible to make their lives *worse* if they misbehave. The anti-social are penalized. A prison record, for example, counts against prospective tenants on many council housing lists. Similarly a bad work record suggests possible unreliability with rent, and so on.

Many of those who actually need help are ignored in favour of those who are most 'visible' and who have given up any attempt to cope with things by themselves. Independence is penalized and helplessness rewarded. People are trained to accept the arbitrary hand out and are made totally dependent on the whims of their well intentioned keepers.

PETER LAURIE, *Meet Your Friendly Social System*

1 What are Rhodes Boyson's main criticisms of the welfare state with regard to the health system, unemployment benefits, education and housing?
2 How far do you agree or disagree with Rhodes Boyson's point of view? Give as many reasons as you can to support your answer.
3 What are Peter Laurie's main criticisms of the welfare state?
4 How far do you agree or disagree with Peter Laurie's point of view? Give as many reasons as you can to support your answer.
5 What are the main differences between Rhodes Boyson's and Peter Laurie's attitudes to the welfare state?

Nick Bond argues that many people who are legally entitled to welfare state benefits fail to receive their rights - partly through their own ignorance - but mainly as a result of bad communication by the state.

The Supplementary Benefit system in this country exists as the final safety net in our income maintenance strategy. The scale rates for benefit are based on estimates of minimum subsistence level needs. Consequently anyone who slips through this safety net, even partially, will be forced to live at a level below that which the State considers no one should fall. The Supplementary Benefit system fails in its purpose, therefore, to the extent to which those who are entitled to receive help through this system fail to receive their rights. Because of its function as the final safety net the Supplementary Benefit system, of all our systems for maintaining income, should be the most sensitive in locating need and the most foolproof in its operations to meet need.

The background to the survey

In June 1970 a shop-front Information and Opinion Centre was opened in Hillfields, an inner-city area of Coventry, chosen as the focus for part of the national Community Development Project. During the first 12 months numerous enquiries and complaints concerning entitlement to Supplementary Benefit came to light at the Information Centre.

As a result of dealing with a number of similar cases, workers at the Centre began to speculate about the extent of ignorance among recipients of Supplementary Benefit of their basic rights to entitlement. Moreover, they began to wonder whether the cases that came to their attention really were the few 'unfortunate exceptions', as often claimed by officials of the Department of Health and Social Security, or whether such cases of claimants failing to secure their full entitlement were in fact more common than generally realized by the public at large and the Supplementary Benefit Commission (SBC) in particular. In an effort to discover answers to these questions it was decided in June 1971 to conduct the action-survey described below.

The purpose of the action-survey

(1)   To discover among a sample of recipients of Supplementary Benefit below pension age:
    (a)   the extent of knowledge of basic rights connected with Supplementary Benefit.
    (b)   the extent to which claimants in this sample were not receiving their rights.
(2)   To help any claimants who were not receiving their full entitlement to Supplementary Benefit to claim it.

Advantage was taken of a sampling frame provided by a 1 in 6 household survey of the project study area conducted by the CDP Research Team. The sample comprised 40 claimants representing 93 per cent of all claimants under pension age identified by the 1 in 6 household survey.

The results of the survey
Knowledge of basic scale rates

The answers revealed an extensive lack of knowledge about this most basic information. Seventeen (42.5 per cent) of the sample did not know if their basic Supplementary Benefit was correctly calculated or not. Thirteen of these did not know how to find out; four thought they could find out by asking at the Supplementary Benefit Office. A further 11 (27.5 per cent) of the sample thought their benefit was incorrectly calculated. Eight of these did not know how to find out; three thought they could find out by asking at the Supplementary Benefit Office. One had tried this but said that he got no satisfaction. Moreover, of the 12 (30 per cent) who thought their Supplementary Benefit was correct, 10 did not in fact know if it was correct; they merely assumed that the Supplementary Benefit Office would not make a mistake.

Altogether only two (5 per cent) of the sample were certain that their Supplementary Benefit was correct; 38 (95 per cent) simply did not know.

No one in the sample suggested writing to the Supplementary Benefit Office asking for a written statement of how their benefit was calculated. None seemed to realize that they had a right to receive such a written statement. None suggested checking with Form S1. This form is obtainable at any post office but not, inexplicably, on display at any Supplementary Benefit Office. Presumably many of the sample were unaware of its existence.

As a result of being interviewed eight individuals wrote to the Supplementary Benefit Office asking for a written statement of how their benefit was calculated. In each of these cases there appeared to the interviewer to be the possibility that the calculation of benefit was incorrect. Only two received a written reply. The others were told verbally by a visitor that their allowance was correct - a procedure which is far more difficult to check or challenge.

Knowledge of the discretionary powers of the Supplementary Benefit Commission to meet need in special circumstances

For the large proportion of claimants who are dependent upon Supplementary Benefit over a long period of time (70 per cent of the sample) it is particularly important that they should be aware of their entitlement to the discretionary grants and additions available, since it is widely recognized that, whilst it may be possible to manage on the basic Supplementary Benefit allowance for a short period, the longer dependence continues the more difficult it is to cope both practically and psychologically.

(1)   Exceptional Needs Payments (ENPs)

These grants are lump sum payments intended to meet need in exceptional circumstances when there is no other way of preventing hardship and to meet the costs of any essential expenditure which is not provided for in the scale rates, e.g. the cost of providing or replacing large items of essential household equipment such as a bed, bedding or cooker.

As revealed in the answers 20 of the total sample (50 per cent) had never heard of these grants. Moreover, of the 19 (47.5 per cent) who had heard of ENPs only 13 (32.5 per cent) of the total knew how to apply for them. Of these 13 only one suggested the method of claiming that would seem to be most certain of response, i.e. to make a written application. Of the remaining 12, 10 suggested asking at the office and two asking the visitor. Altogether 27 (67.5 per cent) of the sample had no idea how to apply for this important discretionary grant.

Moreover, in the sample there appears to be a significant connection between knowledge of how to apply for an ENP and the receipt of an ENP. Of the 13 who had heard of ENPs and knew how to apply, 11 had applied at some time and two had not. Of these 11, 10 had received an ENP at least once.

Similarly, there appears to be a significant correlation between lack of knowledge of how to apply for an ENP and the failure to receive an ENP. Only three of the 27 who did not know how to apply for an ENP had received an ENP as a result of an initiative from the Supplementary Benefit Office. During the survey 15 claimants applied for ENPs (i.e. were judged by the interviewer to have special needs). Seven of these knew in principle how to apply, but had not done so; presumably because they did not realize they could apply (or did not have the confidence to apply) for the particular special need they revealed to the interviewer. The others did not know how to apply.

(2)   Exceptional Circumstances Additions (ECAs).
Ignorance concerning this discretionary benefit is even more widespread than that surrounding ENPs. Altogether only 10 (25 per cent) had heard of this discretionary allowance and only six (15 per cent) how to apply for it. All six suggested contacting the Supplementary Benefit Office in order to claim. Not one suggested the method of claiming that might be thought to be the most dependable - i.e. claiming in writing. As a result of being interviewed four claimants applied for ECAs. None of these four had heard of these additions. These payments are made weekly to the claimant on top of his basic scale rate and are intended to meet the costs of any essential recurring expenditure which it is recognized as not provided for in the scale rates, e.g. the costs of providing a special diet or extra heating for the sick or infirm.

Knowledge of Supplementary Benefit appeal procedure
Seventeen (42.5 per cent) of the sample did not know that they could appeal against decisions of the SBC. Thirteen (32 per cent) thought they knew how to appeal but in fact only 6 (15 per cent) of the total sample knew the correct method of appealing, namely to write to the Supplementary Benefit Office or fill in an Appeals Form. Moreover, only four (10 per cent) of the sample knew that it was possible for someone to speak on their behalf at a tribunal. Altogether only two (5 per cent) of the sample had ever appealed. However it cannot be assumed from this that there is widespread satisfaction concerning Supplementary Benefit payments: when asked if there had been any occasions in the past when they would have liked to have appealed against a decision of the SBC if they had known how to go about it, 12 (30 per cent) quoted specific instances when they would have appealed. It appears that knowledge of appeal procedures is a more important variable in determining whether an appeal is made than whether a claimant feels he has ground for appeal.

Altogether 11 (27.5 per cent) of the sample were thought by the interviewer to have grounds for appealing; eight (20 per cent) actually appealed. A further three were advised to appeal but they preferred not to. Of the eight appeals against decisions of the SBC four were resolved in the claimant's favour without going to Appeal. Four went to Appeal and in three of these cases a determination was made in favour of the claimants (a success rate of 87.5 per cent). These figures compared with a national appeal rate of less than 1 per cent and a successful national appeal rate of approximately 20 per cent of all appeals made.

Extent of unmet need revealed by the survey
Receipt of certain rights associated with the receipt of Supplementary Benefit
(1) Free prescriptions
Eight (20 per cent) of the total sample in fact paid for prescriptions. Two of these knew that they did not have to pay but preferred to do so in order to avoid embarrassment. The other six (15 per cent of the sample) did not realise that they could get prescriptions free.
(2) Free school meals
Of the 19 families with children at school four (21 per cent of those eligible) did not receive free school meals. Of these one did not realize that his children could receive free school meals. One preferred his child to come home to dinner - he thought he was too young to stop. Two said they preferred to pay for school dinners so that their children should not feel different from other school children. Both of these were mothers of adolescent girls.

The total number of children not receiving free school dinners in these four families was five, i.e. 11.4 per cent of the 44 children eligible. This represents a loss of assumed income of 60p per week for three families and £1.20 for one family.

Failure to receive rights as a result of administrative errors
(1) Receipt of free milk tokens
Failure to receive free milk tokens represents a serious loss of income for claimants with children under five. In the sample three (21 per cent) of those claimants eligible had been without milk tokens in the period immediately prior to the survey - two for about three months and one for four weeks. All of these three claimants were unsupported mothers. This represented a total loss of income of 77p for one family, and 38½p each for the other two families. An average loss in income of 51p per week. This failure is a result of simple bureaucratic incompetence. The tokens are given as of right and should involve no need to claim for those entitled. All three claimants successfully claimed payments in cash to the value of the tokens they had failed to receive.
(2) Other administrative errors
One of the sample was found to be receiving an incorrect basic supplementary allowance. This was 45p below the correct scale rate. One severely handicapped man had been granted £10 to purchase a gas fire in December 1970 but the grant had not arrived by the date of the survey (16.6.71). The grant was sent with apologies as soon as the matter was drawn to the attention of the local office.

In total five of the sample (12.5 per cent) were found to be receiving less than they were entitled to as a result of administrative errors.

Failure to receive SNGs in cases of special need
As a result of the survey 13 (32.5 per cent) of the sample applied for SNGs and 10 (25 per cent) in fact received these. However, none of the three whose applications were refused appealed. Assuming two out of three of these would have won their

appeals it could be estimated that 12 (30 per cent) of the sample in fact had a special need at the time of the survey but failed to receive a grant to meet that need.

Failure to receive ECAs in circumstances of special need
Altogether four (10 per cent) of the sample applied for ECAs. Three of these were granted. The other was refused but the claimant did not go to appeal. At least three (7.5 per cent) of the sample therefore were entitled to ECAs at the time of the survey (and at the time of their original interview with an SBC official) but had failed to receive such a grant.

As a result of the survey 16 (40 per cent) of the sample received cash grants either to meet special needs or to rectify mistakes made by the SBC. The total amount of cash received in lump sum payments was £148.27 - an average of £3.70 per claimant in the sample. In addition five claimants (12.5 per cent) had their weekly rate of Supplementary Benefit increased. Three of these had their weekly rate of benefit increased by ECAs averaging 53p per claimant. One claimant had a weekly increase of 45p as a result of the discovery of an administrative error and one claimant received a weekly increase of 25p as a result of notifying the SBC of changes in his circumstances.

Altogether nearly half of the sample - 18 (45 per cent) - received additional resources as a result of being interviewed. In other words, at the time of the interviews approximately half of all the claimants in the sample were failing to receive their full entitlement.

NICK BOND, *Knowledge of Rights and Extent of Unmet Need Among Recipients of Supplementary Benefit* (Coventry Community Development Project)

1   Why is it important, according to Nick Bond, that the Supplementary Benefit System should be 'the most sensitive in locating need and the most foolproof in its operations to meet need'?
2   When and where was Nick Bond's survey carried out?
3   What did the survey aim to find out?
4   Explain in your own words what the survey revealed in terms of:
a   people's knowledge of their basic rights to Supplementary Benefit
b   people's knowledge of special needs grants and other discretionary allowances
c   people's knowledge of the appeals procedure
5   When 'knowledge of their rights' became available to people in the survey, what kind of response did they receive from the Supplementary Benefit Commission?
6   To what extent does this evidence suggest that the Supplementary Benefit system is 'sensitive in locating need' and 'foolproof in its operations to meet need'?

3 Questions and answers

Supplementary Benefits are paid to those people who for one reason or another are unable to work and who do not have enough money to live on. The main groups who get Supplementary Benefits are the unemployed, the sick and disabled, the old and single parents.

Supplementary Benefit is supposed to provide you with enough money to make ends meet without difficulty, but as we have seen, many people find that it does not. Why is this? Is it because 'they don't take the trouble to find out what they're entitled to'? Or, as Peter Laurie suggests on pages 137-8, is the system made 'deliberately complicated' to prevent too many of them finding out?

One way of answering this question is by personal investigation.
1 Imagine you are an unsupported mother of three children aged 11, 9 and 6. Your husband has deserted you. You earn £12 a week as a part-time cleaner. What help could you expect from Supplementary Benefit?
2 Here's a list of things you need to find out:
a whether or not you are entitled to claim Supplementary Benefit
b how to go about claiming
c how your claim will be dealt with
d how you will be paid
e how to check what you are entitled to (in terms of a living allowance, rent allowance, discretionary payments, etc.)
f how to check on any reductions that might be made by the social security officers
3 When you have finished your investigations, make a full report on:
a the amount of Supplementary Benefit you should be entitled to
b the ease or difficulty you found in getting hold of the information and understanding it
c your opinion of the Supplementary Benefit system as a way of helping people

Checkpoints
1 When did Seebohm Rowntree make his first study of poverty in York?
2 When were old age pensions first introduced?
3 What is meant by 'National Insurance' and when was it first introduced?
4 What part did Lloyd George play in the foundation of the Welfare State?
5 When was the Beveridge Report published and what did it recommend?

6   When was the Welfare State in Britain officially established?
7   What is meant by the 'poverty line'?
8   What recommendations were made by the Seebohm Report?
9   When was the government's Urban Aid Programme launched?
10 What is meant by the term 'inflation'?

O-level questions

1   Why does poverty still exist as a problem in Britain?
2   What do you understand by 'poverty'? To what extent has poverty been reduced in the United Kingdom since 1945?
3   'What counts as poverty varies from time to time and place to place.' Discuss.
4   What is the difference between 'absolute' and 'relative' poverty? How has the development of the welfare state affected the extent of poverty in Britain?
5   What is meant by the welfare state? Trace its development in Britain during the twentieth century.
6   What are the major problems facing the welfare state in Britain today?
7   Outline some of the major arguments for and against the welfare state.

6 Work

1 Background information

You may consider that four hours spent digging in the garden is an example of 'hard work'. Or that a housewife who cleans the house, washes and irons the clothes and buys in the family's groceries for the week is engaged in 'work'. But neither of these activities is technically regarded as 'work'. The modern definition of work is not something which demonstrates activity, effort or achievement in itself, but something related specifically to paid employment. Work is something that earns a wage or a salary and which involves being hired by an employer.

For many people work is the least rewarding part of their lives. The hours they spend each week at work are often hours of endurance rather than hours of pleasure. For them work is a 'necessary evil'. Something which has to be done to earn a living but which brings little personal satisfaction. In times of high unemployment many feel grateful to have jobs, even though they do not particularly enjoy the work they do.

Other people find their work interesting and rewarding, especially if it gives them the opportunity to make full use of their skills and abilities. If their wages and working conditions are good so much the better, but often the sense of 'job satisfaction' is an extra bonus which cannot always be measured in monetary terms. In this chapter we shall consider some different types of work, relationships between workers and their employers and some of the effects of changing work conditions on people's lives.

The industrialization of Britain

Britain, as you probably know, was the first industrial nation. The experience of earlier developments provided a number of conditions which made Britain ideally suited to industrialization long before there were any significant changes in technology and production.

Abroad, Britain had built up a considerable empire by the middle of the nineteenth century which provided both cheap raw materials and a range of markets in which to sell manufactured goods. At home the 'enclosure' of agricultural land had made many land-holding peasants homeless and they became the first labourers attracted to the new industries and the towns which sprang up around them.

In the first half of the nineteenth century most manufacturing was still organized on a small scale in workshops, making full use of hand craft and individual skill. But as railways and shipbuilding rapidly developed the possibilities of trade, larger factories were built and machinery was increasingly introduced to speed up and multiply the production of goods.

The spread of machinery, railways and shipbuilding in turn provided a new demand for iron, steel and engineering. Without significant developments in the quality and quantity of iron production, mechanization in other industries would have been greatly reduced. But as a result of technical improvements in mining, smelting and purifying steel, Britain soon outstripped all her rivals in iron and steel production.

The other important innovation was the introduction of steam driven machinery which made it possible for manufacturers to have greater choice in where they put their factories and made them less dependent on water and 'human energy'. The development of steam engines and the increased demand for iron in turn affected the production of coal. Almost without exception, new industries and the manufacturing towns which serviced them grew up near to plentiful supplies of coal. By 1850, therefore, Britain was without equal in terms of industrial production and trade. Her exports multiplied three and a half times between 1850 and 1870, when she was generally considered to be the 'workshop of the world'. In 1870 the total amount of British trade in manufactured goods was greater than that of Germany, Italy and France combined, though industrial developments in the USA and Germany were soon to challenge her supremacy.

Prosperity for the owners of factories and those who profited from trade was not without cost to those who provided the labour, however. Working conditions in the factories and heavy industries were notoriously bad. Women and children were exploited by the same insensitive greed as exploited men. Dangerous conditions, low wages and long hours were common, and in the days before trade unions were well established there was often little that workers could do but complain privately to each other. In the end appalling conditions and repressive measures designed to restrict workers' rights by the employers and government encouraged the development of trade union ideas. Small unions and working men's associations were established and in 1868 the TUC was formed.

Once begun the industrialization of Britain could not be checked. The history of the last 100 years has been one of increasing dependency on machinery and industrial processes - though not always with the same economic success as in the early years of the industrial revolution.

The main concern of sociologists during this time has been with the effects of changing industrial patterns on people's jobs and lifestyles. The main developments have been in mechanization, mass production and automation.

Mechanization

Mechanization is quite simply a method of producing goods or completing tasks with the help of machines - machines which are operated by human beings, and organized in special workplaces. Although mechanization is usually associated with factory production and industry, machines are increasingly being used to speed up and improve office and clerical work and to increase efficiency in the leisure and service industries.

Mass production

Mass production is a term associated with machine-made goods but its added characteristic is that of a moving assembly line. Take radios, for example. Instead of a number of individual workers using machines to make individual radios and being responsible for the whole operation from beginning to end, an assembly line passes the radio along from one worker to another and each is responsible for only a part of its production. This means that workers need to be skilled in only a part of the operation and not all of it. On many assembly lines the different tasks need very little skill at all, since the whole point of mass production is to move from reliance on the craft and skill of individual workers to dependency on machines which can do the job more quickly, efficiently and cheaply. As a result, assembly line work can be boring, repetitive and unrewarding.

Henry Ford was the first factory owner to benefit from mass production by introducing assembly lines into the production of his motor cars at the beginning of this century. The majority of manufactured goods are now made in this way and his simple principle of a moving line has been added to and developed over the years by technical improvements and refinements to speed up and increase the production of a whole range of different products.

Automation

Automation takes the process of mechanization and mass production one step further by the addition of more complicated machinery and computers which are able to produce goods, control the rate of production, feed back information and co-ordinate different processes with very little help from human operators. Automated industries need fewer workers because most of the machines 'work themselves'. They need different kinds of workers on the whole - those who can programme the computers and understand the work process sufficiently to supervise its progress. They need maintenance staff and engineers whose responsibilities are greater than those of assembly line workers and whose status is consequently higher. But working in automated industries can also mean sitting by switches and panels in control rooms far away from where the work process is actually happening, and this can be as boring and unrewarding an occupation as the routine of an average assembly line.

Micro-electronic processors

The most startling development of the 1970s has been the invention and production of silicon chips. These small micro-electronic processors have already revolutionized automation and made it possible for the most complicated of manufacturing production to be directed and carried out by ultra-efficient, robot-like machines, controlled by highly sophisticated computers.

Already in America and Japan, for example, increasing numbers of companies are using micro-processors to automate their industries and experts predict that this development has the potential to double production, increase profit and reduce manpower to a fraction of its present level within a few years.

And it is not only manual jobs that are threatened by this form of advanced automation. Already in America, computers relying on micro-processors are being used to store the information, knowledge and skills held by key professional workers and in the process reducing considerably the need for 'human' doctors, surgeons, teachers, bankers and lawyers.

It is only recently that the British government has acknowledged the potential of silicon-chip technology and during 1978-9, without much publicity or public debate about the issues involved, £400,000,000 was made available to produce micro-processors for use in British industry.

The long-term implications of this decision are, of course, enormous. Scientists predict that micro-processors could, if they were generally developed, make a whole generation unemployed by the turn of the century. Sixty thousand soft-ware engineers employed full-time to programme computers could be all the labour force necessary to organize the whole industrial production of Britain. In the short term, since developments using micro-processors are already established in America and Japan, these will undoubtedly provide a competitive challenge which British industries will be incapable of meeting.

Technological change

The effects of technological change on British industry over the last seventy or eighty years has been to progressively remove work from men and give it to more and more complicated machines. Many workers have benefited as a result and an increased number of supervisors, managers and other white-collar workers have been considered necessary to administer and organize production. But the 'mental' side of production has become noticeably separated from the 'physical' and 'manual' aspects of work. Large concentrations of unskilled and semi-skilled workers have been reduced, as machines have taken over the jobs once done by men. Even one-time skilled workers have had their skills made obsolete by more efficient machines and many have been reduced to the status of machine minders or forced into other jobs as porters, caretakers, cleaners and drivers.

The introduction of mass production and the spread of automation has generally made industry more efficient and more profitable but investment in new machines and the modernization of work processes has lagged behind those other countries, like Germany, Japan and America, so that in comparison to them Britain now has difficulty in competing in international markets.

The invention of the silicon chip now poses Britain, and indeed every industrialized society, with an immense problem. A number of social commentators, including most trade unionists, are opposed to the idea of introducing this development on a large scale. They argue that the social consequences in terms of redundancy and unemployment would cause problems much too horrendous to contemplate. But others point out that if micro-processors are not introduced, British industry will be destroyed anyway by competition from those countries which have automated their industries in this way. In either case, the prospect of persistent long-term unemployment looks to be inevitable.

Multinational industries

The other significant change in industrial societies like Britain has been the growth in the size and the power of industrial organizations. Small and locally based industries have been increasingly bought up and taken over by huge international companies with factories and investments in many different places. Their aim is generally to make as much money as possible and they have no particular allegiance to any country or any workforce. They moved their factories, almost at will, to where labour is cheapest and profits are easiest, and their decisions can have serious repercussions on the neighbourhoods and areas they leave behind.

The social effects of industrial change

It is important to remember that changes in industry do not just affect changes in jobs and conditions at work. Just as manufacturing towns at one time developed in response to new industries, so now are present day communities affected by the kind of work which is available locally. Over the years it is possible to see how many areas have first thrived and then declined in direct relationship to the fate of their local industry (see Table 9).

Different kinds of jobs

There are, of course, a variety of ways of earning a living, and many more different jobs than you could ever hope to count. As we saw in Chapter 2, a person's social class is mainly decided by the job he or she does, and as we saw in Chapter 4, one of the main roles of the education system is to channel members of different social classes into particular types of occupation. In an ideal world, perhaps these different jobs would all be regarded as equally valuable to society. And certainly society needs its lorry dirvers, factory workers, nurses and dustmen just as much as it needs politicians, brain surgeons and businessmen. But in reality, different occupations have different degrees of status. Professional and white-collar occupations are usually thought to be more important than manual jobs. They generally require more education and training and usually command higher salaries. One of the main reasons why professional and white collar employees have been among the last groups of workers to join trade unions is because the status and nature of their work has long protected them against the worst of bad working conditions and low pay. Manual workers, on the other hand, have often been forced into trade union activity to win respect for their skills and reasonable wages for the jobs they do. And although society often appears down on coal miners, service workers and the like, it quickly becomes clear how much we depend on them, when they withdraw their labour.

Job satisfaction

People attach different meanings to their work and get different amounts of satisfaction from doing it. In trying to identify the factors which make for job satisfaction, sociologists have carried out a number of surveys. In general it is thought that people with professional jobs and skilled workers get more job satisfaction than others, especially if they enjoy a fair degree of independence and responsibility. Those jobs which involve a 'caring responsibility' for other people - like nursing, social work and

Table 9 *Relationship between communities and industry*

Industry	Community
Growth Industries are set up in an area using capital which comes from profits made elsewhere. The industries expand and employment grows. All the available land is filled up.	A new population moves into the area in search of work. Houses are built for them. Many have come from other areas where industry/agriculture is in decline.
Maturity Local firms remain profitable. Few firms leave the area and new growth slows down. (Meanwhile a new generation of industrial investments are being laid down elsewhere, partly financed by the profits made here.)	Employment remains at a fairly stable level. The local population settles and amenities develop. Local employment and housing opportunities are still relatively good.
Decline Local industries begin to decline. There is little new investment in existing plant. Employment is cut. The traditional manufacturing sector continues to decline and provides fewer and fewer jobs - especially skilled jobs. Several firms close altogether leaving vacant sites. Vacant sites remain derelict or are developed for warehousing or offices. No new manufacturing businesses are attracted to the area because the sites are relatively expensive, in need of development and because there are now too few skilled workers living locally. But the easy availability of cheap, old premises, together with a pool of poorly paid workers, attracts a number of small scale, low wage, low productivity industries which do nothing to increase the prosperity of the area.	The housing stock begins to deteriorate and many of the better paid and more skilled workers move out to newer working class areas. The reduction in good job opportunities locally also encourages them to move away. The rate of leaving the area increases as local industries continue to decline. Redundant workers remain unemployed or find work outside the area. The housing stock is now in a worse condition. The continued shift to a low incomed population means that the deterioration of the housing is accelerated because residents are less able to afford improvements. The emigration of younger, more skilled workers continues, leaving behind an increasingly ageing, unskilled badly paid and insecurely employed or unemployed, badly housed population.

Based on Community Development Project, *The Costs of Industrial Change,* p. 10.

teaching, for example - are often referred to as 'vocations' and it's assumed that workers like these are more committed to the people they care for than arguing about wages and working conditions. This idea that certain people have a 'sense of vocation' has often been used to persuade workers in these jobs to be less trade union-minded than other employees. In recent years, however, the low pay of nurses and social workers in particular has made many of them feel that their sense of responsibility to their patients and clients is being exploited by employers and they are now much more likely to consider using trade union tactics to improve their wages and working conditions.

Other kinds of jobs which seem to provide a fair amount of satisfaction are those done by skilled workers and craftsmen. Sociologists have found that when a worker is involved in making something himself - like a piece of furniture - which involves judgement and skill, he is much more likely to find that work satisfying than if he is continually pulling a lever or fixing a screw on an assembly line, without ever seeing the finished product he has helped to assemble.

Contact with others also seems to be a crucial factor. If relations at work are friendly and if the employers are considerate and fair, workers are likely to be much more content with their jobs than if they are treated unjustly or if they are working with people they do not like.

For many people, however, work is only a necessary evil which provides little personal satisfaction. They need to earn money to live. When working conditions are bad, wages are low and tasks are routine and boring, it is hard to develop enthusiasm and commitment to what you are doing. Lateness, absenteeism and 'skiving' of various kinds are typical responses to tedious and unrewarding jobs. For many, there is a sense of 'never really achieving anything' and a dreary sameness which makes work something to be endured rather than enjoyed.

Jobs which involve hard physical labour or dangerous and unpleasant conditions, like coal mining and deep sea fishing are hardly likely to provide much job satisfaction either. But sociologists have noticed a special unity and sense of mutual support among workers in such jobs, that spreads over into their family life and leisure time, and is probably a response to the awfulness of the conditions and the frequent dangers they share at work. Although the British trawling industry is now virtually dead, the unemployed and ageing fishermen in ports like Hull and Grimsby still talk with surprising emotion about their experiences at sea. And miners, for many years a badly paid labour force, working in dangerous and unhealthy conditions, have turned their sense of mutual allegience and shared experiences into a particularly effective and militant form of trade union organization.

One of the consequences of automation, as we have already seen, has been the reduction in need for skilled labour and the increasing use of machines and computers to do the jobs once done by men. In terms of job satisfaction such developments have brought mixed blessings. Working conditions have become easier and the working week has become shorter, but many feel reduced to the role of machine minders. Others have experienced redundancy and unemployment for the first time in their lives.

Although work can be tedious, unemployment - in a society in which everyone is expected to work - can be a debilitating and depressing experience. Because the job a person does affects so many other aspects of his or her life, and influences the way in which he or she is regarded by others, to be without work can reduce a person's status, self-image and identity as a 'useful member of society'. The unemployed are so often either pitied or denounced as work-shy and neither stereotype provides a very attractive image to live down.

The influence of work on leisure activities

Ask most people about themselves and they will tell you what job they do. Whether they enjoy their work or not, it certainly is one of the main ways in which people establish their identities.

Work also has a tremendous influence on people's 'non-working' lives in a variety of obvious and less obvious ways. Since a person's job determines his income, it also determines where he can afford to live and how much money he has to spend on furnishing his home and financing his leisure activities. Hobbies like skiing, yachting and scuba-diving, for example, are obviously reserved for the relatively affluent (and energetic!), whereas fishing, watching football, dancing and drinking can be enjoyed by more or less anyone.

For some workers their leisure time seems to be almost an extension of their work. It would be difficult for professional writers and cricketers to know when work stops and leisure begins, for example. For low paid workers, on the other hand, leisure time is often a precious commodity. Much of it gets eaten up by the overtime and shift work that it seems necessary to endure to earn a living wage.

Workers in routine and boring jobs are those most likely to make a clear distinction between their work and their leisure. Many may actually feel that they only really 'come alive as people' when they leave work.

Studies of workers in dangerous and demanding jobs like coal-mining and trawling have shown how the comradeship of working relationships, in which people often have to depend on each other for their own safety, spills over into leisure time friendships. Although Hull trawlermen, in the heyday of the fishing industry and on three-week trips to Iceland, only had a day or two at home with their wives and children between trips, they spent a good deal of it in the local pubs and clubs with their shipmates. And in traditional coal-mining communities, the men's world of the pubs and working men's clubs is still one that is only grudgingly shared with wives and girlfriends on certain days of the week.

For some, leisure time is an escape from the tedium of routine jobs, and most factory labour forces have a surprising number of active sportsmen, amateur gardeners, fly-fishermen and musicians. But for many, the monotony of work spills over into the monotony of leisure, and television viewing and tinkering with the car become the main demonstrations of activity.

Workers engaged in professional jobs and those who experience a good deal of job satisfaction are more likely to have an active and varied social life than manual workers. It is partly a matter of income and the ability to afford holidays and travel for example. But workers in professional occupations are also more likely to have had satisfactory educational experiences in the past. Interests kindled at school or college in the arts, theatre, music or painting may well continue into adult life. Certainly the adults who continue with part-time study, evening classes of various kinds and 'educational' hobbies are more likely to be those who have already experienced a good deal of educational success.

For women workers leisure time is less likely to be something they call their own. As we have seen in Chapter 3, although more women work outside the home these days, and the roles of husbands and wives within the family have had to change as a result, women are still the ones who are mainly responsible for housework and child care. For full-time women workers a good deal of their leisure time is eaten up by catching up with their other work as housewives and mothers. Compared to manual workers, professional women workers may be more fortunate. Their extra earning capacity often allows them to afford domestic help at home or to be able to pay for child-minders and for nursery provision for their children.

It is interesting that when most people, including sociologists, talk about work, it is generally assumed to be a predominantly male activity. We are so accustomed to thinking of 'manpower' as masculine that we ignore the fact that now almost 50 per cent of the labour force consists of female workers. Perhaps it is time to consider some of the special factors relating to the work done by women.

Women in the workforce (Figure 10)

Out of a total workforce of 25.9 million in 1976, 10 million were women. In the twenty-five years between 1951 and 1976 the number of people working rose from 22.6 million to 25.9 million – an increase of 3.3 million. Of the increasing number of workers, 3 million were women and 0.3 million were men.

Of the 10 million working women, 6.7 million were married.

Figure 10 *Women in the workforce*

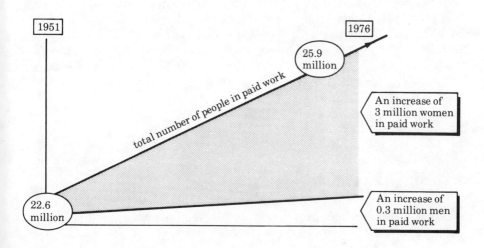

Married women (Table 10)
In 1951 less than 22 per cent of married women were in employment
(either full-time or part-time). By 1971 the number had risen to 42 per cent
of married women. By 1976 the proportion of married women under 60
who were doing or looking for paid work was over 50 per cent in each age
group, and experts were predicting that the numbers would go on rising.

Table 10 *Married women in the workforce*

Married women	1951	% (actual) 1971	1976	% (projected) 1986
16–19	38.1	41.6	51.9	51.9
20–24	36.5	45.7	54.6	55.7
25–44	25.1	46.4	56.3	62.8
45–59	21.5	53.4	61.3	70.5
60+	4.6	14.2	13.5	16.0
Total	21.7	42.2	49.0	54.9

Women's jobs

Eight out of ten women working in Britain today are to be found in one of
four types of jobs and as a result jobs like cleaner, canteen assistant, shop
assistant and typist have come to be thought of as 'women's jobs'.

	% of work done by women
Clerical and secretarial work	30.3
Domestic and catering work	20.4
Unskilled factory work	15.9
Shop work	10.1
Total	76.7

Part-time work

Many women take part-time work because they need to earn money but
still need time to look after children, do the housework, shopping and
cooking, and care for old or disabled relatives.

Because of these other demands on their time they have to be 'less
choosey' than women without such responsibilities or men, and as a
result often have to accept wages which would be unacceptable to full-
time workers. Consequently, most part-time work is badly paid and
unprotected by the legislation and conditions of employment which apply
to full-time workers. Part-time workers are less likely to belong to trade
unions and more likely to be made redundant in times of economic crisis.

Wages (Table 11)

Women's wages in manufacturing industries tend to be higher than in the
Service Industries. In industries in which women are the majority of the
workforce, their wages tend to be lower. Textiles, clothing and footwear
were the three lowest-paid manufacturing industries in April 1976.

In a report published in 1978 by the Equal Opportunities Commission
(a body set up by the Sex Discrimination Act of 1975 to monitor
discrimination on grounds of sex) it was shown that despite Equal Pay
legislation the gap between what men earn and women earn is still
considerable. Although young men and women starting work in their
teens earn about the same, the difference soon begins to show. In 1976 the
highest-paid male manual workers, aged between 21 and 24, were
averaging £80.80 a week, while women of the same age were averaging
£54 a week. Among the same group of non-manual workers, men were
earning £74.60 per week compared with women's £59.10. The report
showed clearly that the lowest-paid section of the workforce was mainly
comprised of women and in 1976 43 per cent of full-time women workers
earned less than £40 a week compared with only 5 per cent of men.

Table 11 *Average gross weekly earnings for full-time manual men and women, April 1976*

	£ women	men
Food, drink and tobacco	39.30	64.90
Chemicals and allied industries	39.40	67.00
Mechanical engineering	41.60	64.30
Electrical engineering	41.20	62.50
Textiles	36.30	58.80
Clothing and footwear	32.60	52.10
Bricks, pottery, glass, cement, etc	39.20	66.00
Papers, printing and publishing	40.40	69.00
Other manufacturing industries	37.30	63.20
Transport and communication	50.80	68.80
Distributive trades	32.80	63.10
Professional and scientific services	39.00	56.40
Miscellaneous services	33.30	50.20
Public administration	42.70	54.70

SOURCE: Department of Employment 1976, tables 54 and 56

Women in the professions
Despite the fact that women now make up between 40 and 50 per cent of the labour force, the proportion of women in top professional jobs is low, as Table 12 shows:

Table 12 *Women in the professions*

Profession	No. of women in 1974-5 (%)
Architecture	4.3
Bar Council	8.0
Institute of Directors	1.0
Medicine	27.0
Law Society	4.0
Engineering and allied industries	2.0
Journalism	23.0
Universities: teaching and research	11.0

Equal pay and sex discrimination

At midnight on 28 December 1975, important legislation affecting women came into force in Britain. The Equal Pay Act first introduced in 1970 finally became law and the Sex Discrimination Act made it illegal, in most circumstances, to differentiate between men and women in work, leisure and educational opportunities. A special Equal Opportunities Commission was set up to hear complaints about discrimination and to make recommendations to the government about future changes in the law.

In some ways the legislation has helped women. It has helped to create a social climate in which women increasingly expect to be treated equally with men and it has prevented some of the more obvious forms of social and legal discrimination. But many people feel that the legislation does not go far enough. Loopholes have appeared which make it possible in practice for employers to find ways of avoiding paying women equal wages, and the Equal Opportunities Commission has turned out to be a rather moderate, secretive body, reluctant to campaign actively on behalf of women or to speak out strongly against continuing discrimination.

Employment legislation

A fair amount of other legislation relating to working conditions and workers' rights has also been passed in recent years – for example, the Health and Safety at Work Act (1974), the Employment Protection Act (1975) and the Trade Union and Labour Relations Act (1974 and 1976). All this legislation is part of an attempt by the government to provide a framework within which employers and employees can protect their own interests at work.

The employer obviously wants workers who will work as hard as they can, as efficiently as they can, for as little as it is possible to pay them. There is no point in paying high wages as an act of kindness if you can get workers to accept less. High wages only mean less profit for the employers. For workers, on the other hand, it is necessary to earn the highest wages possible in order to maintain and improve their standard of living. And since no one enjoys working long hours in dirty or dangerous circumstances, it is important to ensure decent working conditions. Because the interests of employers and employees are different, it is therefore almost inevitable that conflict between the two sides will occur from time to time. Employers may feel that they cannot afford to increase wages or that to provide better training opportunities and longer holidays would reduce their profits. Workers may be anxious about redundancy in times of high unemployment, or find it difficult to make ends meet on wages that seem to lag behing price increases. It is these kinds of conflicting interests which have encouraged the introduction of industrial legislation and the development of associations like the Confederation of British Industry and workers' trade unions.

Industrial relations

A hundred years ago employees were in a fairly weak position when it came to a disagreement with their employers. The trade union movement was very young and many workers did not belong to a union. In many cases people were so afraid of losing their jobs that they felt obliged to accept without question what the employers decided.

During the last 100 years, however, the trade union movement has become much stronger and much better organized. Trade unions are now much better equipped to protect the interests of their members. At local level, shop stewards and trade union officials can sort out problems faced by individual workers and if necessary organize support from other union members. At national level the leaders of some of the larger trade unions are now regularly consulted by the government on a wide range of economic, industrial and social issues.

In present-day Britain the 'power of the unions' is a subject which always provokes heated debate. Some people recognize that stronger trade unions are essential if the interests of workers are to be represented and their rights at work are to be protected. Others believe that the unions have too much power and that their ability to organize large scale strike action puts the rest of the country at their mercy. Of course, no one enjoys the inconvenience that strike action can cause but most people agree that 'as a last resort', when all other attempts at discussion and persuasion have failed, it is the only effective action trade unionists can take to demonstrate the seriousness of their sense of grievance.

Whatever your personal opinions about employers, strikes and trade unions might be, as a sociologist you should try to look beyond the caricatures and stereotypes frequently portrayed by the media and try to identify the social and economic conditions which make for good or bad industrial relations in different places of work. Some of these will be examined in more detail in part 2 (pages 176–81).

Unemployment

The mid 1970s have seen a level of unemployment in Britain which has been higher than at any other time since the Depression of the 1930s. Automation and factory closures have been one cause of the problem, but the dramatic increase in the numbers of people unemployed (almost 1.5 million in 1976) is not only the result of a fall in the numbers of those who are employed. The number of people in employment has decreased in the last three or four years, but at the same time the number of people in the labour force has increased. So unemployment has been added to by the fact that there are less jobs available and more people looking for work.

As unemployment has increased, as a result of redundancies in industry and cuts in public spending, the first workers to be laid off have been those who are most vulnerable – women, school-leavers, young workers and immigrants.

Women are vulnerable because they are often part-time, non-unionized and subject to the familiar prejudice that they only work for 'pin money'. The view is still common among employers and trade unionists alike, that men, as 'breadwinners' in families should have more job security than women. The fact that many women, as single parents, widows and divorcees are frequently the sole breadwinners in families is often forgotten. The official figures show that unemployment among women has increased dramatically during the 1970s but the real extent of the problem is disguised. Many women do not register as unemployed because they have not been encouraged in the past to pay the full National Insurance Contribution which would entitle them to unemployment benefits. Between January and June 1975 unemployment among women rose by 121 per cent. The rise in male unemployment during the same period was 48 per cent. But a survey published by *Woman's Own* in 1976 found that of the women seeking work, only three in ten were registered as unemployed. In other words, the numbers of unemployed women were much higher than the official statistics would lead you to believe.

Immigrant workers are also particularly hard hit by unemployment. Many work in the public services industries like the Health Service and public transport. These are some of the key industries in which jobs are being cut to reduce public spending costs. Others work in small businesses, restaurants and factories, many of which have been forced to close down because of the economic crisis. Whatever the industry, immigrant workers are often the first to lose their jobs because the union has accepted a 'last in – first out agreement' with the employers. Young black workers leaving school know that unemployment is especially bad in some areas but that to be black is an additional disadvantage because of racial prejudice. In the eighteen-month period before May 1975 unemployment rose by an average of 65 per cent for all workers. But for West Indian, Asian and African Britons the increase was 156 per cent, and for young West Indians it was 182 per cent.

Most public attention has been focused on the plight of young people out of work. In 1972 the school leaving-age was raised to 16. Although the official reasons given at the time for raising the school-leaving age were educational ones, many people now believe that this was the first of many subsequent attempts to disguise the real extent of youth unemployment.

Youth unemployment, like unemployment generally, is currently an international problem. At a conference of world leaders held in London in May 1977 it was reported that seven million young people in the rich countries of Western Europe, North America and Japan were out of work. In these countries the under-25s made up 22 per cent of the working population but 40 per cent of the unemployed.

A report from the Common Market at the beginning of 1976 confirmed that in the EEC one-quarter of unemployed workers was under 25. By the end of that year the proportion had risen to one-third and the level of unemployment among the under-25s was double the level for the workforce as a whole.

The British government's response to youth unemployment has been to give financial subsidies to firms offering new jobs to unemployed young people, and to introduce a whole series of job creation schemes and training opportunities. The Job Creation Programme, for example, was intended to provide six months' temporary employment in jobs which would be 'useful to the community'. Schemes for environmental improvements and various sorts of community service have been created by local authorities and various charitable bodies to help keep the youngsters 'off the streets' for a while and to give them something useful to do. But schemes like these have only ever been seen as providing temporary employment; once a youngster's brief experience on a Job Creation Project was over he or she was returned to the dole queue. Work Experience programmes, Community Industry and Youth Opportunities Schemes were also sponsored by the government's Manpower Services Commission to provide other types of temporary employment and further training. The real problem with such initiatives is that although they are apparently designed to make youngsters 'more employable', the number of jobs needed to significantly reduce youth unemployment does not currently exist. And as I have indicated earlier, once the 'silicon-chip revolution' takes hold of British industry, the number will be even fewer.

When unemployment figures began to increase in the mid 1970s, most politicians and social commentators regarded it as a 'regrettable but temporary problem' caused by an economic crisis abroad, inflation and bad industrial relations at home. The view most commonly expressed today, however, is rather different. It is now believed that far from being a passing phenomenon, unemployment at the present level will increasingly become an established feature of industrial society.

2 Looking at the evidence

Working lives

Job satisfaction

The statements that follow are based on data from two sources: surveys carried out by various social researchers, including myself; case studies from *New Left Review*'s two volumes on *Work: Twenty Personal Accounts*. It is hoped that this mixture of the statistically respectable with the humanly interesting will be more acceptable than either source alone.

Let us consider some of the main themes which emerge from people's statements about what makes work satisfying to them:

1. *Creating something.* This is compounded of a feeling that one has put something of oneself into a product and a deep sense of pleasure in the act of creation itself. It is perhaps the most common of all the expressed feelings of satisfaction and felt by the widest range of workers, both manual and non-manual. Referring to steelmaking in the early years of the present century, a steelman writes that 'every pot of steel was an act of creation. It was something derived from the absorbed attention of dedicated men'. An account describes his work partly as 'an act of creation, i.e. if the thing is right there is a form about it, a kind of beauty which comes from its structure; it exists that way because it has been made from the right bits and pieces'. Sometimes the feeling of creating something is linked to how the thing created fits into the scheme of things. Thus toolmaking 'was obviously a source of much ego-contentment and status. Each man made a complete tool, jig or punch and die by himself'. Even a product which is in fact created by a number of people can give satisfaction to the one who can feel that it is really 'his'. A journalist, otherwise indifferent to his work, writes that 'for the time it took me to re-read one of "my" stories in the papers next day, I too felt the satisfaction of having created'.

2. *Using skill.* This is often associated with creating something, but it lays more emphasis on what the work does for the person rather than the product. Again, the use of skill cuts across the manual–non-manual division of work. 'The skilled worker has to work out, from drawings, the best method of doing the particular job; he has to set his own machine, he has to get the necessary tools out of the stores, he has to grind his own tools and so on. Using his ingenuity and his skill, the worker is constantly made aware of his active and valuable role in the productive process.' The bricklayer finding 'a certain joy in being able to do something competently with one's hands and in using muscular force with common sense to overcome obstacles', and the computer programmer delighting in the scope his job has for technical ingenuity are other examples of the different ways in which satisfaction can be gained from the use of skills.

3. *Working wholeheartedly.* Various restrictions on full productive effort by workers (attempting to beat the rate-fixer or time-study man, working to rule, 'go-slows', etc.) are common in industry today. But there is no evidence that these are *preferred* patterns of working. They mostly exist as weapons in the battle to get more money. More enlightened management policies than most existing ones could surely turn to better account the knowledge that most people enjoy working

wholeheartedly provided that they do not feel that they lose financially by doing so. A salesman expresses this idea clearly and simply: 'Like most people, I enjoy working wholeheartedly when I work.' A bricklayer says that 'the jobs I have enjoyed most are those where I have worked the hardest'. A slight variation of this theme is the fact that few people like to turn out substandard work.

4. *Using initiative and having responsibility.* This theme includes a feeling of freedom to take decisions and a certain independence of authority in the sense of people telling you what to do. To some extent the satisfaction derived from a job having these characteristics is a matter of personality and upbringing. Someone who has been raised and educated in the tradition of conformity and subservience to authority may not wish to use his initiative or have responsibility in his job. But it seems that most people value the opportunity to think and act in their work as responsible and relatively autonomous individuals. Even those workers who are 'not paid to think' often find it helps the job to go well if they do. A machine minder will replace the broken part of a machine without calling the supervisor because 'it's quicker and more interesting to do it yourself'. Another aspect of responsibility is well expressed by the doctor's secretary who found that 'one of the chief attractions of the job for me is the feeling of being in charge, feeling that I matter. . . . I would certainly be missed if I left'.

5. *Mixing with people.* This is an outstanding source of satisfaction to people whose work involves dealing with customers or clients. The attraction may lie in the variety of people one meets, the feeling of being able to help or teach others, the use of independent judgement as in casework, or simply the pleasure derived from social contact. A teacher writes that his job is 'concerned with growing and developing individuals who are never predictable, and so provide a variety of experience which is always stimulating'. Those whose work brings them into regular contact with other people may not always feel (as does one minister) 'increasingly refreshed and healed by personal encounter', but at least they will mostly agree with the doctor's secretary that 'it is much more interesting to follow cases than costs'.

6. *Working with people who know their job.* The 'human relations' school of industrial sociology stresses how important it is to have good communication between managers and workers and that it helps if managers show a friendly and interested approach towards their workers. However, if this is merely used as a technique, people tend to 'see through it'. A deeper respect seems to be accorded bosses who really know their job. Among the things that one town planner looks for in a job is the opportunity 'to work for people who know how to get a job done and who are not afraid or ashamed to be seen to be responsible'. Mutual respect is looked for; in the words of a steelman, 'to know that a manager knew his job and that he respected one reciprocally was a good thing all round, good for the metal, good for the melter, and good for the manager'.

So far we have described some of the positive satisfactions that people gain from their work. What can be said of the things that cause dissatisfaction? Obviously some of these are simply the opposite of the things discussed above - not being able to create anything, using no skill, and so on. But the emphases are rather different. Again, drawing on a number of *New Left Review*'s accounts, we can see several themes of dissatisfaction:

1. *Doing repetitive work.* This produces a feeling of never really achieving anything and of failing to use one's human faculties. It has long been recognized as a problem in industry and attempts to ameliorate it include shifting workers from one job to another as frequently as possible (job rotation). The full effects of repetitive work on human beings is incalculable, but we have the evidence of a few articulate victims. 'Nothing is gained from the work itself – it has nothing to offer. . . . Either one job is followed by another which is equally boring, or the same job goes on for ever: particles of production that stretch into an age of inconsequence. There is never a sense of fulfilment.' Sometimes fully mechanical work may be preferred to work which requires a little attention because it enables the person to absent himself mentally from the job. Thus a housewife complains of 'the sameness of jobs that require perhaps less than a quarter of one's mental awareness, while leaving the rest incapable of being occupied elsewhere'.

2. *Making only a small part of something.* Long ago Karl Marx drew attention to what he called the excessive division of labour under capitalism: the forcing of men into a specialisation of function that becomes more and more narrow and less and less inclusive of their various potentials of ability. Despite some attempts to give people more of a whole job to do (job enlargement) there is still plenty of work that in effect makes the worker, in Marx's phrase, 'an appendage to a machine'. One operative expresses the view that 'the worker's role is becoming more and more that of an onlooker and less that of a participant. . . . The loss of dignity and restriction of talent compatible with modern factory life cause a lack of quality in the factory worker'. To a toolmaker, 'the normal lot of the industrial worker is a very unsatisfactory work experience of performing a fragmented task under conditions he can only marginally control.' These observations suggest that fragmented tasks not only mean less participation by the worker in the total work process but also affect his whole way of life and restrict his personal development.

3. *Doing useless tasks.* It can be argued that any work for which someone is prepared to pay or to authorise payment presumably has a use. But this ignores the extent to which the whole system of production and distribution has become remote from direct personal needs as it has become 'mass'. Much of the growth in the service occupations has to do with protecting property. A nightwatchman describes his work as 'a hive of men guarding the sleep of capital. Producing nothing, this labour exists to make nothing happen, its aim is emptiness.' Another type of task commonly felt to be useless is form-filling. In offices, factories, schools and hospitals the amount of paperwork is steadily increasing. The occupations it provides are seldom satisfying to the people concerned. Writing about himself and his fellows, a clerk remarks that 'unlike even the humblest worker on a production line, he doesn't produce *anything*. He battles with phantoms, abstracts: runs in a paper chase that goes on year after year, and seems utterly pointless.'

4. *Feeling a sense of insecurity.* The recurrent economic difficulties of the country, combined with technological and organisational changes, have resulted in an increase in the number of workers being made redundant. This in turn, has

led to mounting fears about the security of jobs. A feeling of insecurity seems to spill over into dissatisfaction with many other aspects of a job. Few people seem able to analyse their feelings of insecurity but many of them mention it in talking about their work. 'There is a general feeling of frustration, a feeling that life has little purpose in such insecure conditions where everyone is threatened with the loss of his job' (warehouseman). Sometimes the loss of a job is at least partly looked forward to. 'You feel dispensable, interim: automation will take (the job) over one day, the sooner the better' (clerk).

5. *Being too closely supervised.* Much has been learned by industrial researchers about the most appropriate and acceptable forms of supervision, but few of the lessons seem to have been learned by management. Office workers are more often the victims of inhuman supervisory systems than are factory workers. The clerk quoted above describes the worst kind, 'those that have you lined up in rows facing the front, with the eagle eye on you and no excuse for moving at all'. In social work and teaching the grievances concerning supervision take a rather different form. A child care officer explains how the 'hierarchy' is a drag on growth and change: 'What each of us needed in the job was the awareness to know what people were really saying, or trying to say, and to then decide how we could help them. To be assigned a role in a hierarchy contributed nothing to that.' Similarly a teacher complains that the bureaucratic structure of the school means that the school governors and senior staff 'wish to supervise the minutest details of the projects they organize'.

The themes of satisfaction and dissatisfaction discussed above cover many aspects of the jobs that most people do today. Perhaps the most remarkable thing about the findings in general is the large gap they show between the most rewarding and the least rewarding kinds and conditions of work - a gap that cannot be entirely justified by the differences in the actual and potential abilities of the people concerned.

S. PARKER, in *Job Satisfaction*, ed. Mary Weir

1 Explain in your own words some of the main work characteristics which give people a feeling of job satisfaction.
2 What are the main work characteristics which cause job dissatisfaction?
3 What does Parker mean by his concluding remark that the large gap between those who find work most rewarding and those who find it least rewarding cannot be explained only in terms of 'the difference in the actual and potential abilities of the people concerned'?

Women and work

Women's work
Women's employment has continued to be concentrated in a small number of industries and confined to a range of jobs which might be described as 'women's work'. Even where women work alongside men, they usually hold positions of

lower responsibility and perform tasks of a less skilled nature . . . men are the employers, managers, top professionals, foremen and skilled workers in our society.

CENTRAL STATISTICAL OFFICE, *Social Trends 1974*

Most employed women in Britain are doing a job that provides a background against which other people can carry out what society believes are the more productive and important kinds of work. The woman employed outside her home is much more likely to be making biscuits than cars, serving coffee than building ships, doing the dry cleaning rather than the dock work.

With few exceptions, most women earn far less than most men. Men have always been considered the breadwinners, which has means that – in terms of cash, training, and promotion – employers have rarely taken women's work as seriously as men's. Neither, until recently, have many unions.

Men and women rarely do the same jobs. The major differences are that women are concentrated in a small number of trades and industries, that they are earning – even with the Equal Pay Act – about three-quarters as much as men do, and that part-time work is almost wholly done by women. (Just over one-third of women workers in this country are employed part-time.) The other difference, which springs from these three factors, is that women workers are mainly unskilled, and the number of skilled women is in fact decreasing.

Most women appear remarkably tolerant of the dreary and repetitive work many of them have to do. 'The best job I've ever had', was how one woman on the assembly line of an Edinburgh bakery factory described her job. What she did was this. She took eight shortbread fingers off the large metal tray which carried them from the oven and placed them in a narrow conveyor belt which deposited them on a cellophane wrapping machine. She was doing what is known as a 'simple repetitive task' – deadening, monotonous and badly paid. But it was far preferable to other jobs in the factory because it was away from the noise and heat of the machinery in the baking section.

The baking industry in Scotland was one of the industries referred to the Industrial Arbitration Board by the Department of Employment in 1975 because of the lack of progress towards equal pay. 'Women have been employed for years in baking as cheap labour', said George Curtis of the Scottish Baking Union. 'They were brought in in the 1920s to do jobs that men once did.' The industry's practices reflect many of the habits that imprison women in the menial, badly paid, and poorly thought of jobs, for the most part working with other women who share the same consciousness, and the same timidity about their potential.

In the Scottish baking industry, for instance, women are not allowed to work in fermentation, that is, with yeast in the early stages of bread production. Like other bans imposed on where women can work, it is a hang-over from the days when considerable strength was needed to handle the flour, to make the dough, and to process it – all done by hand. To exclude women now from these jobs is to exclude them from the higher paid jobs. So they work in other areas of production – either preparing scones, shortbread, cakes, cake decorations or cleaning and greasing tins and doing packing and dispatch.

On the assembly lines, Edinburgh women in 1975 were working beside men earning a fifth as much again as themselves. One middle aged woman said: 'The women put the meat and the onions into the pies and the men put the potatoes on top and for working with onions instead of potatoes the women get 82 per cent of the male rate.' The women resented this, and an added insult was the daily hiring of casual male workers who were paid more than long-serving members of the female work force. The arbitrary nature of the division of labour between the sexes is of considerable concern to the baking union. There appears to be no logic about the ban on women doing jobs that are either too hot, heavy or harmful. In one bakery it was the woman's job to take the newly baked bread out of the ovens and put it on the racks. In another this was designated a man's job.

Just over one-tenth of all women workers labour in the jobs which come under the collective title of the service industries. These million women do the work which is similar to the work they do at home – cooking, cleaning (especially cleaning), serving up the food, getting a place nice. The number of women who clean for a living is unknown because, of all the work women do outside the home, this is the area where they are most isolated, least regarded, and among the least organized in union terms. But cleaning is also a growth industry. The Contract Cleaning and Maintenance Association, which represents 300 members, claims that the industry is growing by between 10 and 15 per cent a year. 'People are more and more putting out their cleaning work to specialists because that relieves them of the whole chore of hiring and firing.' One cleaning combine, Pritchards, the largest in Britain, has a turnover of £325 million annually and operates in South Africa, Portugal, and the Gulf States as well as Britain.

Cleaning is not, in itself, a pleasant or desirable job. Most cleaners are in the job because the work is near their homes and because it takes place either in the early morning or in the evening when young children are asleep or can be minded by somebody else.

At a recent TUC women's conference, one union official suggested that women accept many of the bad conditions of dreadful jobs because they believe that to be aggressive would be to be anti-feminine:

'Women are told so often that they are patient, conforming, modest, good at routine work and so on that in the end they come to believe it themselves: and a very useful belief it is for employers who want an uncomplaining workforce slaving away unambitiously at routine work on low pay, and for those men – and there are many of them – who are afraid of female competition. One woman trade union official recently remarked that the problems with most women is not to make them work harder but to stop them breaking their backs for a pittance. . . .'

MURIEL TURNER, ASTMS

The pride many women in the service industries take in their jobs can seem like an extension of the pride in keeping a home. But there is no reason why this should be used as an excuse for paying badly.

LINDSAY MACKIE and POLLY PATTULLO, *Women at Work*

Part-time poverty

An estimated 2.7 million part-time workers in Britain are earning poverty wages, according to a report published today by the Low Pay Unit. A survey of 351 part-time workers by the unit found that nine out of ten workers were earning less than £1.20 an hour and five out of ten more earning less than 85p an hour.

If the lowest-paid category of part-time workers were working on a full-time basis, the report says, their wages 'would leave them 30 per cent or more below the official poverty line' – a much higher figure than is indicated by official earnings statistics. Only one in ten full-time women and one in 100 full-time male workers are in this same position, according to the report.

The report, 'The Part-Time Trap', says that women part-time workers have been taken on in increasing numbers as a cheap alternative to full-time men. 'Their attachment to work, need for money and potential for workplace militancy were all assumed to be low, compared with full-time male workers', the report says. 'Hence it was thought possible that female part-time workers would accept not only low wages but less favourable conditions of service as well with, at the very least, no sacrifice in productivity.'

The most obvious examples of low pay are apparently in pubs and shops. Three out of four barmaids and half of part-time shopworkers earned less than 85p an hour, according to the report. But low pay is not the only problem. Part-timers have to put up with poor working conditions and they are often excluded from fringe benefit schemes, it says.

The report says that only 10 per cent of workers in the survey were members of a trade union, the majority having no contact with a union and no part in the collective bargaining process. Many part-time workers were anxious to keep their earnings below the national insurance threshold. As many as one in five may be excluded from the Employment Protection Act because they work less than 16 hours a week.

'If part-time work paid better, the poverty of many single parents would be relieved and they would be able to combine employment with child care. Married women's earnings are vital to their families and decent wages for part-time jobs would enable more families to be lifted above the poverty level', it says.

The Low Pay Unit suggests that part-time workers should be encouraged to help themselves by joining a trade union but that legislation will be necessary to help create reasonable conditions.

The report also recommends that the hours qualification in the Employment Protection Act should be reduced to one hour so that all part-time workers are protected.

JULIAN COLES, *Guardian*, 14 February 1978

Women in professional jobs

Anyone reading newspapers over the past five years would imagine that women, rather in the manner of astronauts, had done the impossible. The news of the first woman judge, the first woman to become Prime Minister, the first woman professor of brewing, the first woman rabbi suggests that there is now very little for women to complain about in employment prospects. If one woman can do it so, the feeling goes, can they all. A useful counter to this list of firsts is trying to spot the tenth woman judge, a female majority in the Cabinet, the female vice-chancellors of British universities. Sightings here will be conspicuous by their absence.

There are few women in management posts, the professions or in the higher grades of jobs in industry. Women in the top ranks of the unions do not match the proportion of women union members, women teachers are not promoted to become heads of schools of departments in proportion to their numbers. A third of top nursing posts are held by men, who make up around 10 per cent of nurses. In trades and industries (food, tobacco, clothing, textiles, retailing, and hotel and restaurant management) where women employees outnumber men, women in administrative, managerial, and senior posts can be measured in single figure percentages.

Nor is there anything inevitable about the progress of women towards an equal share of the posts where decisions and policies, which affect male and female employees, are made. In some professional areas, as in skilled, manual work, the proportion of women is actually decreasing.

There have always been a few women who have reached key positions in professional fields, and they have gained enormous respect – often greater than that expressed for their male counterparts – from the public and some of their colleagues. But the gains made by such dedicated professional women in medicine, science, the Civil Service, politics, academic life, and occasionally in business, have not set up a structure in which women are automatically welcomed and accepted in the same way as men. The acceptance gained by professional women in the past has been an acceptance of the exceptional individual rather than the acceptance of women as a professional group.

And this has often been gained after the women made some very harsh personal choices – perhaps giving up thoughts of marriage and children, or deliberately quelling aspects of their personality to fit into a man-made professional structure. The attitudes of men, and sometimes of women, to an enlarged presence of women in managerial professional and senior posts often depend on prejudices, beliefs, and myths, which are hard to disentangle.

And in case there should be any doubt that fierce prejudice exists against women in the fields where women are employed, a timely report (published in International Women's Year) produced for the Department of Employment by Audrey Hunt, paints a lurid picture of the evidence.

'A majority of those responsible for the engagement of employees start off with the belief that a woman applicant is likely to be inferior to a man in respect of all the qualities considered important.' Out of 223 firms studied, the people responsible for hiring proclaimed resoundingly their belief in the inferiority of women. Only 1 per cent of those questioned said that from preference they would hire a woman, 68 per cent said they would hire a man, and 21 per cent said either would do. Only 3 per cent would hire a woman engineer, 80 per cent wanted a male engineer. 15 per cent would have hired a woman to join the sales staff, 45 per cent preferred men. Less than half the managers interviewed thought it would be a good thing if more women occupied senior posts. 'When asked whether there are ... ways in which the performance of one sex is better than the other ... the leading answer in respect of women is that they are better at dull repetitive work. . . .'

Women's special qualities

It is hard to quantify just how different women's 'approach' to work is, or exactly what are the special qualities that women bring to their work. And this is a particularly difficult area since it has been the notion of special 'feminine' attributes that has been partly responsible for putting women firmly into the slots – mostly inferior – thought most appropriate for them. But many women believe that women do bring to their work qualities different from those of men, and that it is time such qualities exerted more influence.

Women's new awareness of themselves and of their potential power is gradually gaining some ground in a cross-section of jobs. The medical profession is not noted for its radical thinking, and its top echelons are still very much a male preserve. For instance, only one in every 130 surgeons is a woman. However, where women doctors practise in larger numbers, that is in family planning, community health, and as GPs, there are some signs of change.

Many women patients prefer to share their problems with women doctors, which goes a long way to explaining the success and importance of the Elizabeth Garrett Anderson Hospital, London. This hospital at the time of writing faced with extinction, is one of the few in the country staffed completely by women for the treatment of women.

Like women doctors, women barristers have tended to be corralled in one area of their profession – namely, family law. This is a branch that has never held high status, but with the introduction of legal aid and easier divorce, work in the Family Division courts has greatly increased. This has broadened the scope, as well as increased the fees, of those practising there. But there is, according to Barbara Calvert QC, a great deal of satisfaction in working in areas of such desperate importance to clients.

Women architects are also beginning to suggest that their experiences as women are valid in a professional context. A special edition of *Architectural Design* (August 1975), which was devoted to women architects, mentioned that 'women have had a more practical and sympathetic approach to housing problems and domestic practice'. Santa Raymond, who has set up a London scheme in which a number of women architects work from home in an informal association, thought that women could communicate with clients who might otherwise be intimidated by the more conventional architectural offices.

However, feminist attempts at changing well-entrenched attitudes in the business and professional world are only just beginning to take effect, and in some areas have little chance of success. Most advertising is aimed at women, and the advertising profession is built around and promotes a facile picture of the average housewife. Women are depicted as almost educationally subnormal, voraciously materialist and immersed in self-delusion. The profession has no wish to change this.

In the whole field of women's employment there is little evidence that serious thought is being given, other than by individual women, to both the needs of women and their contribution to jobs. The passing of legislation of itself does not quickly alter the views of employers, nor of employees, that most fields of employment are literally man made for men. If women are to achieve a more equitable distribution throughout all levels of employment, their work pattern – the years at home and a later return to employment outside the home – needs to be more readily accepted and accommodated. And women themselves need to be less modest in the kind and the level of jobs for which they settle.

LINDSAY MACKIE and POLLY PATTULLO, *Women at Work*

Working mothers
For the estimated 821,000 pre-school age children whose mothers go out to work, there were in 1974, in England, 24,552 places in local authority day nurseries. In maintained nursery schools (run by the Department of Education and Science) there were 15,431 full-time places and 30,401 part-time places. In nursery classes attached to primary schools there were 32,527 full-time places and 51,762 part-time places. The total number of under fives in primary schools (this included rising fives in primary classes) was 301,106 in full-time places and 77,972 in part-time places. Total state provision therefore was 449,462 full and part-time places for the 4,500,000 children under five. Less than one child in ten has a hope of any state pre-school care.

This situation is no accident. For twenty years after the end of the war in 1945, government policy on the care of the children of working mothers was virtually static. Many nurseries closed down so that there were less children in state nursery schools than there had been in 1947. The same thing happened with day nurseries (run by the Department of Health and Social Security), where their numbers dropped from 903 in 1949 to 444 in 1967 (DHSS, *Health and Social Security Statistics*).

The Government gave several reasons for the cutbacks: teachers – then in short supply – were needed for older children; a dramatic rise in the birthrate had created more demand for pre-school facilities than was financially possible: therefore, childcare had suffered from expenditure cuts in the expendable area of the social services.

But the doubts of governments about the wisdom of women with young children going out to work ('abandoning their infants') were also responsible for the cutbacks in childcare provision. This belief had been set aside conveniently in war time, when it became a 'good thing' for married women to go out to work.

However, by 1975, the National Union of Teachers declared that the nursery programme was 'in ruins'. The falling birth rate had been seized by the Government as an excuse for cutting the projection back to 500,000 places. Once again the needs of employed mothers, particularly in a time of economic difficulty, were ignored.

To be fair, the Government drew on and reflected the prevailing views of a host of experts on child development. The best known of these, and the man who influenced a generation of mothers, was John Bowlby, the British psychologist. In a number of books written in the decade after the war he stressed that prolonged separation of a child from its mother in the first five years of life could do irreparable damage. Most of his research was done in institutions such as children's homes, and from this he deduced that a lack of individual and consistent care from one person crippled a child's emotional potential for ever. Despite the fact that he modified his views in 1956, and distinguished between partial and total separation, the conclusions Bowlby drew were interpreted to mean that only the constant presence of the mother ensured the development of a living and adjusted personality in the child. He (and his followers) did more, in fact, to keep mothers at home than any chauvinist husband.

The weight of public opinion also contrived to lay a burden of guilt on the mother who works outside the home. Real guilt is often experienced by mothers over the poor, sometimes disastrous, care their children get while they are at work, but again fewer mothers would be forced into unsatisfactory arrangements if the state did not opt out of its logical responsibilities.

Recent research has now begun to counter the claims of the 'evil working mother' school of thought. It is suggested that the quality of care – from whatever source – and the general home background are the determining factors in a child's happiness. 'Many accusations laid at the door of the working mother are ill founded. Such effects as have been noted are relatively small' (National Children's Bureau 1973).

The majority of employed mothers make their own arrangements for looking after their young children. Audrey Hunt in a Department of Employment Survey in 1968 found that fathers and relatives looked after pre-school age children in over half of the sample while the mother was working. Only 6 per cent of children under two were in day nurseries, and only 12 per cent of two to four year olds were in either day nurseries or nursery schools. Child minders, friends, or simply taking the child to work or working at home were other solutions.

In 1974 the number of children being looked after by registered child minders in England was 85,185 (DHSS, *Health and Social Security Statistics*, March 1974). The numbers of unregistered minders are simply not known, but approximately 100,000 children are left with unregistered child minders each day (Community Relations Commission 1975). The drawbacks of the child minding system are that the quality of care varies enormously and an employed mother is totally dependent on the goodwill and good health of the child minder for the care of her child. The fees charged by minders also vary, and a reasonable fee for good care can often not be afforded by a poorly paid mother. The system is a haphazard one, but the lack of alternatives may force a mother to accept quite unsatisfactory care for her child.

The pressure for places in day nurseries is enormous. In 1974, with 24,000 children in English day nurseries, there was a waiting list of 12,000 – half as many children again. And this list only consisted of so called 'priority' cases. The British day nursery system is intended to be purely a life-saving mechanism for the child or parent in a crisis. Even the often drastic need of the employed mother for somewhere reliable and safe to put her child is not considered a good enough reason for allowing her use of the day nursery system. 'You've got to have a real problem to get your child a place – unmarried, divorced, a battered or handicapped child, a handicapped parent or particularly bad housing conditions. If you can't produce that sort of evidence you haven't a hope.' The deputy matron of a day nursery in the London borough of Hackney who said this, also pointed out that if a mother got married then she was expected to remove her child from the nursery to make way for the product of another crisis-torn home.

The scarcity of child-care facilities for the employed mother is such that the debate revolves only around children under five. The fate of school age children with employed mothers is virtually ignored, as is the fact that the employed mother may then actually have to give up work.' 'When he goes to school I'll have to take a part-time job because of the school holidays and the time between him getting out of school and me getting home. They expect a mother to be at home. I don't know how I'll manage with a part-time job' (unmarried mother, Hackney).

So the employed mother's worries about the care of her child do not end with the arrival of school age. Audrey Hunt's survey (1968) found that there was a greater demand for facilities for children of school age than for pre-school children. Over a third of the women interviewed did not work during school hours, a further third left their child with a husband, relative, or friend, and a fifth said their child could manage alone. During the holidays, a husband, relative, or friend took care of the child in under half the cases, and in over a quarter of cases the child was thought old enough to care for itself. Four per cent employed a minder during the holidays. The use of playgrounds, playgroups, or facilities provided by the local authorities or schools was not mentioned. In fact, when Audrey Hunt asked if any such facilities existed, over 90 per cent of the sample said either that there were not any in their area or that they did not know of any.

LINDSAY MACKIE and POLLY PATTULLO, *Women at Work*

Look back to pages 156–60 for help with these answers.
1 What percentage of the labour force is female?
2 What evidence is there to suggest that more and more married women are going back to work?
3 Why are women, more than men, likely to take part-time employment? Explain why part-time workers are particularly vulnerable and badly paid.
4 Make a list of the main characteristics of women's work.
5 Suggest reasons why women 'appear remarkably tolerant of the dreary and repetitive work many of them have to do'.
6 *a* When were the Equal Pay and Sex Discrimination Acts passed?
   b What improvements were these Acts supposed to ensure?
7 How successful has the legislation been from the point of view of women workers? Give as many illustrations as you can to support your answer.
8 *a* What evidence is there to suggest that women do not have an equal share of professional job opportunities?
   b Suggest reasons why women are at a disadvantage when it comes to choosing a professional career.
9 The view that women are 'better at dull repetitive work' is often given as the reason why women are concentrated in low-status, badly paid employment. How far do you agree or disagree with this point of view?
10 What are the 'special qualities' which Mackie and Pattullo suggest belong to women and which should be recognized as being important in the jobs they do?

11 What evidence is there to suggest that the state does very little to help solve the problems of working men and women with children?

12 Suggest reasons why the state does not make school and nursery provision a high priority at the present time.

13 *a* What are the usual types of arrangements workers have to make for their pre-school children?
    b What are the advantages and disadvantages of these arrangements?

14 What evidence and attitudes have been used to criticize working women who have dependent children?

15 What evidence and attitudes have been used to counter these criticisms?

16 Explain why the problems faced by women workers do not stop when their children reach school age.

17 Do you think, from your own knowledge or experience, that children of single working parents or in families where both parents go out to work are at a disadvantage compared to other children? Give full reasons for your answer.

18 What changes in attitudes and improvements in provision would you recommend for a society like Britain in which married women increasingly choose to go out to work?

Industrial relations

A management view

Some employers have, from the earliest period of factory employment, tried to obtain greater harmony at work, and greater productivity from workers, by improving the physical comfort of their employees. Good standards of hygiene, heating and ventilation in the work-place, planned breaks for rest and meals, are elements in this practice, an approach to human relations which has rudely but not inappropriately been called the 'cow-house' philosophy of management. The supposition is that if physically pleasant and comfortable surroundings are provided for workers, and physical fatigue avoided, the 'problems' of industrial relations will be solved.

A serious revision of this approach was necessary, following the work of a group of psychologists in America during the 1920s and 1930s. They discovered that it was not so much the physical circumstances of the individual worker, but the social bonds which existed between workers in small groups, which influenced attitudes and determined production levels. Workers acting in groups tend to form bonds of loyalty and solidarity, and to make their own rules about what is acceptable on the shop floor. These rules often have little to do with the formal system of management authority and control and may often run counter to management's goal of maximum output.

From these 'discoveries' arose a 'human relations' school of investigators, who were usually employed by management to find 'solutions' to problems of low productivity and lack of 'cooperation' on the shop floor. Their advice to management suggested that if the social relations of work-groups could be understood, they could be realigned or manipulated to achieve labour-management cooperation, improved morale and productive efficiency. Such studies have been greatly refined since the 1930s, and many volumes have been written on the problem of the motivation of workers. The workers' needs for prestige, security and self-esteem have been exhaustively analysed, and the work of behavioural psychologists supplemented by that of sociologists, anthropologists, biologists and engineers. It is an approach which finds a great deal of favour amongst management, and leads – in the context of present-day preoccupations – towards schemes of worker participation and job enrichment. It has found less support amongst trade unionists because it has been seen mainly as a method used by management to solve its problems.

TONY TOPHAM, *Approaches to Work Place Organization in Industrial Studies*

1 What is meant by the 'cow-house philosophy of management'? Why do you think it is called this?
2 What were the important factors discovered by psychologists which encouraged employers to turn to the 'human relations' philosophy of management?
3 What 'management problems' do employers hope to solve by trying to promote better 'human relations' in the workplace?
4 Explain how 'worker participation' and 'job enrichment' schemes can be viewed as a management attempt to solve its problems.
5 Why are trade unions often sceptical about these developments?

A view from the shop floor
The voice of the city is sleepless,
The factories thunder and beat,
How bitter the wind and relentless
That echoes our shuffling feet.

The words of the revolutionary song are still relevant to workers waiting on a cold winter's morning for a bus that is always late. But when a worker is driving to the factory on a fine morning in his own car, as I and hundreds of others in my plant do, the link at first sight may not seem so obvious. Yet if you look below the surface you'll find that the more things change the more they remain the same.

From the Coventry journeymen of medieval times to the workers of 1917 who struck for the recognition of shop stewards, our city has had a tradition of workers' struggle. We are heirs to this tradition; but today, with the development of monopoly capitalism, the struggle is more complex than ever. Attempts to alter the methods of payment, speed-up, mergers and take-overs, wage freeze, unemployment, short-time working, automation – these are among the problems which confront us on the shop floor and which form the core of our struggle.

Since our factory is part of the crisis-ridden aircraft industry, the immediate contradictions are apparent to most of our workers. Advanced technological methods exist in our plant alongside First World War buildings and antiquated managerial ideas, greater output per man is counterbalanced by growing mountains of paperwork and bureaucracy. Overall hangs the lack of planning for the industry and the threat of cancellation of contracts, short time or redundancy. But while these contradictions are obvious, the long-term answers are not so apparent to the same workers.

Our factory is highly organized and highly skilled. Starting as a rather paternalistic concern at the turn of the century, it has grown by a series of amalgamations and take-overs – the latest quite recently when it was swallowed up by its rival – into a combine of some 80,000 workers and technicians in plants all over the country, a size equalled only by a similar concern in the USA. Our plant employs about 4,000 manual workers, over half of whom are highly skilled, and roughly 2,000 staff workers, mainly technicians, draughtsmen and clerical workers.

We start work at 7.30 – the time which was decided by a workers' ballot organized by the shop stewards' committee when the 40 hour week was introduced some years ago – so as to be able to finish early, at 4.15. On Fridays, because the lads like to get away early for the week-end we finish at 3.

Shortly before 7.30 I park my MG in the multi-storey car park which holds 700 cars and go into my shop. I don't have an office, just a desk and a phone; our committee is against the idea of isolating the convenor behind walls from the shop floor itself. I have a quick look at the night book to see if there have been any problems on the night shift, though usually the lads have dealt with their own, and then a glance at the press to see what they're saying about us: the *Morning Star*, the *Guardian*, the *Financial Times*. Usually one or two of the leading shop stewards will come round to discuss any problems.

As convenor, I work full-time on shop-floor problems, though the 170 shop stewards normally do some production work, depending on the amount of union work they have. For some this might be only 5 per cent of their time, for others as much as 30 per cent. My day is fully taken up, usually with two or three meetings fixed in advance with management, plus the day-to-day problems that arise.

To be effective, trade unionism, which is the workers' basic weapon in their struggle, must be militant, immediate and democratic. On our joint shop stewards' committee we are constantly trying to improve the organization inside the plant, to raise the level of awareness to the problems to be overcome and to make a conscious attempt to work out the answers.

We don't believe in lengthy strikes; several short, sharp stoppages are better than one long one.

In a well-organized factory where the strategy is to go for limited advances, long mass strikes shouldn't be necessary. Of course, there are bloody-minded company managements who don't care at all if they are wrong, who prefer a total shutdown to a compromise. But there are many like ours who are not basically bloody-minded and who, though always ready with strong arguments, are often willing to see our point of view. Quite a high proportion of our management is promoted from the shop floor and their feeling that the lads are right, coupled with the economic effects of disrupting production, is generally enough to make them change their minds. These remarks about our management's relative fair-mindedness do not mean that I don't believe in the class struggle, only that our sights should be set higher.

Militancy and class consciousness should not stop at the factory gate. This of course is the hardest task of all to achieve. The same workers who will lose several hours on a question of principle will not always spend several minutes in attending their union branch and voting for a progressive candidate to give them the national backing they need for their shop-floor activity. Irrespective of this, a highly organized plant inevitably widens the workers' vision to more of life than just his work-place. The ideas which really start advancing the workers in a factory, though many are traditional, come from the cooperation of consciously left-wing and communist trade unionists. All the policies that have emerged on automation, resistance to sackings, redundancy, etc. that have been of any use to the working class have come from the left; the growth of this activity is the only guarantee of advance on the shop floor. One aspect of the broader work that really opens the eyes of the worker is the occasional lobbying of Parliament and MPs that takes place amongst well-organized workers. When a worker walks into the House and sees the antiquated rituals, sees with a few honourable exceptions, the fishy-eyed MPs who have no ideas about the problems the worker and his industry face, he comes away certainly a wiser, and often a more cynical, man. But cynicism is of no good to the labour movement, it must be changed to anger and the anger to action to end this farce in which the existing system uses the worker to get what it can out of him.

For myself, and many others like me, there is thus an additional dimension to our work. Seen against a broader canvas, the frustrations of everyday factory life tend to dwindle; the major frustration then lies in not advancing the cause you believe in enough. The satisfaction lies in not being a cipher or a clock number, but in consciously striving to do something for the present and the future.

The present means improving where we can the system we work under and of advancing new ideas; it means high wage-levels and turning the factory to look outward and participate in activities beyond itself. The future is one of building a strong and united movement to bring about a socialist society, so that the final words of the song with which I began can come about:

Yet comrades face the wind,
Salute the rising sun,
Our country turns towards the light,
New Life's begun.

PHILLIP HIGGS, convenor, in Ronald Fraser (ed.), *Work 2*

1 Explain the meaning of the terms: shop steward, convenor, shop stewards' committee.
2 What are some of the main problems which confront workers on the shop floor and which Phillip Higgs believes a well-organized union should deal with?
3 How does Phillip Higgs justify the need for strong, well-organized trade unions? How far do you agree or disagree with his point of view?

4   In what ways does he suggest that trade union activity should be about broader issues than merely the problems which arise at work? How far do you agree or disagree with this point of view?

The great British disease is 'really only a pimple'

Strikes, frequently described as the British disease of the sixties and seventies may be more of a pimple than a running sore on the body of the British economy.

A paper by an official in the Department of Employment due for publication later this month concludes that the effect of strikes on Britain's wage costs does not seem to have been very great and that the direct annual loss to production caused by strikes 'has usually been very small by any criterion.'

The study, by Mr S. W. Creigh, a researcher with the Department of Employment concludes that although a few big strikes have caused exceptional losses these have usually been made up very quickly. 'Really serious disputes are normally limited in number and confined to a few lengthy stoppages in basic sectors of the economy,' he writes.

The study, which will be published in the Industrial Relations Journal, says that the normal public yardstick for the effect of strikes on the economy – the number of working days lost in any given year – is 'inadequate for the task.'

Using this measure, says Mr Creigh, is like 'estimating air-raid damage by reference to the bomb-tonnage dropped, irrespective of target or type of bomb'. It is not clear whether strikes act as an alternative or an addition to less organized forms of industrial conflict, such as voluntary absenteeism, poor time-keeping, 'or even accidents'.

The study comes to the conclusion that stoppages do not harm British industry to any great extent. During 1972, when more working days were lost than during any 12 months since the war, strikes lasting no more than three days accounted for 48.5 per cent of all stoppages.

Mr Creigh backs up the controversial paper written by Mr Nicholas Ridley, MP, accepting that unions in some industries are now too powerful to be taken on by any Government. He identifies seven industries as areas in which strikes would lead to 'emergency conditions'. These are coal, railways, basic steel, port and sea transport industries, gas, water and electricity.

Finally, the study points out that an intensive examination of Britain's motor car manufacturing industry, most strike-prone of all, discovered that most strikes – like British Leyland's toolroom workers' strike last year – happen when the industry was in recession. 'The strike becomes almost a form of work-spreading ... since it is more interesting and sociable than other forms of idleness and helps to keep workers from drifting away to other jobs.'

ALEC HARTLEY, *Guardian*, 17 June 1978

1   Explain in your own words Creigh's conclusions about strikes. Can you provide any other evidence to either support or contradict his findings?

Awaydays

They used to call it 'St Monday' in parts of Britain dominated by the older, heavy industries. It was the day when attendance at work was, well, variable. Nowadays, industrial relations consultants talk pompously about 'ergophobia'. But whatever you care to label it, absenteeism seems to be on the increase. According to a new study from Incomes Data Services (IDS study No. 169, from 140 Portland Street, London W1), total absence in some industries can equal up to 15 per cent of potential working hours. Every year, over 300 million working days are lost through sickness absence, which is a hundred times the figure lost through industrial stoppages.

The study looked at absence rates in 35 companies operating in three industrial sectors – chemicals, motor vehicles and food processing. The chemical industry recorded the lowest absence rate of between 4 and 6 per cent a month, which most personnel managers put down to complicated shift patterns which made attendance at work more vital, and also to better medical facilities keeping workers healthy. Motor industry absenteeism was higher – 6 to 10 per cent – and this was put down to the repetitive nature of assembly line working. Production line operatives had higher absence rates than craftsmen.

More overtime working also led to more absenteeism. In food manufacturing, absence rates ranged from 7 to 11 per cent and this was attributed to the high proportion of females in the workforce.

Absence rates also varied by region, by season, by size of firm, by population denisty and by length of journey to work. Sickness absence, 75 per cent of total absence, was highest in the north of England and south Wales and lowest in the midlands and south east. Winter rates were also higher than summer rates, and there was higher absenteeism around the holiday periods of Whitsun, Easter and Christmas. Firms in large conurbations like Manchester and Liverpool reported higher rates, too, often coinciding with the away games and midweek matches of local football teams.

What makes this study particularly interesting, however, is its evidence that absenteeism has increased quite substantially with the introduction of sick pay schemes under the current incomes policy. The raising of sick pay to equal full pay and the use of 'self-certificated' systems – have been especially important. In Leyland, Lucas, Du Pont and Birds Eye such schemes have doubled sickness absence. This would suggest that manual workers are taking action, on an individual basis, to increase their rewards, with payment now taking the form of increased leisure – or more time for moonlighting and money-saving jobs around the house.

TOM FORESTER, *New Society*, 8 June 1978

1 What were the findings of this study in relation to 'working days lost' by absenteeism as compared to strikes?
2 What reasons were given for:
a low rates of absenteeism in the chemical industry?
b higher rates of absenteeism in the motor and food industries?
3 Why might females be more likely to be absent from work than males?
4 What other factors affected absentee rates according to this study?

Unemployment

On the dole

The dole authorities require that I sign my name on two afternoons of each week. This action apparently proves two things: first, that I am alive; second, that I am open for offers in the line of work.

This I find an intriguing situation in view of the fact that they haven't any work to offer me, nor is it probable they will have any in the foreseeable future because of the desperate nature of things in this part of the country. When I talk about work, of course, I mean work here at home where my roots are and where, if I have any rights at all, I surely have the right to expect it. . . .

Have a brief look at a day in my life on the dole, which, except for slight unsubtle variations, is much the same as any other day.

Up at 7.15 a.m., a smoke and a cuppa, the fire lit, the kids downstairs. See they're washed, given their bit of breakfast, properly turned out, packed off to school. Another cuppa, another smoke, switch on Housewives' Choice, relax, reflect a little on this and that, perhaps play myself a hand at bridge and after about an hour of this lot switch off Housewives' Choice. Get washed, dressed, take dog for a walk by way of the railway line and along by the pit where I pick up whatever bits of coal I can find and put them in a small sack carried for that purpose. Back to the house, dump coal, tell dog to be good, then off down the road to the Miners' Institute where I read the *Express, Morning Star, Scotsman, Guardian,* and, if it happens to be a Tuesday, change my library books. . . .

After leaving the Institute I do my shopping, then back up the road, fix fire, brew another cuppa, this time with a slice of bread and marge (my usual midday repast), another smoke, then start in on the household chores. When the dishes are washed, beds made, etc., down in the chair for a bit of a doze which lasts about half an hour, then it's time to think about getting the kids' tea ready as they will soon be home.

When that's done and they've been fed, there's dinner to fix for self and wife – who, by the way, is earning a welcome pound or two at the potato harvesting – and then, after we've eaten, got selves and dishes washed, it's down in front of the telly for the remainder of the night, except, round about 9 o'clock, for another short walk for the dog.

Coming on bedtime finds wife sound asleep in her chair worn out after her day in the fields; myself bleary-eyed and very often depressed by some of the stuff I've been looking at on the box. . . .

Hectic, isn't it! Lovely life if you happen to be a turnip. But I am not a turnip, mate. I am a thoughtful, sensitive widely-read man, with cultivated tastes in music and the various arts of disputation.

Am I filled with bitterness? Yes indeed! Do I tend to be anarchistic in outlook? Unquestionably! Why am I like this? Is it natural with me, or does environmental conditioning account for most of it? The short answer is, of course, because I am such a bloody pointless waste of a good citizen. . . .

RONALD FRASER (ed.), *Work*

1   Explain in your own words why you think this man is bitter and
    frustrated.

Youth and unemployment in Saltley

In June of 1976 well over half of all young men between the ages of 16 and 19 in
Saltley were either unemployed or in a job that paid them less than £20 a week.

This situation was not just a result of the annual exodus of summer school-
leavers, since unprecedented rates of unemployment prevailed among those who
had been in the labour market for some time.

In addition, many young blacks, who made up the majority of young workers in
Saltley, believed that racial discrimination had been an important factor in
determining their position as unqualified, untrained and unemployed.

The evidence clearly showed that, in terms of qualifications, schooling had
been of little use and served only to reinforce already existing disadvantages. The
jobs that many young lads ended up in involved nothing more than following the
repetitive movements of machines; many of them had hoped to serve an
apprenticeship and become skilled workers but even these modest ambitions were
denied.

For young women the situation was almost certainly even worse. Public
expenditure cuts reduced clerical and service opportunities in the public sector,
and job creation schemes provided more opportunities for young men than
women. In a few cases too the advent of equal pay legislation has closed the door
to some jobs, by preventing women being used as a source of cheap labour.

Since the beginning of the 1970s, in Saltley, the number of female jobs has
declined with natural wastage at Southalls and the closures of the Co-op bakery in
Adderley Road and Hughes Biscuits. Almost a thousand female jobs have gone in
just these three factories.

These young people have a right to question why they should have to put up
with such fate; why they should be the victims of an economic system which
throws one and a half million out of work and which gives rise to such uneven
development that areas like Saltley can lose one third of its manufacturing jobs
over a period of ten years.

Yet for all young workers the Youth Opportunities Porgramme is supposed to
herald a bright new future; like North Sea Oil, a sign of better things to come. The
introduction to 'Young People and Work' claimed that the programme 'aims to
demonstrate by deeds rather than words that society cares about them. . .'.

In the summer of 1977 thousands of school-leavers in Birmingham joined the
dole queues and most of them had to wait six weeks or more before they received
any supplementary benefit. They could be excused for thinking that no one cared
very much about their position. In a situation of such massive unemployment no
amount of temporary 'work experience' or charitable labour will ease the
problems of youth unemployment.

Moreover, the Government's policy of reducing public expenditure has not only
increased unemployment but also aggravated the problems in areas like Saltley.
Educational resources are increasingly unable to cope with the problems of young
people in these areas. The housing stock continues to deteriorate despite the
enormous sacrifices made by local residents.

What is needed at a minimum level if places like Saltley are not simply to slide unpleasantly to disaster is a large scale (and expensive) campaign of improvement. A real 'war on poverty'. A properly organized programme of public works, organized by the council or central government with the full involvement of local residents, which started at one end of Saltley and worked its way through to the other could begin to solve the problems – could begin to provide adequate housing and other facilities for its inhabitants, as well as jobs for them.

Of course, such a policy (particularly if repeated throughout Birmingham's inner cities and decaying council estates, never mind those of the rest of the country) is incompatible with a policy which hopes to restrain public expenditure, but the choice is there to be made. We can no longer pretend that problems can be solved by marginal shifts of spending from one area to another.

Other suggestions have also been made about how to help cut the level of unemployment. Many of them have great merit, but their achievement, too, would require huge policy shifts. Jack Jones, for example, in a T&GWU pamphlet entitled 'The Case for the 35 Hour Week' has said that the introduction of a basic 35 hour week (brought about by a reduction of eight and a half hours in the normal working week) would provide 700,000 new jobs.

The idea of early retirement has also been put forward as part of a solution, and certainly the opportunity to retire early would no doubt be grasped willingly by older workers up and down the country. We should be careful, however, that the problem is not just shifted from young to old. Early retirement would be a prison sentence, not an improvement, if it meant attempting to live on very low incomes.

Unless the campaign to create more jobs is taken up more convincingly the experience of the youth of Saltley will become commonplace.

BIRMINGHAM COMMUNITY DEVELOPMENT PROJECT, *Youth on the Dole* (Report 4)

1 Why were girls and young blacks particularly badly affected by unemployment in Saltley?
2 Explain why schooling and qualifications had little effect on the situation in Saltley.
3 What suggestions do the writers make about how the problem of youth unemployment should be tackled?
4 What are the drawbacks to their suggestions?

3 Questions and answers

Checkpoints

1 Why was Britain ideally suited to becoming the first industrial nation?
2 What is meant by the terms mechanization, mass production and automation?
3 What is a silicon chip?

4   What is a multinational industry?
5   Approximately what percentage of the workforce is female?
6   What is the Equal Opportunities Commission?
7   Which groups of workers are most vulnerable in times of high un-
    employment and why?
8   Explain what is meant by the Job Creation Programme.
9   What is meant by piecework?
10 What is meant by the 'cow-house philosophy of management'?

O-level questions

1   'Automation is the name given to industrial processes which use
    machinery and computers not only to make goods but also to control,
    by 'feed-back' mechanisms, the rate of production, the input of raw
    materials and the co-ordination of separate processes. In automated
    factories less manpower is needed, but workers have to understand the
    whole process and their responsibility is much greater.'
       Why are sociologists interested in automation?
2   Newspapers talk of 'latch key' children as though children whose
    mothers go out to work are necessarily neglected. What evidence is
    there to support or contradict this opinion?
3   'Work is crucial in that it is a source of income. But the work a person
    does is also important in other ways. . . .'
    Why is work important in other ways than as a source of income? Give
    three examples to show the importance of work in an individual's non-
    work behaviour.
4   What is the difference between automation and mechanization? What
    effect is automation likely to have on the lives of employees?
5   If a sociologist were asked to find out the reasons for a high number of
    strikes in certain factories, what kinds of research methods could he
    or she use?
6   The steelman and the assembly line worker might both be described as
    working class. Explain the difference in lifestyle, general values and
    behaviour which exist between them despite the fact that they are
    members of the same social class.
7   Study Table 13 (page 186).
a   What changes in the occupational structure are indicated by Table 13?
b   How would you explain these changes?
8   Study Table 14 (page 186).
a   Outline the changes indicated by the table in working hours and paid
    holidays of manual workers since 1951.
b   What factors have caused the changes and what are the
    consequences?

Table 13 *The occupied population of Great Britain by major occupational groups 1911–66*

	1911	1966
	(%)	
Employers and proprietors	6.7	3.4
White-collar workers	18.7	38.3
Managers and administrators	3.4	6.1
Higher professionals	1.0	3.4
Technicians and lower professionals	3.1	6.5
Foremen and inspectors	1.3	6.0
Clerks	4.5	13.2
Salesmen	5.4	6.1
Manual workers	74.6	58.3
Skilled	30.5	28.1
Semi-skilled	43.4	26.1
Unskilled	9.6	8.5
All occupied	100.0	100.0

SOURCE: D. Weir (ed.), *Men and Work in Modern Britain*

Table 14 *Weekly hours of paid work and holidays: manual workers United Kingdom*

	1951	1961	1966	1971
Men (21 years and over) working full-time				
Normal basic hours of work	44.4	42.1	40.2	40.0
Actual hours worked including overtime	47.8	47.4	46.0	44.7
Percentage of all full-time workers having a basic entitlement to annual holidays with pay of duration:				
Two weeks or less	97	97	63	28
Between two and three weeks	2	1	33	5
Three weeks	1	2	4	63
Between three and four weeks	–	–	–	4
Four weeks and over	–	–	–	–

SOURCE: Central Statistical Office, *Social Trends 1973*

9 Study Figure 11.

a What information can be obtained from the graph?

b What explanations do sociologists offer for the situation shown by the graph?

Figure 11 *Absence from work in England and Wales, by sex and job satisfaction**

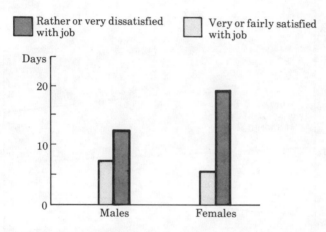

* Average number of working days lost per employed person per year

SOURCE: Central Statistical Office, *General Household Survey* (1973)

10 'It has been suggested that automation will bring a new golden age of leisure and plenty for everybody. It has also been suggested that automation poses the greatest threat to our standard of living and way of life since the Industrial Revolution.' (adapted from E. Kristenson, *Automation and the Workers*)

What are the possible consequences of automation?

11 Study Figure 12.

a Outline the changes indicated by Figure 12 (page 188).

b How have these changes affected women's work patterns?

12 A person's occupation influences his whole way of life. Select two examples which demonstrate this and show how they relate to this suggestion.

13 In times of high unemployment which sections of the labour force are most vulnerable?

14 Explain why 'the interests of employers and employees are frequently in conflict'.

Figure 12 *Women's changed living pattern*

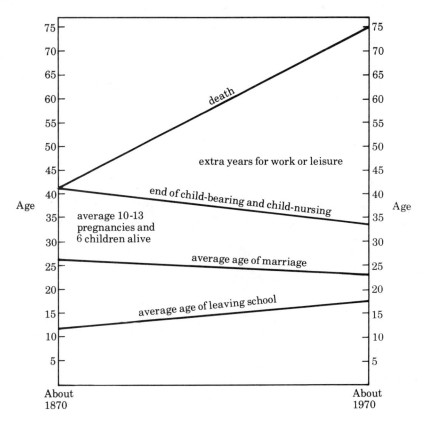

SOURCE: C. Hambling and P. Mathews, *Human Society* (1974)

7 Population in perspective

1 Background information

Technical terms

In the study of population characteristics and trends you will come across a variety of technical terms. Here are some of the most common ones.

Demography

Demography is the word used to describe the study of population characteristics. Those which particularly interest sociologists are the *birth rate*, the *death rate*, the *infant mortality rate*, the average age of *life expectancy, fertility* and *migration*.

Birth rate

The birth rate is a figure used by sociologists to compare the number of people being born each year in different societies. It is of little value to compare the total number of births in Britain and America, for example, without taking into account the fact that America has a much larger population than Britain to begin with. To arrive at a birth rate which can be compared, it is first of all necessary to know the size of the population in thousands. The number of births in any one year is then divided by the number of thousands of people in the populations. For example, in a town of 320,000 inhabitants, say there were 3520 live births recorded in one year. The birth rate would be obtained by dividing the number of births by the number of thousands of population: 3520 ÷ 320 = 11. The birth rate in such a town would therefore be 11.

Population increase can partly be measured by the rate at which the birth rate increases every year. It is in the developing countries of Asia, Africa and Latin America that population is growing very quickly. Some countries in these regions have a growth rate of around 3.5 per cent, which means that their populations will double in twenty years or less. It has been estimated that seven-eighths of the expected increase in population in the next thirty-five years will take place in countries which are economically less developed. By contrast, the rate of increase in European countries is about 1 per cent a year.

Death rate
The number of people alive is affected not only by the number of people born, but also by the number of people that die each year. We call the number of people dying (per thousand of people alive) the death rate.

Infant mortality rate
If the death occurs within the first year of a baby's life, it is called infant mortality. The infant mortality rate for any one year is calculated by dividing the number of infant deaths by the number of thousands of live births.

In 1901 the infant mortality rate in Britain, for example, was 185, which meant that for every 1000 babies born, 185 died during the first year of life.

By 1973 it had dropped to 19: for every 1000 babies born, 19 died during the first year of life.

Life expectancy
This refers to the estimation made at birth about how long people can be expected to live and is based on information about existing patterns of infant mortality and death. Over the last 100 years in Britain there has always been a difference between the life expectancy of different sexes. Women have always had a higher expectation of life than men.

Fertility
This is usually expressed as the number of live births per thousand women of child-bearing age and the age is usually reckoned to be between 15 and 45.

Often a distinction is made between legitimate fertility and illegitimate fertility and in each case the rate is calculated in relation to each thousand married and unmarried women of child-bearing age.

The phrase 'illegitimacy rate' is sometimes misleadingly used to mean the percentage of births to unmarried women. It would be more accurately called the 'illegitimacy percentage'.

Migration
Migration is the term used to describe the flow of people from one area to another. When people are leaving an area or a country to set up home somewhere else, the movement is called emigration. Movement into an area or country is called immigration.

The term 'net migration' is a confusing one. It's used to indicate the flow of people from one area to another, with the reverse flow subtracted, and is calculated from those migrants still alive at the time of the next census. In practice it ignores the true extent of population movement as well as all those who moved but died before another census could be taken.

Population increase

Consider the population of Britain. Which of the following statements do you think is true?

The number of babies born in Britain each day is

a   the same as the number of people who die
b   bigger than the number of people who die
c   smaller than the number of people who die

If you thought (b), then you were right. Each day in this country about 2740 babies are born and about 1720 people die. This means that today there are about a thousand more of us than there were yesterday. But this is only what is happening in our country. Each day in the whole world there are about 180,000 people more than there were the day before. (That is like adding a city the size of Dundee every day.)

Over 70 million people are added to the world each year. While it has taken the whole of man's history to reach the present world population (about four thousand million people), experts predict that there will be twice as many people on earth by the year 2000 as there are now.

Developing countries

Eighty-five per cent of the population of the world live in developing countries, that is, in those countries which are in a state of transition from an agricultural, non-technological economy centred on traditional and rural life to a technological, industrialized economy, based on urbanization and rapid social and economic change. Not all of these countries are at the same point of transition, because their industrialization and development occur at different rates and were begun at different times.

The remaining 15 per cent of the world's population live in the rich countries of North America, Japan, Europe and the USSR and share between them about 90 per cent of world income, about 90 per cent of the world's gold reserves, and nearly 95 per cent of the world's scientific capacity. This rich minority also enjoys 50 per cent of the world's wheat, 70 per cent of its total meat production and 80 per cent of protein foods.

Population changes in developing societies

Societies can be said to be in one of three stages of development (see Figure 13):

Type A societies are undeveloped, agricultural and non-technical. Their demographic characteristics are a high birth rate, a high death rate, a high infant mortality rate, and a short expectation of life.

Type B societies are developing countries in a stage of transition from a backward agricultural economy to an industrialized urban way of life. Their demographic characteristics are a high birth rate, a declining death rate and infant mortality rate, and an increasing expectation of life.

Type C societies are industrial technological societies, which make up the rich 15 per cent of the world's population. Their demographic characteristics are a low birth rate, a low death rate, a low infant mortality rate, and a long expectation of life.

This movement from Type A to Type C societies, producing these different age structures, is called the 'ageing of population'.

Figure 13   *The age structure of societies*

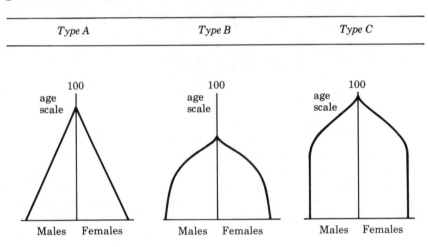

Medical science

Discoveries in medical science have the effects of reducing disease and preserving life. When Britain first experienced medical improvements it, too, suffered a rapid population increase, but this was soon checked by limiting family size. Britain now has a low death rate and a low birth rate, so that the population increases only very slowly. In developing countries, however, little advance has been made towards encouraging the people to limit the size of their families, while medical improvements have been able to cut down the high death and infant mortality rates. In

Guyana, in 1945, for example, two scientists went across from Trinidad on a weekend visit. The medical officer told them about the exceedingly high infant mortality rate - one child in four died before the age of one year. The deaths were almost entirely due to insect-borne diseases. They mentioned the use of DDT, then becoming publicly available, which had proved its worth as an insect-killer in the war. They helped the medical officer to get it and he was able to spray an area of ten square miles, including Georgetown, by aeroplane. The results were amazing. By 1948 the infant mortality rate had dropped from 250 per thousand to 67 per thousand. In Ceylon, DDT used on the malaria mosquito halved the death rate in seven years, a process which had taken seventy years in Britain.

Problems arising from the population explosion in developing countries

1   The rapid growth of population in many of the developing countries means that a large proportion of the inhabitants are young and dependent upon the work of others. In most of these countries, 40-50 per cent of their population are under 15 years of age, compared with 25-30 per cent in developed countries. The burden of feeding, clothing and educating this large number of children can be a serious handicap to improving the social and economic conditions in poorer countries. In 1975 the total number of children in the world exceeded 14,000 million, with 1130 million of them in developing countries.

2   Abortion is one of the world's most common ways of limiting family size, even though it is frequently illegal, expensive, and medically hazardous. In five countries of western Europe it is estimated that there are as many illegal abortions as live births. In India, the estimate is that each month a quarter of a million women undergo illegal abortion. In Latin America, illegal abortion rates are among the highest in the world. In one country they are said to total three times the live birth rate: in another, to be the cause of two out of every five deaths of pregnant women. Where public authorities will not assist parents to avoid unwanted births, the parents will often take matters into their own hands - at whatever cost to conscience and health.

3   The problems of feeding, educating and providing work for the extra people vary from country to country. In countries already densely populated like Korea, Lebanon, and islands like Mauritius and some of the Caribbean islands, the world population explosion has real meaning. There may be actual land shortage, and there is always shortage of capital to develop the land intensively. People flock into the cities to look for work, all too often merely increasing the urban unemployment problem. The immigrant communities in our own country are witness of these pressures. They have come because there is a better chance of a

livelihood here than there is in their own country. Calcutta, with nearly seven million people crowded into the 400 square miles of its metropolitan area, is a frightening example of a city growing too rapidly:
More than three-quarters of the population live in overcrowded slums.
More than 57 per cent of the families have only one room for their home.
In the slum areas each outdoor water tap is shared between thirty people and each lavatory between twenty people. Rubbish is dumped in the streets and left uncleared. Open sewers are common and people often use untreated water for cooking and drinking. Despite the efforts of the World Health Organization, cholera cannot be kept in control for long.
4   The pressure on food supplies is the most immediate and serious of the problems arising from the rapid growth of population. The Far East, the Near East, Africa and Latin America contain over 70 per cent of the world's population, but they produce only about 43 per cent of the world's food supplies. Agricultural production is going up only gradually in most of these areas, and every year there are more mouths to feed.

Family planning

One of the only acceptable ways to defeat the population explosion is to encourage and provide for the practice of family planning. But this is by no means a straightforward procedure.

In many of the developing countries family planning activities are handicapped because of religious or political opposition. Many countries in Latin America are predominantly Catholic, and family planning work has encountered considerable church opposition. In Africa and Asia there are religious beliefs which encourage people to have large families.

Many countries in Africa have low population densities. Their governments tend to discourage family planning as they feel that a high rate of population growth will help their development, without realizing the implications of a disproportionate number of young people which the country has to support. Some African nationalists use family planning as a political weapon, saying that it is a device invented by their former colonial rulers to limit the number of African people.

Such beliefs indicate how far family planning is from being universally accepted. If family planning programmes are to earn the support of the people in developing countries, they must be carried out by local organizations.

The major obstacle to family planning is the lack of adequately trained personnel. The development of different methods to limit family size has been the result of research carried out only recently, and practical application of these methods on a large scale requires the training of many thousands of medical personnel in a very short time.

Population trends in Britain

The census

In 1801 the first national census was carried out. In 1971 a minor public outcry condemned the government's support of a similar survey to calculate the number and characteristics of the population today. Except for 1941, in fact, an official census has been taken every ten years since 1801. Critics in 1971 complained about what they called government snooping into people's personal lives and feared that vast dossiers of private information about individuals were being built up, which could be used against them in the future.

The reasons for the census are in reality much less sinister then this, but are none the less extremely crucial in the planning of a complex industrial society like our own. Governments must know, for example, what proportions of the population will be at work and how great the number of dependents will be; what school provision must be made for the future; what facilities are needed for the elderly. Information about the geographical distribution of population will reveal where population density is greatest and where the centres of unemployment and hardship are likely to be. Details of family size and housing conditions pinpoint the extent of redevelopment that is needed; car ownership has implications for road and motorway building and for town planning; hospitals and nurseries must be related to the areas in which the need is greatest.

For all of these reasons the government needs accurate statistical information which can only be obtained by a compulsory national census.

Population growth in Britain

Since 1801 the population of Great Britain has increased steadily as Figure 14 shows. Many factors have contributed to this growth, the most important ones being the changing rates of births and deaths.

The birth rate

In the first half of the nineteenth century children working from an early age in factories and mines were undoubtedly an economic asset, and while this must have been one factor encouraging the production of children, a more likely reason for the steady increase in the number of babies alive at the time was the reduction in the infant mortality rate (IMR). It has been estimated that up to 1750 nearly three-quarters of all children died before the age of 5, but with medical and scientific improvements this high rate of child mortality was cut to under one-third 100 years later. From about 1870 until more recently, the birth rate has been declining steadily and the average family size which was between

Figure 14 *Population growth in Britain, 1801-1976*

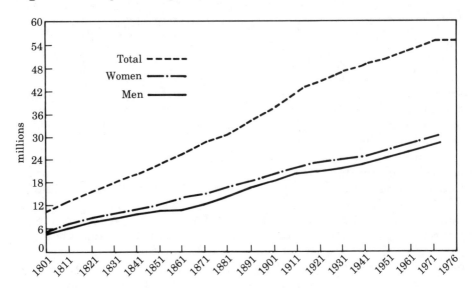

Figure 15 *Birth rates (per 1000) in Great Britain 1901-73*

1901	1911	1921	1931	1951	1961	1971	1973
29	25	23	16	16	18	16	14

five and six for couples marrying in 1870 is now more like two. Figure 15
shows the birth rates for Britain in the twentieth century.

Changes in family size
The trend towards smaller families began in the late nineteenth century,
but was largely confined to middle-class families. These were the people
who had experienced rapid prosperity in the industrial heyday of
Victorian England, or the traditionally privileged minority which still
enjoyed inherited wealth and patronage. With increasing foreign
competition profits began to decline, however, and at home education
became increasingly necessary for entry into hitherto middle-class
occupations like the army and the civil service. As the cost of living,
including servants and household expenses, rose, and since education

had to be paid for, the one practical way of preserving standards was to limit family size and preserve the excellent opportunities for a few children which had once been provided for several. At this point, the idea of family planning was being publicized by Annie Besant who, despite Victorian prudery, helped to influence the practice of middle-class parents in limiting their family.

As child labour was reduced and compulsory education spread, large families began to be an economic liability for the working class. Even though more children survived birth and were economically dependent on their parents for longer, the working class enjoyed no marked increase in wages to ease their situation. Despite all this, the conscious decision to limit family size had no place in working-class behaviour. Perhaps the main reason was that poverty and hardship, plus overcrowding and ignorance, were not conducive to the foresight and logic that contraception and family planning demanded. The working-class culture still defined sex as the man's right and the woman's duty; children were her responsibility and she was left to make the best of her lot. It was not until vast numbers of working men were lost in the First World War, followed by a massive slump and period of depression which exacerbated poverty that, belatedly, the working class followed the middle-class example and began to reduce family size. As women received the vote, and their status improved because of increased educational and occupational opportunities, they were progressively emancipated from their purely reproductive functions and the birth rate continued to decline until at least the mid 1950s. This trend has continued and became partiularly marked in the late 1970s as more easily available contraception, economic problems and unemployment all contributed to a further fall in the birth rate.

Mortality

Despite the reduction in the birth rate and the size of families, the population has still been increasing steadily over the last 100 years. This is mainly because the IMR has been considerably reduced and children who would have died in infancy 100 years ago now live on into middle and old age.

While the death rate has also declined gradually, it was not until the inter-war years that a significant decrease began to take place. The decline is usually attributed to medical improvements and the reduction of disease by sanitary reforms, but while these undoubtedly played a part more credit must be given to the overall rise in living standards and especially to improved and more nutritional diets. The extent of the reduction in mortality is shown in Table 15.

Table 15 *Death rate in England and Wales 1850-1976*

Year	Deaths per 1000 persons	Infant mortality per 1000 live births
1850	20.8	162
1860	21.2	148
1870	22.9	160
1880	20.5	153
1890	19.5	151
1900	18.2	154
1910	13.5	105
1920	12.4*	80
1930	11.4	60
1940	14.4*	57
1950	11.8	30
1960	11.5	22
1968	11.9	18
1976	11.0	16

* civilian deaths only
SOURCE: *Annual Abstract of Statistics*

Life expectancy

The high birth rate and death rate of the nineteenth century meant that the majority of the population was young. As both of these rates were reduced, the overall age structure of the population began to change. Social changes also meant an increase in the expected age of life, as Table 16 shows. The changes which have brought about an increased expectancy of life are:

a Improvements in medical science, reducing in turn the IMR and the spread of disease.

b Improved education, increasing the desire for better hygiene and public health, plus also providing a better informed public opinion demanding welfare legislation and social reforms.

c A greatly improved standard of living providing a better diet, and amenities and appliances which make life easier and physically less arduous.

d Improved working conditions, shorter hours and more leisure time making work physically less demanding.

e Increasing state intervention in the social welfare of its citizens through the welfare state. Also, development of the National Health Service, making medical treatment more widely and freely available.

Table 16 *Expectation of life at birth in England and Wales*

Year	Male	Female
1841	40	42
1871-80	41	45
1881-90	43	48
1901-10	49	52
1910-12	52	55
1920-2	56	59
1930-2	59	63
1950-5	66	72
1960-2	68	74
1964-6	69	75
1974-6	69	76

The elderly

The fact that people live longer today also means that the number of elderly people in the population is growing. If we define elderly as all those men over 65 and all those women over 60, then the numbers increased from 2.9 million in 1911 to 8.9 million in 1971 (see Figure 16). Experts predict that the numbers of elderly people in the population will go on rising over the next twenty years or so and that they will also live longer.

The current emphasis, in a rapidly changing society which thrives on material consumption and competition, is to place a high premium on the

Figure 16 *The elderly in Britain (population in 1000s)*

		1911	1931	1951	1971
Men (aged 65 and over)		964	1470	2251	2757
Women (aged 60 and over)		1915	2950	4599	6141
Total		2879	4420	6850	8898
Elderly as a percentage of the total population		6.8	9.6	13.6	16.0

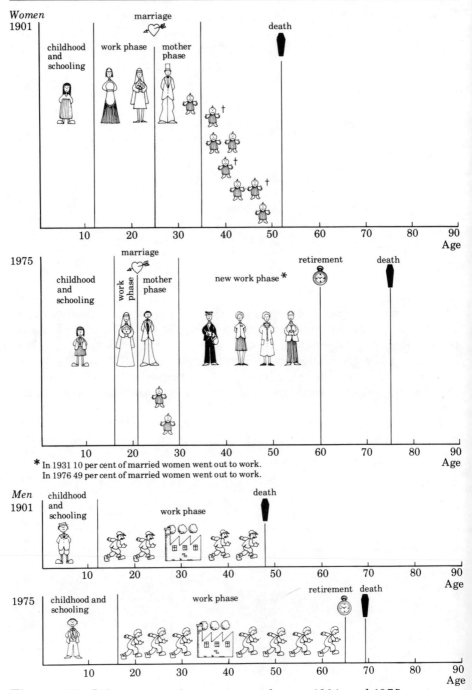

Figure 17   *Life patterns for women and men, 1901 and 1975*

young. In this situation the old rapidly become obsolete and the skills of their youth are no longer wanted. The change in family structure also tells against them, because there is no place for the elderly in the nuclear family as their children's social mobility leaves them behind. Despite improved health and living standards, retirement is compulsory at 65 and many people who are doing an active and economically productive job one day are considered to be old age pensioners the next. The problem of an increase in numbers is not that old people are financially dependent upon the state, but that many of them have no meaningful role to play. Once they begin to feel unwanted or useless, then loneliness, depression and other forms of psychological illnesses can develop.

The changing patterns of life (Figure 17)
If we put all this information together and add a few other details about the age at which people usually leave school, start work, get married and have children, we can see just how much the pattern of people's lives has changed since the beginning of the century.

2 Looking at the evidence

Changes in fertility and family life in Britain

Demographers have developed the quaint custom of comparing fertility rates with the even quainter customs of the Hutterites - a flourishing community of agrarian fundamentalists in North Dakota. Demographers have chosen these people because they have the highest known levels of what is termed 'natural fertility', that is fertility which is not affected by fertility reducing social practices. They have no deliberate birth control within marriage. On average their families have over ten children. Against the Hutterite yardstick, Britain and Europe have low reproductivity. Even in the 1870s before the onset of widespread fertility control, Britain recorded little more than one third of the Hutterite rate. By 1931 fertility had plunged still further by more than half of the 1871 level.

This remarkable demographic transition is not peculiar to Britain: it happened in other European states and is currently happening in developing countries today.

The demographic transition in Europe had three stages. In the pre-industrial stage, a slowly growing population was maintained by a balance of high death rates and high birth rates. In the second stage of early industrialism, extending well into the 19th century, fertility habits remained from the first stage, while a growing array of life preserving practices reduced mortality. Then in stage three, fertility declined at a rate which overtook the still falling mortality rate, until a new equilibrium was reached, by a balance of low birth rates and low death rates.

The trend towards smaller families was started by the professional and middle classes. It may be that it took time before people realized the full implications of lower levels of mortality, and that the middle class did so first and responded by planning and reducing their fertility within marriage. Working class men and women followed more slowly. But as the twentieth century has developed, all social classes have adapted to a small family pattern. More people have gained greater freedom and virtually all can now choose the timing of their parenthood.

The burden of childbirth is central to the story. In 1900 in Britain, one quarter of married women were in childbirth every year. Thirty years later that proportion was down by one half to one in eight. At the beginning of the century a British woman aged 20 could expect to live 46 years longer. But approximately one third of this life expectancy was to be devoted to child bearing and maternal care of infants. Today a woman aged 20 can expect a further 55 years of life. Of this longer expectation, only 7 per cent of the years to be lived will be concerned with child bearing and maternal care. But no less important than the virtual slavery of Edwardian working class women on the wheel of childbearing was the relation of women to the economy and the state. In the earlier decades the great majority of families depended entirely for their material support on male employment. The establishment of a new position for the mother, independent of her link to the economy through her husband, was therefore a prominent theme of feminist reform.

The state has contributed indirectly towards the liberation of women, especially through the expansion of health services and education. But the lonelines of mothers with young children is still attested and the absence of communal child care provision for such women remains an unsatisfied need. Meanwhile more direct emancipating influences have come from developed methods of birth control and, more important, the gradual movement of women, including married women, into employment. In the first two decades of this century, less than 10 per cent of married women in Britain went out to work: in 1951 the percentage was 21.74: by 1966 it had risen to 38.08 and by 1976 to 49%. The slow spread of affluence has also played its part in combination with the invention of power appliances to relieve some of the drudgery of housework.

The parallel trend which is less frequently noticed is the one affecting the roles of husbands and fathers. Seventy years ago working men typically lived in local communities in which they all shared the same kind of work. Mining and dock work are classic examples. Such communities evolved essentially male public organizations - the pub, the betting shop, the football club: organizations which loosened marriage bonds and took resources away from women and children. But the more recent patterns of industrial development and geographic mobility took their toll on the old male domination. Particularly after the Second World War hours of work were reduced, holidays lengthened, home ownership became more common, children were less ever-present and men were drawn into a more intimate relationship with their wives than their predecessors had ever known.

The third estate of the nuclear family the child has been the chief beneficiary of these developments. Individualism is the motif that has increasingly informed every aspect of child rearing, whether in the family or in the public sphere of playgroups, clubs, schools, holiday camps, juvenile courts or borstals. There has been a general trend in the small family towards higher standards of upbringing. For example, of those children born in the decade around the First World War, only one fifth grew up in owner occupied houses. Those born in the decade after the Second World War belonged to smaller families and well over a third of them were owner occupiers. Most children in the early years of the century grew up in the streets of industrial cities, while there has been a more recent move to the suburbs in council estates and private dwellings. A working class area is not now, as it once was, a kind of dormitory annex to the work place. The working class family has become less closely geared to the factory hooter. This combined with the shorter hours of work may well have increased the amount of attention men give to their children.

Children are more likely now to come from middle class families. The working class has fallen and the middle class have risen as suppliers of children. Before the First World War more than two thirds were of working class origin. But though the standards and expectations of childhood have undoubtedly risen in the lifetime of the oldest Britons left alive, we must not forget that the probability of membership of a large family, and of a low income, poor housing, illness, and early death, have continued to mark off the social classes from each other. In December 1975 there were 380,000 families with children who were normally on supplementary benefits. The number of children involved was 810,000. And though the average size of completed families among manual workers has fallen, a description of the childhood circumstances of those living in the Birmingham educational priority area in 1969 showed that no less than 91 per cent came from families of three children or more.

Adapted from A.H. HALSEY, 'Between the generations', in *Changes in British Society*

1   Who are the Hutterites?
2   Why are demographers particularly interested in the Hutterites?
3   What kind of population characteristics are typical of pre-industrial societies?
4   How do population characteristics change as societies become more industrialized?
5   Which social class group in Britain began the trend towards smaller families? Can you suggest any reasons for this?
6   What difference has the reduction in family size had on women?
7   Explain in your own words how changes in the economy, health and education have affected the role of women in our society.
8   What factors have influenced the changing role of men in our society?
9   How have children benefited from being brought up in smaller families? Do you agree that small families are more beneficial than large families so far as children are concerned? Give full reasons for your answer.
10 Explain in your own words why Halsey says 'children are more likely now to come from middle-class families'. Does he mean that more people are middle class these days?

Demographic review 1977

There are likely to be more bachelor uncles than the traditional spinster aunts, in the future, according to the 1977 Demographic Survey published today. Single men under 45 years old now outnumber single women by about 5 per cent - a proportion which could well rise.

This switch in the balance of the sexes could have tremendous implications for social behaviour and customs. But no one has yet really begun to assess the possible impact. 'It's not a matter to which the people give a great deal of thought, rather to my surprise,' said Mr Eugene Grebenik, consultant on demographic research to the Office of Population Censuses and Surveys, who compiled and wrote the report.

He told a press conference that there might be changes in the sexual dominance of marriage, in the sex of the person initiating a union, and in the age groups men search out for their partners. They might prefer, or be forced, to marry older women, as was common in agricultural countries in the seventeenth and eighteenth centuries, instead of generally marrying someone younger.

Certainly, women would be able to exercise greater choice. Once they realized the shift they might choose to postpone marriage until later in life instead of taking the plunge early for fear of being left on the shelf.

The report points out that the once natural biological surplus of male births over female - 106 boys for every 100 girls - has now been eroded.

In the late 1940s women formed a majority from about the age of 18, or about 25 if British forces stationed abroad were included in the home population. The new marriage squeeze has already resulted, according to the report, in an increase in the marriage rates of women relative to those of men.

'Unless the imbalance is redressed by migration - either emigration of men or immigration of women - there will be an appreciable number of men for whom no marriage partners are available at what is today regarded as the normal marriage age.'

Detailed tables show that for people born in 1900, 93 per cent of men and 85 per cent of women married at least once before the age of 50. Now the comparable figures are 91 and 92 per cent respectively.

The lengthening interval between marriage and the arrival of the first child indicates that people are not marrying just to provide a secure base for children. 'It seems likely that social and other pressures may be more important than the decision to start a family in converting a pre-marital relationship to a marriage.' the report comments.

The demographic review assesses other aspects of population trends and their possible implication for future planning and use of resources.

There will, for example, be an increase in the numbers of very elderly people, the numbers of men and women of working age and the numbers of women who could be mothers, in the next 15 years. This does not necessarily mean that there will be more children.

At the end of this first major review for 30 years - the experts say it is quite impossible to be definite about future fertility. Tomorrow's younger women may or may not choose to have large families. There will be about 10 per cent more potential mothers and the possibility of another peak in births at about 1990.

JUDY HILLMAN, *Guardian,* 20 June 1978

1   What was the main population change reported in the 1977 Demo-
    graphic survey?
2   What might the effects of this change be in the future?
3   What other population trends did the report comment upon?
4   Who produced the report?

The elderly

A major social problem today is how to provide for the large number of elderly
people. Over the last fifty or so years the elderly population has grown
substantially faster than the population of younger ages, both on account of the
fall in the birth rate in the early nineteen twenties, and on account of general
improvements in health and social conditions which have led to increases in the
proportions surviving to old age. At the same time, the rise in the general level of
economic prosperity has enabled more people to set up their own households so
that, while the nuclear family has increased in importance, the elderly on the
whole now receive less support from their families.

In 1971 there were 2.8 million men in the UK aged at least 65 and 6.1 million
women aged at least 60, in all 8.9 million elderly persons. This contrasts with 2.9
million in 1911, soon after the Old Age Pensions Act 1908 introduced a non-
contributory pension of 5 shillings a week to persons over 70 and on an income
less than £21 per annum. Since that time the number of elderly people has risen as
in the third row of table A.

Mainly on account of the high numbers of births in the years up to 1921, the
number of elderly people in the population will increase for the next two decades
or so, before the lower annual numbers of births between the wars lead to a slight
decrease in the elderly population, until the end of the century. One of the effects of
these changes, in combination with other factors, is that over the next ten years,
the number of persons of retirement ages will grow faster than the population of
working ages, though not as fast as in recent decades. Past and projected moves in
the ratio are shown in table A. One implication of the increasing ratio of elderly

Table A *Elderly persons, 1911-2001, United Kingdom*

	Actual				Projected	
	1911	1931	1951	1971	1981	2001
Elderly population (1000s)						
Men aged at least 65	964	1,470	2,251	2,757	3,166	3,139
Women aged at least 60	1,915	2,950	4,599	6,141	6,545	6,313
Total elderly	2,879	4,420	6,850	8,878	9,711	9,452
Elderly as a percentage of total population	6.8	9.6	13.6	16.0	16.8	15.0
Elderly persons per thousand population of working age	110	145	213	267	280	244

people to the numbers of working ages is that if the standard of living of the elderly is growing in line with earnings, an increasing proportion of each worker's earnings is required to support them. The average age of the elderly will increase over the next few decades, adding considerably to the demands on the health and personal social services for the elderly, both statutory and voluntary. The percentage of elderly women aged at least 75 is projected to rise from 28% in 1971 to 32% in 1981 and to reach 37.6% by 2001. Table B also shows how the proportion aged at least 85 will increase. The proportion of elderly men aged at least 75 is likely to rise from 29.2% in 1971 to 36.3% in 2001, but movements in this proportion and in the proportion aged at least 85 are substantially affected in this period by casualties in the First World War.

As women tend to outlive their husbands the problems of loneliness and adjusting to new circumstances faced by the elderly are confronted more frequently among women than men. Table C shows a considerably higher proportion widowed (or divorced) among elderly women than among elderly men. There are also substantial differences between age groups, especially for women. As may be seen from table C over 80% of women aged 75 or over are single, widowed or divorced. The proportions in each age group have varied noticeably in recent years, partly on account of war deaths.

As many more people have been able to establish separate households for themselves and their dependent children and more retired people are able to afford homes of their own, the proportion of elderly people who live alone has steadily increased (table D). In addition the pressures on working people to move to other areas where better opportunities exist have contributed to a situation in which families are less likely to provide company and care for the old. Thus gradually the state and the community have taken over more responsibility, and considerable efforts are made by social service departments to provide old people with company and activities outside the home in order to dispel the social isolation, boredom and vulnerability of many elderly people living alone.

Table B *Age structure of the elderly population*

United Kingdom   *Percentages*

	Actual			*Projected*	
	1951	1961	1971	1981	2001
Men aged at least:					
85	3.1	4.4	4.4	3.8	5.5
75	30.7	32.7	29.2	31.3	36.3
65	100.0	100.0	100.0	100.0	100.0
Women aged at least:					
85	3.4	4.5	5.6	6.0	8.7
75	24.0	27.1	28.0	32.0	37.6
65	70.3	71.3	72.4	76.3	77.7
60	100.0	100.0	100.0	100.0	100.0

Table C *Elderly persons by marital status*

United Kingdom   *Percentages*

	Married		Single		Widowed and Divorced	
	1951	1971	1951	1971	1951	1971
Men						
65-74	72.2	78.9	8.9	7.5	18.9	13.6
75 and over	50.0	61.6	8.2	6.2	41.8	32.2
All elderly men	65.4	72.4	8.7	7.1	25.9	20.5
Women						
60-64	56.6	64.5	16.1	11.9	27.3	23.6
65-74	42.2	46.0	16.1	13.9	41.7	40.1
75 and over	19.8	18.1	17.0	16.2	63.2	65.7
All elderly women	41.2	43.3	16.3	14.0	42.5	42.7

Table D *Elderly population in private households[1]*

Great Britain   *Percentages*

	Living alone[2]			In married couple without others[3]
	1951	1966	1971	1966
Men				
65–74	6.5	9.0	10.9	52.2
75 and over	10.5	14.7	17.7	38.4
All elderly men (%)	7.7	10.8	13.0	48.6
All elderly men (1000s)	168	265	354	1,190
Women				
60–74	15.6	23.1	27.0	34.7
75 and over	23.1	31.4	37.5	12.6
All elderly women (%)	16.8	25.4	30.0	28.7
All elderly women (1000s)	749	1,417	1,813	1,603

1 Excluding persons in household where no member was present on Census night.
2 One person households as defined in the Censuses.
3 The partner may not be of pensionable age, e.g. men 60-64 married to women in the same age group.

SOURCE: *Social Trends 1973*

1   Why has the number of elderly people in population increased over the last fifty years?
2   How has the development of nuclear families affected the lives of old people?
3   What effect will the increasing proportion of elderly people in the population have on working people over the next ten or twenty years?
4   Suggest reasons why women tend to live longer than men. What effects might this have on elderley women who outlive their husbands?
5   In what ways has the state become more involved in the lives of old people these days?

Survey of the elderly in East Hull

The purpose of a survey, conducted jointly by the College of Education and David Lister School in Hull during the first two weeks of July 1970, was to find the number of old people living in the vicinity of the school and the addresses where they lived. A sample of these was then interviewed to find out about their way of life and their social needs. The school already did much to help the elderly in its area, and the information from the survey was to enable this work to be extended, either by the school itself or by other agencies.

Census
College student and school sixth-former worked together in pairs and located initially the places of residence of all persons aged 60 and over who lived adjacent to the school; the area covered was bounded by Holderness Road and Southcoates Lane and was equivalent to one ward in the city. The Register of Electors gave 7,270 adults aged 18 and over as living in the area, and the census located 1,350 elderly, which was almost 20 per cent of the adult population.

Sample
A sample of the elderly was chosen by taking every sixth name from the census list giving a sample size of 226. These were then interviewed by a student and sixth-former together. The response rate was rather disappointing: 163 interviews took place, which was 72 per cent of the sample size. Much of the non-response was due to the elderly person not wanting to be interviewed, some was the result of absence in hospital, etc., and some interviews could not be completed because the interviewee was too ill or senile to answer the questions. However, apart from the sex balance, the people interviewed appeared to be representative of the population, as the following shows:

Age and married status	Sample of 163	1966 National Census: Hull
% Aged 60–69	56.4	57.6
% Aged 75 and over	24.5	24.1
%Married of all 60+	57.1	54.5
% Single of all 60+	9.2	9.6
% Female of all 60+	66.9	60.0

The sample had an over-representation of females, which could be the result of women being more likely to be at home when the interviewers called during the day.

Main findings from the sample inquiry

This area in Hull is predominantly working class. Only 9.2 per cent of the sample were salary-earner status or equivalent; 89 per cent were wage-earner status; 3 people were not able to be classified. Nearly all the sample left school when they were 14 or less; 94 per cent came within this category, leaving 6 per cent who stayed at school until they were 15 or older.

Household arrangements

A large number of the elderly lived alone or just with a husband or wife. Not a large proportion lived with a daughter or son; only about 24 out of the 163 (15 per cent) interviewed lived in this kind of household. The following gives the two main types of household arrangement:

Persons aged 60+ living alone or with spouse

	Number	Percentage
Living alone	51	31%
Living with spouse only	69	42%
Other household arrangement	43	27%
Total	163	100%

This shows that nearly three-quarters (73 per cent) lived alone or just with a spouse. When those aged 70 and over were considered separately, the preponderance of this type of household is even greater: 47 per cent lived alone and 31 per cent lived just with a spouse (over three-quarters (78 per cent) of this age group). Thus for the older people in the sample, the commonest arrangement was a single person household and this seemed to increase with age. There were 18 people in the sample who were aged 80 or over, and of these 12 or two-thirds lived alone.

Household amenities and home entertainment

Basic household amenities

% of dwellings with:	1966 National Census: Hull	Sample
No inside lavatory	33%	36%
No fixed bath	26%	44%
No hot tap in dwelling	21%	52%

In 1966, one-third of the dwellings in Hull had no indoor lavatory, one-quarter had no fixed bath and 1 in 5 had no hot tap in them. According to the sample, the elderly in this part of Hull are without an indoor lavatory in over one-third of their dwellings and in over one-half of old people's homes there was no hot tap – a very large proportion compared with the rest of the city. In marked contrast, the elderly in the sample fared well for entertainment at home: the vast majority had TV and radio and took newspapers. 87 per cent had a TV set and over 90 per cent had a radio; only 17 people said they did not get a newspaper every day, and only 2 people in the sample never received a daily newspaper.

Going out

The elderly were asked how they had spent the previous 7 days. Sixteen (10 per cent) had not been out of their house during the previous week. The remaining 90 per cent had been out of the house at least once that week. The typical outing was to go to the shop, or for a walk, or to make a call on a relative or friend. Other types of outing were made by only a minority of the elderly; 38 had attended a club, 15 had been to church, and 12 had been to bingo.

Contact with relatives

Old people in this part of Hull saw a lot of their relatives, and they feature in their lives a great deal. If an old person who lives alone does not belong to a club or go to church, and does not see much of neighbours, then relatives can be his only regular social contacts. They were asked how many of their relatives they had seen in the 7 days prior to the survey ('seen' included contact by letter or telephone) and whether or not it had been a typical week for contact.

Taking the 70+ age group, of which half lived alone, the average number of relatives seen was just over 4 (4.2 per cent).

Help from social services and other organizations

Sixty-two of the sample belonged to some club or society, and for 15 of these it was the Old People's Club run by the School. However, when the old people were asked if they had ever had any help in their homes from such as health visitors, meals-on-Wheels, social workers, or from vicar of minister, 123 or 76 per cent said no such help had ever been given. Sixty-six per cent of the sample said they thought that not enough was done to help the elderly these days, and when they were asked whose responsibility they thought it was to care for them, only 18 per cent said they thought it should be their relatives: 62 per cent expressed the opinion that the state should take responsibility.

Conclusions

There is obviously much that could be done to cater for the social and other needs of the elderly in East Hull. The majority of the sample (62 per cent) did not belong to a club or society, but the unsatisfied need for this kind of social life may not be great as only 49 of the 163 said they enjoyed old people's gatherings usually, and 47 said they did *not* enjoy them.

What would seem to require attention, however, was indicated by the fact that the large majority had never had any assistance from those agencies which exist to help the elderly. Perhaps the greatest need in an area like this is for organised visits to the homes of the elderly and advice given on where and how they can get help when it is required. Visiting old people, armed with basic knowledge of the state and voluntary services that are available so that they can be informed of the facilities provided for them in the community, would, the researchers concluded, be a valuable service for the elderly.

1 What was the purpose of the survey?
2 Explain carefully:
a what is meant by a sample
b how the sample of elderly people was drawn up
c why the sample response rate was rather disappointing.
3 Explain in your own words the difference between people of 'salary-earner status' and people of 'wage-earner status'.
4 *a* What seems to be the normal pattern of household arrangements for the elderly in this area? Give statistical evidence from the survey to support your answer.
   b Suggest reasons for this type of household arrangements.
5 *a* How did the basic household amenities of the sample compare with those of Hull as a whole?
   b What does this tell you about the kind of area investigated?
6 How do the elderly in the area spend their leisure time?
7 Give some examples from your own knowledge or experience to show how relatives feature a great deal in the lives of the elderly in an area like this.
8 What percentage of the elderly had been offered help in their homes by the state or voluntary organizations?
9 What recommendations does the survey make in the light of its findings?

Population 'problems' in developing countries: two common mistakes

One common view of the population problem appears to be as follows. In most developing nations the birth rate is far too high with the result that there is population pressure – in other words, just too many people. This inevitably has vast social, political and economic effects, most, or all of them, for the worse. The area that seems to spring most readily to mind here is South Asia, particularly India. The solution seems obvious. What is needed is for Western nations to propagate birth control methods in such countries in order to limit the birth rate. Without this people in India and other underdeveloped areas will continue, from both ignorance and unwillingness to change, to breed to the limit, and the resultant population pressure will inevitably bring disaster.

The picture is of people subject merely to uncontrolled biological forces, living somehow on the threshold of nature. Such people, according to this view, must be instructed in the idea of birth control and taught how to use appropriate devices. Otherwise they will continue to breed unchecked.

Now this view is in fact false. *All* populations already have their own norms for regulating both fertility and the size of the resulting population. It used to be assumed that 'primitive' populations bred to near the biologically possible maximum. Recent study, however, of the demography of such communities has shown that this belief is unfounded: 'the influence of social and perhaps even psychological factors becomes dominant. In all the communities studied the average number of children born to women over the reproductive period is much lower than the maximum possible.' The point is that fertility is always to some extent a *socially* controlled process, both because of social norms regulating fertility in general, and because having children is in all societies a motivated act.

In various areas of the world, for instance, social controls were and are applied to population growth by such socially approved customs as lengthy suckling, spacing children through deliberate abstinence (especially in polygynous societies), infanticide in certain circumstances, whether overt or disguised, or abortion. Other social norms have encouraged a high birth rate, like, for instance, the prestige or economic value of a large family. Many other social factors too are almost certainly correlated with the birth rate, even though the exact relationship may be unclear – like religious beliefs, for instance, age of marriage, social class, economic background, amount of education. With changes in these factors, furthermore, it seems that demographic patterns are also liable to change. Even when the exact relationships are unclear, it is certain that fertility is in all countries very much a socially controlled process.

Population in India can be taken as one example. If we are to understand the process of fertility in India, we have to consider a large number of *non*-biological factors. We must also consider social factors like, for example, the near-universality of marriage, which is a quasi-religious duty, and the generally early age of marriage. There is also the social ban on the re-marriage of widows and the value placed on the tradition of the Hindu joint family. Again, there is the emphasis placed on having sons, partly for religious reasons, partly for economic, for in many peasant-farming situations the labour provided by family members represents one of the main forms of wealth. There are also locally held ideas about the ideal size of families probably at least partly related to the known high rate of death among young children, so that to achieve even a moderately sized family it is not unreasonable to adopt the insurance policy of a large number of births.

Now these social factors – among others – cut several ways, even though the main emphasis is, in practice, on the factors encouraging fairly high fertility. Some, like the ban on widow re-marriage, may reduce over-all fertility, while the preference for sons rather than daughters (and therefore probably greater care – and thus lower mortality – of male than female children) may help to explain the higher number of men than women in the population over-all.

A further point should be added here. This is that the over-all population size (and hence rate of increase or decrease) is not merely a function of fertility (and mortality) rates, but also of population movement. Migration, whether internal or external, can affect the 'population pressure' in any given country, and this too is a process that is clearly socially rather than a biologically controlled one.

So it is far too simple and misleading a picture merely to think of people in underdeveloped (or any) nations somehow breeding unchecked, subject to biological not social forces, with the implication that certain contraceptive techniques must be introduced from the outside, i.e. from Western nations.

As already argued, such an assumption mis-states the 'problem'. People in all populations already have their own means of controlling births (whether at a relatively high or a relatively low level, depending on the society), through norms about the ideal family size or through various other social factors (perhaps not consciously recognized) that affect fertility. The 'problem' of changing fertility patterns is not, then, only or primarily a biological one – a matter of the innovation of new mechanical techniques. It is, more significantly, a matter of the accepted norms, and other social factors which, in a number of developing countries (at least at certain points in history), encourage high fertility. Without a change in these, techniques of whatever kind can have little effect. Obviously, then, if the 'problem' is seen as high fertility, the solution has to be seen in terms of changing the social norms and social conditions which make for high fertility. In such a change, particular techniques of birth control, from wherever they are imported, are only one factor. To concentrate exclusively on this is to fall into what has been well termed 'the technological fallacy which has long marked Western thinking in this area . . . in other words, a kind of blind faith in the gadgetry of contraception.' What the sociologist can contribute in this situation is to try to isolate other social factors as well which affect fertility so that, if government or other agencies wish to influence the birth rate, they can pay attention to these as well as (or in addition to) the currently fashionable mechanical techniques.

The Population Explosion: An Interdisciplinary Approach (Open University D100)

1 Explain in your own words what is meant by the terms 'developing country', 'polygynous societies', and 'infanticide'.
2 Explain in your own words the 'two common mistakes' people make when describing 'the population problem' in developing countries.

3 Describe some of the ways in which people in some developing societies choose to control fertility.
4 Give examples of social factors which in some societies encourage a high birth rate.
5 Explain in your own words why 'a blind faith in the gadgetry of contraception' is an inadequate solution to population problems in developing countries.

3 Questions and answers

Look back to the survey of the elderly in East Hull (pages 210–13). How does the life of elderly people in your area compare with the findings of this survey? The only way to find out accurately would be to conduct a survey of your own. Discuss the size of your sample with your teacher. How will you draw it up? How many people will you interview?

Here is a questionnaire to help you. Add any other questions which you think are important.

(Explain to each person interviewed on first meeting: 'We are from .... college/school and we are conducting a survey about elderly people in this area. We want to obtain some general facts about older people as part of our studies and should like to ask you some questions about your way of life. If it is not convenient to talk now may we call again in the next few days?')

Sex of respondent   M( )   F( )

1 First could we ask your opinion about whether you think enough is done to help the elderly these days?
Yes( )
No( )
Don't Know( )

2 Could you tell us if you live alone, or if anyone else lives with you?
Parent( )   Grandchild( )
Spouse( )   Great-grandchild( )
Sibling( )   Child( )
In-law( )   Lodger( )

(Tick or put number in brackets)
Other ....

3 Could we now ask you about your home: Have you any of the following in your house?
Radio( )
TV( )
Telephone( )
Indoor lavatory( )
Bath which is fixed( )
Hot water( )

4 Do you get a newspaper?
Every weekday( )
Sunday( )
Sometimes( )
Never( )

5 Have you ever had any help from
 any of the following?
    Meals-on-wheels( )   This year( )
    Home help( )   This year( )

 Have they helped you at all this
 year?
    Health visitor or home nurse( )
                   This year( )
    Social worker( )   This year( )
    Vicar, Minister( )   This year( )
    Voluntary community Worker( )
                   This year( )

6 How long have you lived in this
 home?
    Over 30 years( )
    Between 11 and 30 years( )
    Between 6 and 10 years( )
    Five years or less( )

7 *(If less than 11 years in this home)*
 Where did you move from when
 you came here?
    This neighbourhood( )
    Elsewhere in the city( )
    Outside the city( )

8 Can we ask your opinion about
 whether the state or relatives
 should mainly care for the elderly?
    State( )
    Relatives( )
    Don't Know( )

9 Finally, would you mind telling us
 your age, whether married or not, and
 your occupation?

a Which age group do you belong to? 60–64( ) 65–69( ) 70–74( )
    75–79( ) 80–84( ) 85 or over( )

b Are you, or have you been,
 married?
    Married( ) Single( )
    Widowed( ) Divorced or Separated( )

c *If man:* What was your occupation
 just before you retired or what is it
 now?

 If married woman: What is, or was,
 your husband's occupation?

 If single woman: What was your
 occupation?

 If widowed/divorced/separated:
 What was your former husband's
 occupation?

    (Occupation): ....
    ....
    ....
    ....
    ....
    ....
    ....

Thank you for letting us interview you and for your co-operation
        Interviewer's name ....
        Date of interview ....

Interpreting your findings
1 When you have completed all the interviews and collected all the
 information together, you can best interpret your findings by
 answering the following questions:

a   What percentage felt that not enough was being done for the elderly
    today? Did the majority feel that relatives or the state should be
    responsible for the care of the elderly?
b   What percentage of the elderly in your sample:
    lived alone?
    lived with spouse?
    lived with relatives?
c   What percentage lived in houses which lacked basic amenities?
d   Give statistical evidence to show how much help the old people got
    from social services and voluntary organizations.
e   How long had they been living in their present homes?
f   What percentage of the elderly in your sample were:
    married?
    single?
    widowed?
    divorced or separated?
g   From the information given about their occupations and the type of
    housing they were in, say what percentage of the sample were working
    class and what percentage were middle class.
2   Now look again at the results of the survey carried out in East Hull to
    assess how your findings compare with the findings of the East Hull
    survey. Then write a careful and detailed report to compare the two
    pieces of research.

Checkpoints

1   What is meant by the term 'demography'?
2   What is the difference between the 'death rate' and the 'infant
    mortality rate'?
3   What is meant by the term 'developing country'?
4   What percentage of the world's population lives in developing
    countries?
5   Why is there a 'population explosion' in many developing countries?
6   When was the first British census carried out?
7   Why do we have a compulsory national census every ten years?
8   Who was Annie Besant?
9   Why has the population of Britain continued to increase despite the
    fall in the birth rate?
10 Who are the Hutterites and why are they of interest to
    demographers?

O-level questions

1 Study Figure 18.
a What is meant by 'expectation of life'?
b Comment on the differences shown between women and men.
c Comment on the changes since 1870 and suggest reasons to explain them.
d What problems are caused by changes in expectation of life?

Figure 18 *Expectation of life*

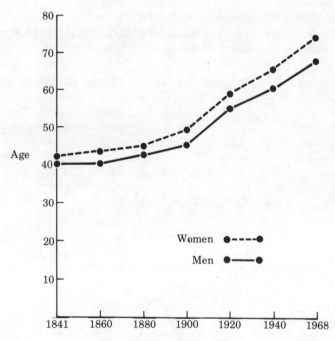

SOURCE: Ian Martin, *Workhouse to Welfare* (1971)

2 Study Table 17 (page 220).
a What is meant by the term 'birth rate'?
b What is the difference between the 'birth rate' and the 'fertility rate'?
c Why has the population continued to rise although the birth rate has fallen?
d How would you account for the fall in the birth rate since 1871?

Table 17 *Birth rates and population of Great Britain, 1871–1970*

Year	Birth rate (per 1000)	Population (millions)
1871	35	27
1901	27	37
1950	16	50
1970	18	55

3 Study Table 18.
a What is meant by 'birth rate' and 'death rate'?
b How is population increase calculated?
c What explanations do sociologists offer for the change in the rate of
    increase in the population of the United Kingdom?

Table 18 *Birth and death rate (per 1000), United Kingdom, 1931–71*

	1921	1931	1951	1961	1971
Birth rate	32.1	16.3	15.8	17.9	16.2
Death rate	12.4	12.5	12.6	12.0	11.6

SOURCE: Central Statistical Office, *Social Trends 1972*

Figure 19 *Net migration, United Kingdom (thousands)*

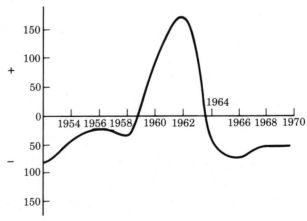

SOURCE: Central Statistical Office, *Social Trends 1972*

Table 19 *Population of Great Britain: people born overseas*

Birthplace	No. of people (thousands) and % of population they represent			
	1931	1951	1961	1966
Foreign countries	347 (0.8)	722 (1.5)	842 (1.6)	886 (1.7)
Canada, Australia, New Zealand	75 (0.2)	99 (0.2)	110 (0.2)	125 (0.2)
Other Commonwealth	137 (0.3)	218 (0.4)	541 (1.1)	853 (1.6)
Irish Republic	362 (0.8)	532 (1.1)	709 (1.4)	732 (1.4)
Total	921 (2.0)	1571 (3.2)	2202 (4.3)	2596 (5.0)

SOURCE: Adapted from Central Statistical Office, *Social Trends 1972*

4 Study Figure 19.
a What is meant by 'net migration'?
b What trends in migration does the graph show?
c Describe some of the consequences of these changes.
5 Make use of the figures in Table 19 to write an essay on immigration and population in the United Kingdom.
6 'Of all the problems which face mankind today, perhaps the greatest is the so-called "population explosion". Over large areas of the world populations are now growing faster than ever before. Often these areas are the poorest either because they have few resources or lack the capital and knowledge to exploit them. Often too they have political and social systems that appear quite inappropriate to deal with the variety of problems associated with rapid population growth. In this situation, what can the social scientist offer? At first glance the answer might appear to be – not very much. In fact, however, the social scientist can offer a greater understanding of what is involved in the problems associated with population growth. He can define them more precisely, clarify the issues and so lay the foundations for more enlightened policy.' (Open University, *Understanding Society: Readings in the Social Sciences*)
Comment on the above passage and explain in more detail the kind of work sociologists do in this field.
7 Study Table 20 (page 222).
a What are the causes of the changes in the birth and death rates since 1902?
b Discuss the important consequences of these trends.

Table 20   *Vital statistics United Kingdom (per 1000 population)*

	1902	1932	1967
Birth rate	28.6	16.3	17.5
Death rate	17.3	12.2	11.2

SOURCE: Registrar General UK

8   Study Figure 20.
a   What is meant by the term 'Expectation of life at birth'?
b   What trends does the graph show?
c   Explain the trends shown in the graph.

Figure 20   *Expectation of life at birth in England and Wales, 1871–1971*

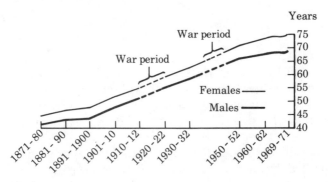

SOURCE: HMSO, *Britain 1974*

9   The population of the United Kingdom is now about 56 million.
Describe some of the important differences it would make if the
population rose to 80 million.

Table 21   *Family size*

No. of live births   Proportion of women (per 1000), according to date of first marriage

	1870–9	1900–9	1925
0	83	113	161
1 or 2	125	335	506
3 or 4	181	277	221
5 to 9	434	246	106
10 or more	177	29	6
All	1000	1000	1000

10   What does Table 21 tell you about family size in Great Britain since 1870? How would you explain this change?

11   What are the causes of the increase in population in this country during the last fifty years? What problems have arisen as a result of this increase?

12   Explain as fully as you can the meaning of the term 'developing country', giving examples of societies which could be labelled in this way.

13   Explain in your own words, with examples, the meanings of the following terms:
     birth rate
     death rate
     infant mortality rate
     life expectancy
     net migration
     ageing of population

14   Explain fully the meaning of the term 'population explosion'. What are some of the main problems faced by countries experiencing a population explosion?

8 British politics

1 Background information

In our society the political system is based on the principle of democracy. Democracy means, quite simply, that the government of the society should be undertaken by the people of that society – either directly, by people making their own decisions; or indirectly, by choosing representatives to make decisions on their behalf.

In small organizations like clubs or neighbourhood organizations, it is quite easy for all those involved to discuss together and make decisions about policies, but not everyone can be involved when it comes to larger organizations like local and national government. What happens, in fact, is that we hand over the power to make decisions on our behalf to elected local councillors and members of Parliament.

This system of 'representative democracy' means that we give our elected representatives a good deal of authority. They are expected to take their responsibilities seriously and not to abuse the power we give them. If they fail, or if in time we feel that other people will do the job better, they can be removed at the time of an election by the people they represent deciding to vote for someone else.

In principle the idea is a fair one, but politics is a controversial business and there are enough flaws in the democratic system to displease a lot of people. In any election there are losers as well as winners, and those who have voted Labour in an election won by the Conservatives, for example, may have just cause to feel dissatisfied with the policies which are then introduced and the decisions which are made. Members of minority groups who disagree with the views held by the majority of people in the country may feel they have no way of influencing political activities.

But the strengths of democracy are also important. The notion of democracy also implies free speech, legal protection and the freedom of choice about who will represent us. These are all very different characteristics from the widespread tyranny and restrictions imposed in societies governed by dictators.

The political system in Britain

All adults over 18, except members of the House of Lords, those who are
insane or in prison, are entitled to vote in parliamentary and local
elections. For parliamentary elections, the United Kingdom is divided
into 635 constituencies, each represented by one MP. The MPs generally
belong to one of three major parties – the Conservative Party, the Labour
Party or the Liberal Party, although some belong to minority parties like
the Ulster Unionists and the Scottish and Welsh Nationalists. The party
returning the most MPs to Parliament in any one election forms the
government from that time and until another election is held. So far as
local politics are concerned, each local authority area is divided into a
number of wards which are represented by one, two, three or even four
local councillors, depending on the local circumstances.

The electors

Sociologists are interested to discover and to be able to explain the
reasons why people vote the way they do. Investigations into voting
behaviour have continually revealed the importance of the following
factors: social class, sex, age, tradition and environment, trade union
membership and the mass media.

Social class
Generally speaking the well-to-do are more likely to vote Conservative
and the less well off are more likely to vote Labour. The Labour Party
developed at the beginning of this century as the party of the working
class. While its appeal has now broadened considerably, the majority of
its supporters can still be classified in this way. Yet it is also a fact that
many working-class people vote Conservative. Since manual workers are
in the majority in our society, no Conservative government would ever be
returned to power unless it could rely on working-class votes. Working-
class support for the Conservative Party is usually explained in one of
three ways:
1 People who *call themselves* middle class are more likely to vote Conservative than those who call themselves working class, but their
   ideas of what constitutes being middle class often do not agree with
   the classification sociologists would make. As the standard of living
   and environment of many working-class people improve, they begin
   to consider themselves middle class and in so doing start to support
   the Conservative Party.
2 Some working-class people, especially the elderly, still feel that the
   Conservative Party is made up of leaders from a natural ruling class
   who, by birth and breeding, are most fitted to govern the country. This

is born of a traditional respect for the upper classes now disappearing as present generations are brought up without such a sense of deference.

3 The swing of support from one party to another after a spell of unpopular government is also used to explain working-class votes for the Conservative Party after a period of Labour rule. Politicians encourage the uninformed to think selfishly and personally about political matters – 'the what's in it for me' approach – and those whose attention can be drawn to rising prices or heavy taxation can be easily persuaded to change their political allegiance in the following election.

Altogether, almost one-third of working-class people vote Conservative, and this makes up one half of the total Conservative votes. Percentages of Conservative and Labour support among the various classes all indicate similar results to those found by R. Rose (Table 22).

Table 22 *Social characteristics and voting behaviour*

	Middle class (AB)	Lower middle class (C1)	Skilled working class (C2)	Unskilled and very poor (DE)
		%		
Total population	(15)	(22)	(32)	(31)
Conservative	72.5	54.0	40.0	35.5
Labour	20.5	37.0	50.0	52.5
Others	7.0	9.0	10.0	12.0
Total	100.0	100.0	100.0	100.0

SOURCE: R. Rose, *Electoral Behaviour, A Comparative Handbook*

Sex

Women over 21 were given the vote in 1928 and since that time the sex of the voter has played a significant part in voting behaviour. In all the voting studies quoted, women in all classes and age groups continually vote more conservatively than men. The middle-class behaviour is perhaps easier to explain. It is likely that a conventionally middle-class upbringing, with its stress on deferred gratification, standards of quality, achievement and stability, will all imply conservative ideals. Working-class women are more likely to be apathetic, not to vote at all, or to do as their husbands say. Women more than men are pressurized by the consumer society 'to keep up with the Joneses' and, stripped of all other roles but the domestic, are likely to become houseproud and status-conscious. This again often leads to conservative voting.

Age

Age also seems to have a significant effect on voting behaviour in that the older a person is, the more likely he is to be conservative. This is usually explained by the fact that the Labour Party is traditionally seen as the more radical of the two major parties and radicalism is associated with youth. The young are more concerned to make sweeping changes and care more about inequalities and injustice, or so the argument goes. Middle age brings greater financial security and compromises in idealistic views. The competitive society encourages selfishness and conservation and in the process a swing away from radical politics. This is an argument which relies heavily on generalizations, however, and you must be careful of accepting such hypotheses too uncritically. First, it assumes that there is a significant difference in values between the two major parties; second, it assumes that all young people are radical. It could, however, be argued – and research has proved this – that many young people have the same political opinions and prejudices as their parents and are no more tolerant or idealistic in political matters than the previous generation.

Tradition and environment

Tradition and environment can play a significant part in voting behaviour among sections of the population where there is little social and geographical mobility. For instance, young people who are not exposed to any other political opinions but those of their parents will tend to vote similarly and will, in addition, tend to reflect the predominant voting habits of their social class. Environment also affects voting habits. For instance traditionally industrial areas will vote Labour, while comfortable suburban sprawls will more likely be Conservative. People will tend to conform to the predominant influence of the area in which they live so that, for example, manual workers will be more likely to vote Conservative in a middle-class environment than if they lived in a working-class environment.

The influence of class background and environment both break down with the increase of social and geographical mobility, however, as people moving up the social scale and into a middle-class environment tend in turn to vote Conservative. Even within groups which can still be classified as working class, improved standards of living tend to encourage increasingly conservative voting behaviour.

Trade union membership

National surveys have shown that manual workers who are members of trade unions are usually twice as likely to vote Labour as Conservative. Almost half of the manual workers in this country do not belong to a trade union, however, and since they form an unidentifiable group without any particular shape or form, they are frequently overlooked in studies of voting behaviour. It could well be that for various reasons a sizeable proportion of this group are persuaded at election time to vote Conservative. Table 23 shows Rose's 1974 findings on trade union membership and voting patterns.

Table 23 *Trade union membership and voting*

		Con-servative	Labour	Other	Total
Middle class	Member of a trade union	58	32	10	3
	Non-member of a trade union	73	20	7	12
Lower middle class	Member of a trade union	45	46	9	6
	Non-member of a trade union	51	33	10	16
Working class	Member of a trade union	31	60	9	31
	Non-member of a trade union	44	44	12	33

SOURCE: R. Rose, *Electoral Behaviour, A Comparative Handbook*

The mass media

The mass media have an influential part to play in shaping public opinion. In three specific areas this influence directly affects voting behaviour.

Newspaper bias

Newspapers are aligned to major political parties and their interpretation of political events tends to be biased in favour of the party each supports. It is likely, therefore, that the people who read a certain newspaper will tend to take over its political opinions.

Table 24 shows the total circulation of British national newspapers in 1974. The ownership of the press is more restricted than this variety of newspaper suggests, however. In 1961 three groups of newspapers (Daily Mirror, Associated Newspapers and Beaverbrook Newspapers) owned between them two-thirds of the circulation of daily newspapers. They also had extensive control of local papers.

Table 24 *Total circulation of British national newspapers, 1974*

Daily	(millions)	Sunday	(millions)
Mirror	4.3	News of the World	5.9
Express	3.3	Mirror	4.6
Sun	3.2	People	4.4
Mail	1.8	Express	4.1
Telegraph	1.4	Times	1.5
Guardian	0.4	Observer	0.8
Times	0.4	Mail	0.8
Financial Times	0.2	Telegraph	0.8
Morning Star	0.5		

SOURCE: Institute of Practitioners in Advertising, *National Readership Survey*

In 1974 Associated Newspapers owned the *Daily Mail*, the *Evening News*, fifty-one local papers and had an interest in Southern Television.

Beaverbrook Newspapers owned the *Daily Express*, the *Sunday Express*, the *Evening Standard*, Beaverbrook Western Provincial Papers and interests in ATV, Capital Radio and Radio Clyde.

News International owned the *Sun*, the *News of the World* and twenty-six provincial papers.

International Publishing Corporation owned the *Daily Mirror*, the *Sunday Mirror*, the *Sunday People*, the *Sunday Mail* (Glasgow) and over seventy magazines and journals.

Table 25 shows the general allegiance of national newspapers to different political parties.

Television
TV provides an immediate and powerful means for politicians to put themselves and the policies of their parties before the electors. The way in

Table 25 *Partisanship of the British press (national dailies)*

Partisan Conservative	Moderate independent Right	Moderate independent Left	Partisan Labour	Partisan Communist
Daily Telegraph	The Times	Guardian	Daily Mirror	Morning Star
Daily Mail		Sun (?)		
Daily Express				
The Financial Times				

which they do so, in particular the images they are able to present, plays a significant part in influencing voting behaviour. Here is what P. J. Madgwick has to say about it:

Since 1955, television has transformed electioneering. In the election of 1959, both the BBC and commercial television began broadcasting news reports of electioneering, press conferences, interviews and discussions, as well as the special broadcasts allocated to the parties themselves. The coverage was intensive and was broadcast to a high proportion of the electorate. In 1966, when over 90 per cent of homes had television sets, 85 per cent of the electorate claimed to have seen at least one of the party television broadcasts. By then television seemed to have replaced the press as the major source of political information and opinion.

This conclusion is highly significant because television operates in this field under quite different rules from that of the press. Newspapers are commercial enterprises involved in severe competition for readers and following a tradition of political partnership. Television on the other hand is much less competitive, there being only two contestants, and observes statutory rules of fairness and non-partisanship, and a tradition of impartiality and integrity. Broadcasting time of television or radio is not open to purchase, but some time is allocated to the parties (in proportions determined by the votes received at the previous election) for party political broadcasts. In consequence the background and style of a British general election no longer derive from the screaming headlines of the popular dailies, but rather from the comparative reasonableness of the television screen and studio.

This is not to say that the mass media have little effect on elections. The *form* of the campaign is now largely determined by the operation of the media. This means not simply that parties must organise press conferences, 'walk-abouts', and so on, to catch the camera's eye: it means also an emphasis on party leaders and the central campaign; a playing up of 'personality', conflict and news.

P. J. MADGWICK, *Introduction to British Politics*

Advertising

Advertising is increasingly playing an important part in electioneering. The techniques commonly used to sell consumer goods are now being utilised to 'sell' politicians and to create favourable impressions of political parties and their policies.

The Conservative Party has used the techniques of persuasive advertising more than any other party. Before the 1959 election, market research surveys confirmed that the Tory party was associated with privilege in the minds of many ordinary people. An advertising campaign, mainly in the press, concentrated on showing working class people who would vote Conservative. After the campaign was over, further research showed a drop of 7 to 8 per cent in the association of the Conservative Party with privilege. More recently the Conservative Party has hired the big advertising agency, Saatchi and Saatchi, to help make the image of Margaret Thatcher more acceptable to public opinion and to produce more entertaining political broadcasts and publicity campaigns.

Non-voters

The rate of voting in General Elections is usually between 74 per cent and 80 per cent of the registered electors. In by-elections and local elections the rate is much lower, falling to 50, 40 and even 30 per cent of those who could vote.

Given the assumption that democracies, to survive, must make full use of their political machinery, why does this degree of abstention or non-voting occur?

Some people abstain from voting for well-considered reasons: they do not approve of the policies of any of the parties or they have no respect for the candidates seeking election in their area. The majority of people who do not vote have less positive reasons, however. They are not interested in politics, they cannot be bothered to make the effort to go to the polls, and they are poorly informed and have no particular political opinions. Non-voters are usually to be found among women, the old and the poor; these are members of the population who are least socially encouraged to be politically aware.

Floating voters

These are the small groups of voters, perhaps only as much as 15 per cent of the electorate, who have no strong party loyalties and who are likely to change their votes in every election. These are the voters who determine the political 'swing' and are therefore extremely important.

Yet floating voters are not the most rational of electors and do not seem to be aware of their responsibilities:

They do not seem to be drawn from the most politically conscious section of the community. The reasons for their change of allegiance are often trivial. They seem to be less committed, not because of a genuine independence of mind, but more out of apathy. They resemble abstainers more than they resemble the image of the perfect voter. Indeed, since many floaters are, or have been, abstainers, there is a natural similarity between the two groups. [J. Blondel, *Voters, Parties and Leaders*]

During the period between general elections when political propaganda is less intense, the size of the group uncommitted to any party, and that unwilling to be politically involved, seems to increase. The rate of abstentions in by-elections is twice that of general elections and the swing to a particular party in local elections tends to be directly against the interests of the government elected in the previous general election.

When such a large proportion of the electorate is politically uncommitted and relatively casual about its voting responsibilities the arena is left open for those groups which are best organized and most active.

The political parties

People with the same political opinions and policies join together in large groups to form political parties. These parties select candidates for elections in both local and national politics and offer the electorate a series of policies which have been adopted and are supported by the party as a whole. To win electoral support on a national scale, political parties need to be highly-organized associations with hundreds of thousands of members and with hundreds of paid officials. In the study of political parties sociologists are interested in the following factors:

1 Whether the ordinary paid-up members of political parties are representative of the electors as a whole. Whether they come from the same social classes and whether they hold the same views.
2 Who the local leaders of political parties are, since they have the power to choose the parliamentary and local council candidates.
3 Who the regional leaders of political parties are, since they are the link-men between the local and national party organzations.
4 Who the national leaders are and how far they represent the rank and file, and the local leaders.

Let us look at these factors in a little more detail and try to analyse the composition of the two largest political parties in Britain, Labour and Conservative.

Rank and file

Not everyone who votes Conservative or Labour becomes an official member of the party, paying a weekly subscription and taking part in its activities. Those who do, however, help to make British political parties among the largest in the world. The Labour Party is much larger than the Conservative Party because of its many trade union members, but a good proportion of these take little direct interest and merely contribute to the funds. Roughly one in every five Conservative electors is also a member of the party. They organize themselves into local associations or clubs, which, unlike the Labour Party meetings, provide a social and recreational emphasis rather than just a political one.

The social structure of the membership seems closely to reflect that of the electors. Members tend to be slightly older than electors, however, but the sex distribution is about the asme – the Conservative Party attracts more women members and the Labour Party more men. When we look at social class and occupation, however, the situation becomes more interesting. We should expect the Labour Party membership to be almost entirely made up of manual workers, which it is. The Conservative Party, however, should have about half and half manual and non-manual members if it is to reflect the Conservative electorate. In practice this is not so; the working-class Conservative is, in fact, unlikely to become a party member and spend his leisure time drinking and socializing at the Conservative club.

Local leaders

Just as not all electors are politically involved enough to become party members, so the majority of members are less active than the minority. This minority, therefore, because of its interest and involvement, has more say in decision-making and the election of local leaders. For instance, when it comes to choosing a parliamentary candidate, the short list is drawn up by a handful of people and most of the selection has already been done before the general members are consulted.

The local leadership of both parties is more middle class than the membership. In Glossop, for example, manual workers formed 50 per cent of the Conservative voters but only 8 per cent of the leaders; in Greenwich the lower income groups formed 60 per cent of the voters but only 9 per cent of the Conservative Party officials. One reason for this is given by J. Blondel:

It must be remembered that Conservative associations are perhaps primarily social organizations. They are rightly called 'associations' and not 'parties'. These social organizations have a definite middle class atmosphere. Whoever comes and acquires the tastes and values of these middle class clubs is certainly welcome: the associations are not closed societies. On the other hand, those who do not have these tastes and values are barred, not by any conscious decision taken against them, but simply because these individuals are unlikely to feel at home in a society which behaves in a manner which is somewhat foreign to them. [*Voters, Parties, and Leaders*]

Local Labour Party leaders are not representative of the whole of the membership either. A bigger percentage of manual workers are officials than in the Conservative Party, but the balance of power also swings towards the middle classes. They are a different type of middle class to the businessmen who dominate local Conservative associations, however. Many are white-collar workers from working-class origins, others are teachers and social workers. Although the local Labour leadership is not entirely representative of members and electors, it does follow the traditional alliance in Labour Party history between the workers and trade unionists on the one hand, and the intelligentsia on the other.

Figure 21 shows the electors, members and officers in Greenwich. Note the social composition changes as power increases:

Figure 21

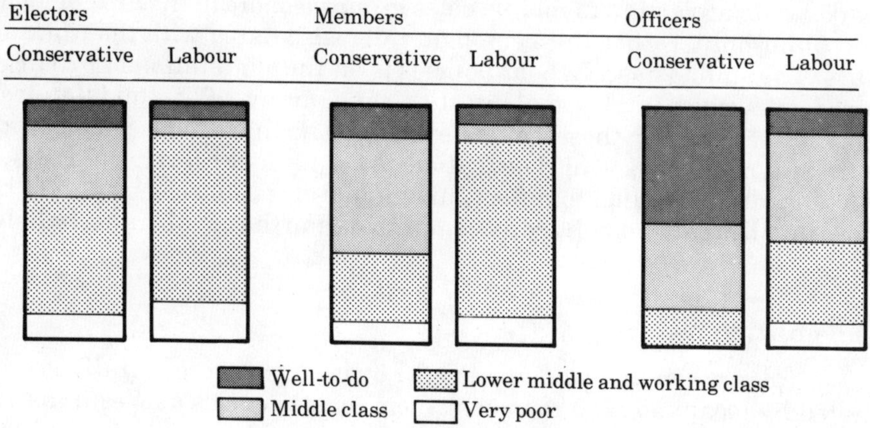

Electors		Members		Officers	
Conservative	Labour	Conservative	Labour	Conservative	Labour

Well-to-do   Lower middle and working class
Middle class   Very poor

SOURCE: J. Blondel, *Voters, Parties and Leaders* (1969)

Regional and area leaders

The regional organizer of a party is appointed by head office and is supposed to co-ordinate the activities of local constituencies in his area. He is supported by a council of regional officers elected by local party branches. The most important elected officers are chairman, vice-chairman and treasurer, and in the Labour Party these positions are usually held by members of the middle class and influential trade union officials.

Power in the Conservative Party at a regional level is concentrated in the hands of an upper-middle-class minority recruiting leaders from big business, the professions and the officer class of the armed forces. Oxbridge and public school education figure predominantly in their backgrounds, both indicating a certain exclusiveness of upbringing far removed from the 50 per cent manual working-class backgrounds of Conservative electors.

National leaders
British political parties can best be described as pyramids. Neither the Conservative nor the Labour parties are as open as their large membership suggests they could be.

A definite class barrier exists within the Conservative Party – the more elevated the leaders, the more exclusive is their background. Thus, at a national level, the Conservative leadership is recruited from a much more selective group than the electorate as a whole.

The barrier in the Labour Party is a more subtle one. It is not one of class so much as of the possession of a certain kind of expertise and professionalism. Since the party is almost entirely made up of manual workers, its attraction to middle-class groups is more in the area of ideas and philosophy rather than common interests shared with the working class. The emphasis in Labour policies is on the elimination of privilege based on wealth and social prestige, and many of its middle class members champion these beliefs even though they themselves do not suffer financial or social deprivation. At a national level, the Labour Party leadership tends to reflect this middle-class conscience and to be more intellectual and politically committed than the members as a whole.

The politicians

These are the men and women selected by local party organizations and elected by local voters to represent their constituencies at Westminster. Sociologists are interested to know how representative they are of the voters who elect them.

The socialization of politicians
The politicians can never be totally representative of the electorate as a whole because they are not selected at random and one person, so far as being a politician is concerned, is not as good as another. Blondel suggests some of the conditions in upbringing which tend most commonly to produce future MPs:

A man who comes from a family where politics are never discussed is at a disadvantage compared to a man who comes from a background where politics matter. If this family has friends or relatives among politicians, there will be an added incentive to enter politics and entrance in the job will be made easier. Background does not mean only family, it also means contacts outside the family: for instance in the trade union movement.

Education adds to the influence of the environment by providing contacts and character training as well as intellectual training. Contacts come through the better public schools, through the older universities. Character-training also comes through the public schools: they tend to inculcate a certain philosophy of the public service, as a result of which politics and the civil service come to be considered as worthwhile careers. Most important of all, the intellectual training of the best public schools, of the older universities, as well as, to a lesser extent, of grammar schools and other universities, is a preparation for the job of politician.

Thirdly, the occupation which one exercises before entering Parliament is also important. An administrator, a secretary, an organizer is more likely to become political material than a person engaged in a routine job: this is why the trade union movement is an almost essential channel for manual workers who want to enter politics.

Because of the existence of these conditions, an unskilled manual worker, working in a trade where employees are not organized in strong unions, starts with a great handicap against a non-manual worker with a university degree or against a professional worker with a middle class social background. Whether one likes it or not, politics is a middle class job and the training appropriate for middle class jobs is also a training for politics. The dice are loaded by the present structure of society as well as by the natural conditions which govern the job of politics in any society. [*Voters, Parties and Leaders*]

The candidates

In each general election about 1500 candidates compete for 635 seats in Parliament. The majority of these (1200) belong to the two main parties. In Britain as a whole, two-thirds of the population are manual workers but only 200 out of the 1500 candidates belong in this category. At least half of the candidates will have a university degree and a third will have been to public school. In the nation generally, 5 per cent of each age group goes to university and 3 per cent goes to public school. Even though women were given political equality with men in 1928, they will make up only 5 per cent of candidates for Parliament.

There are, of course, variations between parties. The Conservative Party has at most only 1 or 2 per cent manual-worker candidates, while professional men and businessmen with public school backgrounds are predominant. It has as many old Etonians as Labour has candidates from all the public schools put together, usually about ninety.

The majority of manual worker candidates come from the Labour Party, but even here, three-quarters of Labour candidates are from the middle classes.

Members of Parliament

The candidates who are successful enough to become MPs are drawn from more exclusive backgrounds than those who fail. This means that there is an even higher proportion of professional people, ex-public school men and university-trained politicians than among the candidates as a whole. In fact a gradual sifting-out process is taking place: the higher one goes up the political ladder the further one moves away socially, educationally, and economically from the people being represented. *The Times Guide to the House of Commons* in 1966 and 1974 revealed the statistics summarized in Table 26.

Table 26   *Educational background of MPs, 1966 and 1974*

	1966		*1974 (October)*	
Education	*Labour*	*Conservative*	*Labour*	*Conservative*
All universities	52	67	60	76
Oxford and Cambridge	24	58	26	55
All public schools	20	77	8	63
Eton	1	21	0	17
Elementary only or elementary and adult	21	1	19	1

There is one big exception to this process and that is within the Labour Party. More workers are included in the parliamentary party. This is largely due to the influence of trade unions which, because of the vast financial support they give to the Labour Party and the contributions they make to election expenses, are allowed to nominate and sponsor trade union candidates, frequently in 'safe' electoral seats. These MPs are classified as manual workers because that is what they originally were but in fact the majority of them have been trade union organizers and so are likely to be white-collar workers or even managers.

All the evidence confirms, therefore, that the majority of MPs are middle class, but it is important to notice that the Conservative middle class and the Labour middle class are very different groups of people. Labour MPs are more likely to be teachers, journalists and lawyers; those who, if not intellectuals, are at any rate more concerned with ideas than with making money. The Conservative middle class is more likely to be made up of businessmen, farmers, accountants and even regular soldiers. About one-third of Conservative MPs start out in business and about

Table 27 *Occupational groups within the Labour and Conservative parties*

Occupations	1966		1974 (October)	
	Labour	Conservative	Labour	Conservative
Barristers, solicitors	15	22	14	21
Journalism	10	8	9	8
Teachers, lecturers	15	1	24	3
Farmers, landowners	1	15	0	8
Company directors	1	28	1	26
Management, executive administrative	7	3	9	7
Clerical, technical	8	2	5	1
Trade union officials	11	0	6	0
Manual workers (incl. miners, railwaymen)	14	1	9	0

SOURCE: *The Times Guide to the House of Commons*

three-fifths eventually have some connection with business concerns. Table 27 indicates the occupational breakdown of the two main political parties in 1966 and 1974.

Over the years the percentage of Labour MPs with a working-class background has declined considerably, falling from 87 per cent in 1918 to 43 per cent in 1945 and 27 per cent in 1970 (W. L. Guttsman in P. Stanworth and A. Giddens (eds.), *Elites and Power in British Society*).

Party loyalty
Because the background of Conservative MPs is fairly similar and because the heirarchy within the parliamentary party embodies the tradition, values and common experience of them all, there is a strong sense of unity which prevents clashes with leadership on policy issues. The parliamentary Labour Party has three different centres, however: the manual workers coming from the trade unions; the established professions with strong middle class backgrounds and traditional educations; the less-established professions achieving their status through more democratic educational opportunity. These differences in upbringing, education and occupation are immense. They provide no social unity born of a common social environment, but rely on a belief in a set of political ideals. It is logical, therefore, that when the ideals are

questioned, or changed, there is often considerable internal difference of opinion about the emphasis and interpretation of policy. Appeals to party loyalty are frequently made when divisions become a threat to government or party solidarity, but the basic difficulty of uniting all three elements is never wholly eradicated.

Parliamentary leaders and ministers

As you can see from Figure 22 the Conservative parliamentary party is a hierarchy with the majority of power and influence concentrated in the few hands of a socially unrepresentative elite. The large majority of the Conservative senior ministers of the 1951-61 government went to public school, and three-quarters of them were educated at Oxford and Cambridge. Old Etonians are traditionally overrepresented in Conservative governments, sometimes providing as many as one-third of the cabinet. Neither the Conservatives nor Eton seem to feel any need to conceal this tradition and boast quite openly, 'Eton, cabinet makers to the Queen'. Six 'old Etonians' were included in the 1979 Conservative Party cabinet. In fact all but two of them went to public school and seventeen were graduates of either Oxford or Cambridge.

In the Labour Party, the hierarchy is more complicated. The need for administrative ability tends to tell against manual workers whose education is likely to have been restricted. Members of the newer professions are also underrepresented in positions of authority, largely because they tend to be more radical; and in office leaders rarely appoint left-wing members to positions of influence. The older professions therefore benefit from both these trends and while in background and education many of them have more in common socially with the Conservatives than members of their own party, their ideals and objectives differ considerably.

Pressure groups

Political pressure on the government does not only come from MPs and members or political parties. It also comes from pressure groups – or associations of people concerned to promote or defend a special interest. They differ from political parties in that they do not want to govern – merely to exert pressure and win influence on behalf of their particular concerns.

There are countless numbers of pressure groups in Britain. Some are large and powerful like the Confederation of British Industry (CBI) and the trade unions. Others try to influence legislation and get more resources for the deprived (for example Child Poverty Action Group) and

Figure 22 *School background of MPs and of ministers*

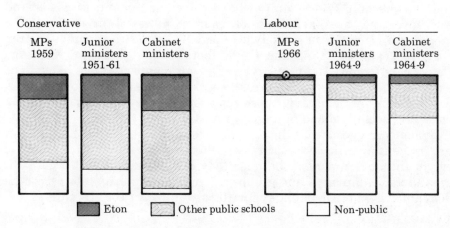

SOURCE: J. Blondel, *Voters, Parties and Leaders* (1969)

the homeless (for example, Shelter). Some are concerned to publicize a specific issue, like their opposition to the building of a new airport or motorway. Others want to influence public opinion about, for example abortion, racial prejudice or homosexuality.

Pressure groups are usually divided into two types according to their main aims. The first type seeks to *protect* certain groups in society. For example, trade unions defend the workers, professional associations protect the interests of business groups. In the same way other protective pressure groups defend the rights of specific groups of people, for example Consumers Association, the RAC and Alcoholics Anonymous.

The second type of pressure group is *promotional*. They try to promote a cause by not appealing to only one section of the community, but to everyone. Some, like Shelter, may want to protect a special group of people, but they do this by appealing to everyone who is concerned about the plight of the homeless, rather than just those who share the experience of homelessness. Other examples of promotional pressure groups are the Anti Nazi League, the women's liberation movement and the Friends of the Earth.

Pressure groups use a variety of methods to publicize their causes and to exert influence on local and national governments and public opinion, through petitions, letters to councillors and MPs, media coverage in the press and on radio and television, the writing and publishing of reports and by holding meetings, conferences and demonstrations.

The opportunity to influence government in this way is said to be one of the strengths of the British democratic system in that it gives everyone 'an equal opportunity' to make their views known. But it is also the case that all pressure groups do not have the same amount of power and influence and are therefore not equally powerful in society. The government is much more likely to take notice of the trade unions and the CBI, for example, than the Gay Liberation Front or the Old Age Pensioners Union. And Conservative governments are more likely to be sympathetic to conservative pressure groups while Labour governments will be more influenced by those representing the interests of working class and socially disadvantaged groups.

Evidence suggests that the pressure groups which are most influential are influential either because they wield economic power, they have the ear of the government or because they are incredibly well organized. Small local campaigns and groups defending a minority interest which does not attract much public sympathy are unlikely to be very influential.

2 Looking at the evidence

Voting behaviour

If you take a map of Britain and shade the Conservative constituencies blue, the Labour constituencies red, and the Liberals and the nationalist parties by some other colour, a clear pattern emerges. Whilst there are exceptions, it is *broadly speaking* the case that the inner cities, the heavily industrial areas and the under-developed areas of the country will be shaded red, whereas the residential outer-city areas, the affluent South-East and the wealthier farming counties will be shaded blue. (The nationalists, of course, figure only in Scotland, Wales and Northern Ireland, and the Liberal strength is mainly on the Celtic fringes.)

If you focus on Greater London, you will see that it is nearly all red in the centre and all blue round the perimeter. *Broadly speaking* (and I am deliberately emphasizing those words) you can say that many of those who live in the blue circle on the outskirts of London are middle class and professional people living in more or less solely residential areas, many of them owner-occupiers, and most of them believe their way of life is best defended and represented by the Conservatives. Still broadly speaking, it can be said that many of those living in the red centre are less likely to be home-owners, more likely to be council tenants or sharing accommodation, more likely to be working in the service industries, and believe their cause to be best defended and represented by the Labour Party.

If you wish to approach the question from a different direction, walk into a factory and take a poll of the directors, executives and managerial staff, and then a poll of the 'shop-floor' and manual workers, and once more you will discover that, while there are exceptions, they broadly divide as Conservative in the first instance and Labour in the second.

It is class-inspired party loyalty that causes so many constituencies to be safe seats. Nearly every study and survey of voters' behaviour indicates that most people, consciously or subconsciously, identify with a class and many (but by no means all) vote for the party they believe serves that class best. The Conservatives, conscious of their middle class and professional support, are the party most likely to be heard criticizing the trade unions or defending the hierarchical education system, whereas the Labour Party is the one most likely to be attacking property developers or the City of London, whilst supporting comprehensive education. The Labour Party has been the one most committed to council housing. If class is still a significant factor, however, it is by no means the only factor. If it was, Labour would be permanently in office, for there are still nearly twice as many people in traditionally working class occupations as there are in traditionally middle class occupations. As we base our decision less and less on traditional class loyalties, one overriding factor has emerged: it can be simply defined as a concern for *competence.*

The issue of competence has become even more important as the differences (in practice, if not in theory) between the major parties have decreased. It could be said that the fundamental difference is that Labour believes in a greater element of State intervention, whereas the Conservatives believe in creating the incentives and opportunities for private enterprise. Perhaps the major difference in the economic field is in industrial relations, for there is no doubt that there is a greater sympathy between the Labour Party and the trade unions than between the Conservatives and the trade unions, and when it comes to competence to manage the economy, this would surely be one of Labour's more convincing points. On the other hand, the Conservatives could point to the failure by British industry to invest at times of Labour administration, and say that they alone can inspire the necessary confidence.

It is surely possible to argue that the elections of 1970 and 1974 were won and lost on the issue of competence. Few expected the Conservatives under Edward Heath to win the 1970 election; indeed, few commentators saw any reason why Labour deserved to lose at that time. But commentators don't spend much time in the supermarkets buying food, and voters do, and once Edward Heath and the Conservatives decided to concentrate on food prices, the lead that Labour had clearly established, according to the opinion polls, dwindled away and they became the shocked losers. Rightly or wrongly, the voters had decided the Conservatives could manage things better. Likewise, in 1974 when the country was on a three-day week and Heath went to the polls to seek public confidence in his confrontation with the miners, he was in fact judged by the country to be mismanaging things - lacking in competence - and he was dismissed.

But let's return to the factors that can affect the way we vote, for there are others:

First, there is the growing influence in Wales and Scotland of Welsh and Scottish nationalism. While as far as its leadership is concerned, this may have its origins in a sense of historical destiny, its success with the ordinary voter in those countries has probably much more to do with their greater levels of poverty, unemployment and economic and environmental neglect, and a feeling of remoteness from Whitehall and Westminster. A substantial vote for the nationalist parties is a recent phenomenon, and one that has forced the major parties to pay more attention to the administrative and economic needs of those two countries.

Another, and particularly sad, influence on British elections in recent years has been the question of race. Race, and in particular, immigration, dominated the campaign of one Conservative candidate in 1964. Peter Griffiths, who won the constituency of Smethwick by surprisingly defeating Patrick Gordon Walker, the man destined to be Foreign Secretary in the Labour Cabinet. The vote was inconsistent with the national swing, and afterwards Labour accused the new Conservative MP of conducting a racist campaign.

But race and immigration really became a big political issue in 1969 when, also in the Midlands, Enoch Powell (then a Conservative shadow minister) made his now famous speech saying that unless immigration was more controlled the streets of Britain would be 'like the River Tiber, foaming with much blood'. Edward Heath immediately dropped him from the Shadow Cabinet, but Powell had struck a chord with the latent fears, prejudices and even racism that existed under the surface of the community. Significantly, Powell, and other Conservative politicians in the Midland areas near by, achieved better election performances than the Conservative performance in the country as a whole in both the 1970 and 1974 elections. Indeed, Powell has often said that it was he who won the 1970 election for the Conservatives, claiming that race and immigration were much bigger issues than was generally realized.

The issue came alive once more in February 1978 when Margaret Thatcher, interviewed on a television programme, newly voiced the alleged fears of the British people about the number of coloured immigrants in the country. The issue once more hit the headlines, and opinion polls showed an immediate and dramatic swing from a Labour lead to a Conservative lead.

It is a sad fact that in a country that prides itself on tolerance, prejudice on race cannot be ruled out as a factor that can swing votes, particularly in some parts of the country. It is also a sad fact that there are politicians who will take advantage of this.

An increasingly important factor in British elections has been the personality and popularity of the leaders of the major parties. Indeed, many feel that Britain is moving closer to the presidential-style elections that take place in the United States, and that this is stimulated by the way the media tend to portray the party confrontation as being a clash between leaders. We need look no further back than 1978-9, when the Labour Party was leaning considerably on the image of James Callaghan as a national elder statesman, father figure, uncle, family doctor, or even the village bobby, whilst trying to accentuate fears about Margaret Thatcher's inexperience, alleged extremist views, and perhaps even the fact that she was a woman.

This leadership factor is related to the issue of competence – all parties seek to present their leader as the kind of man or woman we can trust to manage our affairs best.

Just how important the personality and record of the leader is when it comes to election time we cannot be sure, but clearly, now that television creates the opportunity for all voters to have the rival leaders in their homes, observe them closely under fire from interviewers and make personal judgements about them, this has probably become a significant factor in helping voters to decide between the competence of the main parties.

Another factor that can influence our votes is the behaviour of the media. The majority of voters pick up what they know or think they know about politics and politicians from the media – from their newspapers, from radio and, increasingly, from television. This being the case, the way the media treat politics has a profound effect on the kind of politics we have. There is much truth in the argument that the media, instead of just reflecting the way people behave, can influence the way they behave. Many believe that the obsession of the media with personalities has the effect of reducing politics to personal attack and confrontation at the expense of intelligent discussion of issues; that the media's liking for confrontation and conflict forces the political parties and political leaders into what are often artificially opposite camps; and that the obsession of the national media with London has been a contributing factor to political neglect of the regions. But the main criticism by politicians of media coverage is that it is biased. Newspapers, for example, are privately owned, and in some cases their proprietors have strong political views and expect their newspapers to further them. For instance, the Daily Mail, the Daily Express, and The Daily Telegraph consistently support the Conservative Party. Between them they have a huge circulation, and thus their readers are fed a diet of political opinion that is consistently supportive of the Conservatives. The Daily Mirror tends fairly consistently to support Labour. The allegiances of The Times and Guardian are less pronounced, though the former is probably at heart more disposed to Conservative policies and the latter is traditionally liberal in policy and more likely to support Labour or Labour with a Liberal influence on its policies, as in the period of the Lib-Lab pact in 1977-8. Local newspapers over the country as a whole would show a bias towards the Conservatives, if only because their proprietors are in most cases businessmen who believe themselves to be best served by the Conservative Party.

DES WILSON, *So You Want to be Prime Minister*

1 Which areas of the country *broadly speaking* are most likely to vote Conservative, Labour, Liberal, and Nationalist? Suggest reasons why you think this is so.

2 Why are middle-class people more likely to vote Conservative and working-class people more likely to vote Labour on the whole?

3 What is the fundamental difference these days between the philosophy of the Conservative Party and that of the Labour Party?

4 What does Des Wilson mean by 'competence'? Can you give any examples, besides those mentioned in the passage, to illustrate a government's possession of, or lack of, competence?

5 Why has there been an increase in Scottish and Welsh Nationalist voting in recent years?

6 Why does the discussion of race at election time usually encourage support for the Conservatives? What are your own views on Des Wilson's comment that there are politicians who take advantage of racial prejudice to win votes?

7   Suggest reasons why the personality and popularity of politicians seems to be a growing factor in deciding their success or failure in elections.
8   Explain in your own words why the media, instead of just reflecting the way people already feel about politics, can actually influence the way they feel.

Six weeks or so before the 1979 general and local elections, Peter Jenkins assessed the relationship between social class and political allegience:

We have been so obsessed as a nation with the idea of social class that it is scarcely surprising that myths sprout faster than the sociologists and political scientists can hack them down. That widely held beliefs are unscientific does not make them any the less powerful and the way politicians behave depends a great deal on how they see the state of the class struggle.

When Mr. Harold Macmillan led the Conservative Party to their third successive victory at the general election of 1959, people searched for an explanation rooted in the theory of class. The result was *embourgeoisement* which chimed well with their famous election slogan: 'You've never had it so good.' The idea was that a washing machine in every kitchen (together with a telly in every parlour and a car in every garage) was turning the British worker into a respectable middle class citizen whose material stake in the nation's gadgetry gave him better reason to vote Conservative than Labour.

The theory took a knock when Labour swept to power in the 1964 and 1966 elections. These made it seem more likely that it was the government of the day which benefited from increases in prosperity and not the Conservative Party as such. The *embourgeoisement* thesis was further battered by the Oxford sociologist, John Goldthorpe, and his associates whose studies among Luton car workers suggested that affluence had very little effect on class allegiance, voting behaviour or trade union activity.

A somewhat different explanation was required to account for Labour's four out of five election wins between 1964 and 1974. This was that although class was becoming a decreasingly important factor in determining voting behaviour this was hurting the Conservatives more than it was hurting Labour. While Goldthorpe's affluent workers went on for the most part being Labour, at Essex University, Professor Ivor Crewe was discovering that middle class voters were becoming less reliable Conservatives. By 1974 about a third of the middle class were Labour which was roughly the same proportion of the (of course, much larger) working class as was traditionally Conservative.

In all discussions on the subject of class and politics a caveat is necessary and we must enter it here. However fascinating may be the changes or trends in class formation and attitudes they are glacial compared with the avalanches of opinion which take place at election times. As Dr David Butler has put it: 'Social mobility can make only a small contribution to the fact that more than a quarter of British electors fail to vote in accordance with their class.' Winning election issues are the ones which cut across class lines.

Should Labour win this year's election people will be turning to the political scientists, such as P. J. Dunleavy of Nuffield College, Oxford, who have been pointing to the growth of a new Labour constituency in the expanded public sector. Two major industries have been brought into public ownership – shipbuilding and aerospace – and there has been a vast expansion in local authority, hospital and other forms of public employment. These days one in three employees works for the state in one guise or another and it is thought that a majority of trade unionists are now public sector workers. Dunleavy suggests that Labour's appeal in the public sector could at least compensate for an erosion of support among private sector manual workers.

If Mrs Thatcher wins the election the notion of Labour as the national party embracing all the vested interests of a burgeoning welfare state will be pushed aside to make way for a resurgence, I would guess, of the *embourgeoisement* thesis in an amended form. Indeed, this is already available in a pamphlet by the veteran Polish-emigre student of the British working class Ferdynand Zweig, and published, interestingly, by Sir Keith Joseph's Centre for Policy Studies. Zweig contends that the working class has become the dominant or standard class of affluence and is converging with a *debourgeoised* middle class into a single, new class which is inspired by a spirit of 'Collective acquisitiveness'. Remaining down below are the poor, who are always with us to the tune of, say, 20 per cent.

Meanwhile, more work has been done at Oxford by Goldthorpe and his friends. Its political significance is long range, and in any case a matter of speculation, but it certainly does not confirm the prejudices of either political party. Goldthorpe still sees no signs of *embourgeoisement* in the sense of workers becoming middle class in attitudes or behaviour as a result of affluence. What he does see is a great deal of social mobility as a result of a changing occupational structure. Most of the mobility is upward, very little downward. The result is a net expansion of what he calls the 'service class' – that is the people who run the mixed economy. The old manual working class has diminished to 45 or 40 per cent of the population.

The expansion of the middle class is a secular trend helpful in the long run to the Conservatives but because it is recruited in large part from the working class it becomes, as a class, less and less reliable. In other words, the most probable explanation of the growing number of middle class Labour supporters, and perhaps also of the upsurge of 'middle class trade unionism' or militancy, is the influx of working class recruits who do not shed their attitudes and allegiances on admission to the middle class.

The picture which generally emerges from the Nuffield researchers is of an economy whose entire occupational structure is shifting upwards without much effect on the class structure or attitudes of the society.

A possible conclusion is that we still live in a class society but in one which can no longer be governed by class politics. A Conservative government would be making a great mistake if it tried to govern according to the slogan that we are all middle class now, all living in an open and acquisitive society, a dwindling proletariat, which feels itself culturally isolated, will not make the country any easier to govern – especially if job securities are felt to be threatened.

In Labour's case the error would be to suppose that the support of its dwindling working class base depended upon the pursuance of socialist policies. The evidence of the Essex researchers suggests that the leftward lurches of the Labour movement in the early seventies did more to alienate its traditional working class support than its growing middle class support. As to the election, my own guess is that it will go to whichever of the parties, and whichever of their leaders, can most effectively mobilize the forces of working class conservatism.

PETER JENKINS, *Guardian*, 16 March 1979

1 Explain in your own words what is meant by the term 'embourgeoisement'.
2 Which important sociological evidence has been used to discredit the theory of embourgeoisement?
3 Whose research has shown that not all middle class people vote Conservative?
4 What proportion of the British population do not vote in tune with their class position, according to Dr David Butler?
5 Explain in your own words Zweig's latest theory to explain the relationship between voting and social class.
6 Explain in your own words Goldthorpe's latest theory to explain the relationship between voting and social class.
7 What was the result of the last general election? What influence, if any, did social class have on the way electors voted?

Parliament and politicians

Being elected to the House of Commons is sometimes said to be like becoming a member of an exclusive club. It is exclusive in the sense that it has only 635 members out of a population of over 60 million. Its club headquarters, the Palace of Westminster, on the banks of the Thames, is one of the most imposing buildings in Britain. Its rules and traditions reinforce its exclusivity – for instance it does not have mere members, but 'honourable members'. In practical terms, the 'club' has such benefits as immunity from arrest while in the precincts of the 'club-house', and immunity from prosecution in the courts for whatever members say in the 'clubhouse'. Members are paid salaries and expenses, travel free back and forth from their constituencies, and can refresh themselves and entertain guests in their own bars and restaurants. They even have their own gymnasium. But, with exceptions, the men and women at Westminster do not become members for these fairly modest benefits: they have come to Westminster, usually with a real sense of exhilaration and anticipation, to make the world a better place to live in, and the biggest disadvantage of the 'club' is that its power to do that is much less than either many of its would-be members or many of public realize.

The most common misunderstanding about the House of Commons is that it governs the country. It does not. The *Government* governs the country, and the Government is not the House of Commons, but rather the Prime Minister and the one hundred or so members of the House of Commons and House of Lords who have been appointed ministers, together with the Civil Service and, to some extent, the courts. While it is the case that only Parliament can create new laws, and that the Government is said to govern with the consent of Parliament, the reality is that the Government decides what it wishes Parliament to consent to and can usually insist upon it by imposing discipline on members of its own party.

It follows that any new Member of Parliament who arrives at Westminster believing that he or she has a hand on the levers of power is bound to be disillusioned, and many have been. The ordinary Member of Parliament, the backbencher – so called because it is ministers and their opposites who sit on the front benches on either side of the gangway in the House of Commons – has to accept that one of his or her functions is literally to make up the numbers when the votes take place. Embittered backbenchers have sometimes described themselves as 'lobby fodder', especially when they feel that all they are called upon to do is go into the voting lobby to support the Government or the Opposition, even when sometimes they believe in the opposite to what they are voting for, and when sometimes they don't know what they are voting for at all.

While most Members of Parliament have to be in the House of Commons most days, and there is always activity in the Chamber between 2.30 and 10.00 p.m., there is much more to an MP's life than participation in the debate in the Chamber. They spend time in committees. They spend time meeting with colleagues and discussing how they can influence one policy or another; they meet visitors from their constituencies, journalists, and other lobbyists. They have to visit their constituencies regularly, and while this may not be a difficult matter for MPs with constituencies in or within easy reach of London, it can be a time consuming and tiring business for MPs representing far-flung corners of the UK. Many of them also earn part of their income from another source – as consultants to industry, advisers to pressure groups, or in any form of business. There are differing views on whether this is a good thing; some believe it makes MPs less dependent on their salary and thus more independent in the House; others believe that being an MP should be a full-time job.

Some MPs believe that, once elected, their responsibilities lie in the House of Commons, dealing with national and international matters, and that local problems are for their local authorities. Some have been known to admit that they hate every minute they spend in their constituencies. Others, such as Cabinet Ministers, have relatively little time to spend in their constituencies and depend on their local parties, their local agents or administrative staff to keep an eye on constituency matters. But the good constituency MP will keep in close touch with the people, so that he can both reflect their opinions in the House of Commons and further their interests. Close partnership between a Member of Parliament and a local council can be highly effective.

DES WILSON, *So You Want to be Prime Minister*

1   Why are MPs not as powerful as many people think, according to Des Wilson?
2   Explain in your own words the difference between 'government' and 'Parliament'.

3 What is meant by the terms 'frontbencher' and 'backbencher'?
4 What do some backbenchers mean by the term 'lobby fodder'?
5 What do MPs do besides debating policies in Parliament?
6 Suggest why there are 'differing views' about whether or not MPs should earn money from other sources.

First impressions

My first impressions of the House of Commons were of a kind of living museum. The Speaker was dressed as he would have been in the eighteenth century, the Serjeant-at-Arms and his deputies were also in antique dress, and in the members' cloakroom, beneath each hook, a loop of pink ribbon was religiously renewed whenever it faded, for each member to hang up his sword!

Nearly everything is connected with tradition. I learnt that while it is correct to refer to members of the same party as 'Honourable Friends', those on the other side are, normally 'Right Honourable Friends', 'Gentlemen', or 'Members', according to whether they sit on the same or opposite side of the House. Retired Officers of the armed forces are 'Right Honourable and Gallant'. Lawyers are 'Right Honourable and Learned'. Peers are 'Noble Lords'. And you're supposed to refer to members' constituencies too. For example, my 'Honourable Friend the member for Kingston upon Hull East'.

I was surprised to find that heckling and jeering in the House are quite common. Shortly after I first arrived, one of Harold Wilson's speeches was made almost completely inaudible by the noise from the Conservative benches. Seeing a piece of paper being passed from hand to hand on the other side of the House, I enquired, amid the hubbub, what was going on. The MP next to me explained that it was probably instructions for everyone to talk and to create such a row that Wilson wouldn't be heard. 'Disgraceful', I commented in anger. 'If only the Public could see this!'

'Don't get so excited,' my colleague replied. 'After all we do it to them as well!'

I soon learned that shouting out is traditional in the House. 'Answer', is shouted when speakers try to evade questions. 'Sit down', if somebody with whom you disagree is trying to intervene when a speaker from the front benches is speaking. 'Rubbish', and 'Disgrace', when things you disagree with are being said by the other side.

Amidst all this tomfoolery the Speaker has to try to keep order and is continually reprimanding the members for their flippant and school-boy-like behaviour.

Constituency work

Most of my work isn't done at the House at all but in my constituency. I am a kind of local ombudsman, to whom all and sundry come when they are in difficulties, with government offices, local authorities, the police, the Inland Revenue, their own relatives or anyone else.

If a constituent is unable to obtain a house, if he has been refused a pension, if his neighbours' teenage son is taking potshots at the washing on the line in his garden with an air gun, he comes to me. I am deluged the whole year through with a range of problems which concern almost every aspect of life, from the most public to the most intimate of issues.

On the first Saturday of every month I have an advice bureau. A steady stream of constituents keeps me busy from 9 a.m. to about 7 p.m. Every day I receive about twenty letters. I am telephoned at home at all hours of the day and throughout the weekend. I am never without some work waiting to be done.

Some of the problems are hardly those you would expect an MP to tackle. I have been asked to pursue a missing letter, or deal with the problems of burst pipes, to take action about the wallpaper being used by Council decorators, and even to help a man who thought his brain was being controlled by a transmitter in outer space. The case of a lady who lost her false teeth whilst being sick involved me in a long correspondence with the National Health Service about getting them replaced!

Postscript

The work of an MP is hard and never-ending. The pressure is such that I never have time to read books, study the news or see television programmes as I did in the past. It would be very easy to lose sight of the original reasons which led me into the Labour party – the need for fundamental social changes to make a fairer Britain for all. Now that I have the opportunity to meet my political opponents face to face, I find many of them to be likeable and humane people of the highest principles. The atmosphere of the bars which don't keep normal licensing hours, the dinners and social functions which cut across party lines all tend to blur the differences of principle with genuine ties of friendship and respect.

At the same time, it's easy to become cut off from your roots. Evenings are spent in the House or at meetings and social functions. Less and less time is available for meeting with and talking to ordinary people. I feel drawn away from the working class background of my past.

Compromise – the toning down of extreme points of view – seems much more reasonable than before. It's easy to conclude that class barriers are a figment of the imagination of the immature and those with a grievance, and to fit cosily into your new environment.

But, frustrated as I am, I still believe that my work as an MP is worthwhile. Whenever I'm asked, I'm reluctant to concede that I enjoy being in parliament. But for the present, I'm glad to be there and intend in the future to do all I can to remain there.

Adapted from STAN NEWENS, MP for Epping, in Ronald Fraser (ed.), *Work 2*

1   Explain as fully as you can why Stan Newens thought the House of Commons was like a 'living museum'.
2   What does he mean by 'I'm a kind of local ombudsman'?
3   Why does he find it difficult to remain true to his background, the people he represents and his political principles?

Pressure group politics

Gingerbread

I do not want to recite here the innumerable problems facing one-parent families. Anyone who wishes to know that in detail can find official information between the covers of the Finer Committee Report on One-Parent Families, now gathering dust in the archives of Whitehall with hardly any of its 230 recommendations implemented. But there are a few facts which readers must understand; more and more people will at some time in their lives be part of a one-parent family, and find out what it is like living in a society designed exclusively for the nuclear two-parent family. At any one moment, one out of every ten families with dependent children have only one parent to look after them, and the total number of children is more than a million, about as many as the population of a city such as Birmingham.

Divorced or separated women are the largest group of single parents, widows make up the next largest, and single, never-married mothers are the smallest group. Five out of six lone parents are women, but there is a growing number of fathers caring alone for their children.

Much of the hardship facing lone parents and children is directly related to the economic exploitation of women and to the fact that women in general and mothers in particular are still treated as if they were economically and socially dependent on men. Day-care provisions for working parents are virtually non-existent and where they do exist are usually inflexible and often expensive. The average income of one-parent families is under half of that of two-parent families' average income. A great many one-parent families have to depend on Supplementary Benefit. Housing is a nightmare – often substandard accommodation at punitive rents. Finally the legal system, both the laws and the courts, are experienced as a bewildering, absurd machine, perfectly designed to foster as much bitterness and frustration as possible among people trying to extricate themselves from their marriages.

Faced with an intractable problem of finding somewhere for herself and her two small boys to live, with the Social Services Department threatening to take the children into care if nowhere adequate could be found, a lone mother feels embattled and desperately isolated. Just such a mother wrote to a Sunday newspaper, setting out her own difficulties and suggesting that if there was anyone out there in the same boat, she would like to join up to organize for a better deal for one-parent families. A flood of 300 letters came in from all over the country, and in January 1970 Gingerbread began, to 'ginger' the government for more 'bread' (money) for one-parent families.

Gingerbread has expanded enormously. In January 1972 it won a grant and free office accommodation from the Joseph Rowntree Social Service Trust. By April 1972, thirty-five local self-help groups were running, many of them based on contacts made initially as a result of the response to the newspaper letter. Three years later there were 150 groups and in 1975, more than two groups a week started up throughout Wales, Scotland, Northern Ireland and England.

The groups are open to anyone who brings up children alone. They hold regular meetings and arrange social activities for parents and children, as well as running second-hand clothing and toy pools and arranging baby-sitting. Fund raising depends on the usual jumble sales. Although the local group and its activity remains the core of the association, there is a flourishing pen-friend scheme, run from the national office, for those who live too far from a group ro participate. There is also a thriving magazine, 'Ginger', which comes out six times a year.

The association also runs, through its national office which is staffed by six people, an advice service for lone parents, writing and telephoning to give information about welfare rights and other matters. Leaflets are also available on topics such as social security, eviction and family law.

As the organisation has consolidated and developed it has become increasingly important as a focus for political pressure at a national level. Through struggle, members acting together have become quite militant about the lack of government action to help them, and this anger culminated in an unforgettable demonstration through London in July 1975. Five thousand parents and children, the majority of whom had never taken part in any form of protest before, marched to Parliament and ventilated their anger on bewildered MPs.

This national demonstration was important for two reasons. Many MPs and government representatives were undoubtedly taken aback at such vehemence and militancy from people they had been used to consider as inarticulate and passively unfortunate – from a section of the community about whom they could wax eloquent but to whom they had never had to listen. And for many lone parents, both those Gingerbread members who marched and those who didn't, as well as those who had not yet heard of Gingerbread, the demonstration proved resounding evidence of the potential for lone parents who could come together, with a dignified and positive identity, to fight for the right to a decent standard of living and for their children and themselves. There need be no more isolation and hiding away in shame, cringing gratefully for the humiliating pittance of Supplementary Benefit, simply because they had 'made a mess of their marriage'. Now, instead of having to mumble an explanation of 'one-parent families' when strangers asked, 'Gingerbread, what on earth is that?', lone parents heard people saying, 'Yes, I've heard of that, you fight for one-parent families.

JANET HADLEY, in *Women in the Community*

1 Why is Janet Hadley disillusioned by the Finer Report? Try to find out what kind of recommendations the report made.
2 What proportion of Britain's families are one-parent families according to Janet Hadley?
3 What proportion of one-parent families are headed by women?
4 What kind of problems do one-parent families face in our society?
5 When and how was the pressure group Gingerbread founded? What is the significance of its name?
6 How has Gingerbread developed over the last ten years or do?
7 What kind of activities do members of Gingerbread take part in?

8   How has Gingerbread tried to exert pressure on national government and why?
9   How has Gingerbread managed to change the public image of one-parent families?
10 Is Gingerbread a protective or a promotional pressure group?

Old Age Pensioners' Union

Betty Harrison has been a full-time trade union official for twenty-five years, first in the Fire Brigade Union for seven years and from 1946 to 1964 in the Tobacco Workers' Union. As a national organizer at a time when very few women reached a national position in any job, Betty says she 'had to work twice as hard as a man to prove she was half as good' — but she and the women in other trade union jobs fought their way through these prejudices. Since retirement, Betty has been very active in the old age pensioners' movement. She has been treasurer of the Camden Old Age Pensioners' and Trade Union Action Association, and claims that her trade union experience has been invaluable in her work in the old age pensioners' movement.

Could you describe how the branches of the Old Age Pensioners' Union were set up and organized in Camden?
We held a meeting in the Town Hall, where a lot of people came, and we signed them up. We agreed that we should make a charge of 5p a year. We then had to go out to try to get members in other ways. The first meeting was organized by the Camden Trades Council and Camden Borough Council. The Trades Council invited people and I think that there were almost more Trades Council people and Labour Councillors there than pensioners. The information had also gone round by word of mouth, and we had a few names and addresses of people who were interested.

We then went to luncheon clubs and talked to people, many of whom joined. Then, during the summer of 1972, some members stood outside the Post Office in Kentish Town on the days when the pensioners went to draw their money, and gave out duplicated forms. The first part of these forms said who and what we were, and what our objectives were; the bottom part was an application to join, and we signed some of them up there and then outside the Post Office. When we had quite a number of addresses on these forms, we called a local meeting in Kentish Town. Then Task Force and the Neighbourhood Centre in Malden Road started to form a branch in that particular area. They took a leaf out of our book and went outside the Post Offices and they had one or two big blocks of flats which they could canvass for members. They called a meeting at the Neighbourhood Centre and asked me to go and speak when their branch was formed.

Local branches have been formed all over north-west London now, and I have been along to speak to them. The only trouble as far as I am concerned is that because I am articulate and have some experience of organization through my trade union background, anybody who's starting up a new branch wants me to go and talk to them, and this has meant quite a bit of work.

How do you recruit new members, and how do you organize the meetings to keep up their interest and active participation?
We keep getting new members all the time: not so much by standing outside shops and post offices: in the winter, anyway, old people can't really be expected to do that: but by people who are already members bringing in their neighbours and friends. One of the things we've done in our Kentish Town branch, which I think has kept the branch going very healthily, is that we have had a succession of speakers on various subjects. If we have to call a special meeting to discuss any particular problem, we get out a circular – I usually do that – but we don't have to post it. I give a bunch of notices to various people in different parts of the area we cover and they deliver them in person.

Out of all the issues you take up, could you rank them in order of their importance for your organization?
Well, all these social problems, however important in themselves, are incidental to the main work of the organization. The main issues are usually connected with housing – lack of hot water, workmen taking weeks to come along and do repairs – but the real issue is lack of money. Our main aim is to increase the pensions of old people with the ultimate objective of getting a pension related to the average earnings in industry. We want two-thirds of the average male earnings in the country. We are working for this because we want to do away with people going to Social Security to ask for the money to buy another blanket. We don't want them to have to ask for the telephone to be paid for, either, or the television licence. All these demands are also in our programme. But we are different from other organizations such as Care for the Elderly and Good Neighbours because we don't want these things as charity or handouts. We feel that the old age pensioner has earned them as a right, particularly this generation of OAPs who fought and won two World Wars for this country, who suffered unemployment and came out of that, who fought for, and won, a Health Service and the Beveridge Insurance Plan. These things had to be fought for, too, they were not just handed out as a generous bonus. Now our generation of pensioners built up the wealth of this country in order to be able to do these things, and therefore we are entitled as a right to a sufficient pension to live a decent life in the community with dignity.

What kind of support have you had from other parts of the organized trade union movement in this campaign?
As I have already mentioned, our Camden Pensioners' Association is sponsored by the Trade Council, which sends a representative to our Committee. They have given us money from time to time, because the 5p from the members doesn't go very far and we have to get money from other places, too. We have also had money from the Co-op Political Committee. In our Association, we have organized deputations to the Social Services Minister, and have had a demonstration outside Buckingham Palace. Together with other pensioners' organizations from all over the country, and the TUC, we also organized a lobby in November 1972 at the House of Commons, with a big meeting in the Albert Hall and, of course, we received a good deal of publicity for that. Well, we had 1,800 by the end of the day! We got the Mayor to come along and speak, and we kept having to rush out to buy

bread and cheese as we kept running out of supplies. We had OAPs standing at the stations with banners telling people where to go and several taxi-drivers gave free rides to the pensioners – this got us a lot of publicity, too. Arising out of the lobby, we made contact with people all over the country who, like us, were trying to organize pensioners' organizations with a militant outlook. We'd already got the support of the Transport and General Workers' Union and the Engineers' Union, but we wanted all the other unions as well, and something more than just a token 'Yes, we support you'.

Has this political campaign involved you in any difficulties with some of your members because you might be seen to be too closely identified with one particular political party?
No – we haven't had the problem of some of us thinking we are becoming too much identified with the Labour Party. Most of our people just feel that they want this decent pension so much that they are prepared to let anybody or any party help them. I think they have only sorrow that the other parties haven't identified themselves as much as with their cause. Some of the unions, particularly the Transport and General Workers' Union, have also set up OAP committees of their members because the pensioners themselves have not become more active and have forced the unions to accept that they must help the pensioners. We have said to them that they will be OAPs themselves one day and have an interest in organizing to rectify the present position before they get to that stage. On this point of links with the unions, it has been infinitely important that people like myself have been active trade unionists and known how to talk to trade unionists. In fact, most of the people active in the OAPs' organization up and down the country have been ex-trade-union officials.

Wales has started a very active OAPs' association with another miners' leader who is also a Communist Party member. In the Coventry area the key organizers are ex-Transport and General Workers' Union members as in the Birmingham area, while in the Manchester area, they are ex-textile workers. And it has been this influx of experienced people who started their organizations from the grass roots, like we did in Camden, who have bow built up our big pensioners' association which has induced, if not forced, the TUC and the Labour Party to come out in our favour. A terrific step forward for the pensioners.

BETTY HARRISON, 'Camden Old Age Pensioners', in *Community Work 2*

1   What is a 'trades council'?
2   How did Betty Harrison go about setting up the Camden branch of the Old Age Pensioners' Union?
3   What are the main issues which the OAP Union has to deal with?
4   What are the main aims of the union?
5   Why is the OAP Union more of a pressure group than a charity?
6   Which other organizations and pressure groups support the OAP Union?

7 Why is it particularly important for them to get this support, do you think?
8 Is the OAP Union a protective or a promotional pressure group?

3 Questions and answers

Pressure group project

1 Make a collection of two or three different daily newspapers over a period of a few days. Read them carefully to find any reports on the activities of pressure groups.
2 Make a list of the pressure groups involved.
3 Do their aims and objectives appear to be:
a to protect the interests of a special group of people?
b to promote a cause and gain public support for it?
4 What methods is each group using?
5 Is there any evidence to suggest, or do you imagine that the groups:
a will be successful and get their way?
b will have quite a big influence on government policy or public opinion?
c will have their point of view taken seriously?
d will have almost no effect at all?
6 Are the newspaper reports sympathetic or unsympathetic to the groups' behaviour?
7 Choose any of the groups which particularly interests you and find out as much as you can about its activities.

Checkpoints

1 What is the difference between direct and indirect democracy?
2 Which groups of people are not allowed to vote in an election?
3 Which political party is usually associated with business interests?
4 Which political party is usually associated with trade union interests?
5 Which four companies controlled the majority of British newspapers in 1974?
6 Which political party is generally supported by *(a)* the *Daily Express*, and *(b)* the *Guardian*?
7 What is the difference between a non-voter and a floating voter?
8 What is the difference between government and Parliament?
9 What is the theory of embourgeoisement?
10 When was Gingerbread founded and whose interests does it represent?

O-level questions

1   Does political freedom involve more than the right to vote?
2   What relationships have been discovered between voting intentions and social class? What explanations do sociologists offer of the working class Conservative vote?
3   'During the General Election of 1959, Trenaman and McQuail surveyed the political opinions and exposure to the mass media of a sample of electors, who were interviewed before and after the campaign. Although they detected a campaign swing of attitudes in favour of the Conservative Party, they reported that the political viewing engaged in by the sampled voters had made no difference at all to the outcome. In the words of Trenaman and McQuail, '. . . political change was neither related to the degree of exposure nor to any particular programme or argument put forward by the parties" ' (J. G. Blumer, 'The political effects of television', in J. Halloran (ed.), *The Effects of Television*)
a   Before accepting or rejecting the findings of the above research, what questions would you like to ask about it?
b   If you were satisfied that the research was acceptable, what explanations might be given to account for the lack of influence of the television programmes on the voters?
4   What are pressure groups? Give two examples of influential pressure groups in this country, describing their aims and how they try to get what they want.
5   *a*   What is the role of pressure groups in our society?
    b   Describe, with examples, two types of pressure groups showing how they differ from each other.
6   'It has been suggested that the Labour Party represents the interests of the working class and the Conservative Party represents the interests of the middle class. On the basis of this assumption one would expect the Labour Party to win every General Election.'
    What explanations are offered for the fact that the Labour Party do not always win general elections?
7   'Generally speaking, social class and the way one's parents and neighbours vote both have a strong influence on political leanings. Until quite recently it was usually supposed that people who saw themselves as manual workers, or as coming from a working class home, would vote Labour, and those who considered themselves middle class would vote Conservative. . . . One of the key facts about British politics is that about one third of those *who think of themselves a working class* usually vote Tory.' (Crick and Jenkinson, *Parliament and the People*)

a What is the importance of the phrase 'who think of themselves as working class'?
b What explanations do sociologists offer for the working-class Conservative voter?
8 Discuss the view that 'politics is a middle-class profession'.

9 Mass communication and the media

1 Background information

In pre-industrial societies, communication between people is relatively simple and direct. Children learn the behaviour, values and attitudes expected of them from their family, relatives and neighbours. Communication happens usually in face-to-face situations in which information, advice, stories and experiences can be shared easily and directly. In practice the rate of social change tends to be slow in pre-industrial societies as one generation transmits its way of life to the next in a traditional and fairly predictable way. So long as other values and outside influences do not intrude, then life goes on in much the same way for generations.

In industrial societies face-to-face communication still occurs between people in families, at work and in day-to-day contacts, but the role of supplying information, transmitting values, conveying messages and putting widely differing groups of people in touch with each other, in a complex and rapidly changing world, is increasingly taken over by more sophisticated methods of mass communication.

The main media of communication will be very familiar to you – television, radio, advertising, newspapers, film and recordings. Their significance in a society like ours is obviously important. Certainly with the introduction of sophisticated media, designed to communicate information and messages to a large number of separate individuals simultaneously, an important change takes place in the relationship between those who are communicating. Mass communication no longer represents a face-to-face exchange of information. Mass media imply the production of information, news, ideas and entertainment by a source such as the BBC, a publishing house or a recording company, and then directed towards a mass audience. The source gathers the information, decides what will be passed on and how it will be passed on, and the audience, with few exceptions, does little more than receive what is sent. In other words, those who are in control of the various mass media initiate and process the communication of messages to a large and essentially passive audience.

Clearly this situation is one which intrigues sociologists. They are interested to know what effects, if any, the various media have on people generally and whether or not they reflect the social, economic or political interests of certain groups at the expense of others in society.

One-way communication

The view that the mass media only provide for one-way communication, to an audience who have little influence or control over what they receive, is obviously a controversial one. It implies that the relatively few people who control the media and who work as journalists, film-makers, record producers and advertisers, have enormous power to decide what the majority of us will read, look at and listen to.

Clearly an audience has the right not to watch television or to choose one newspaper in preference to another. Television viewers, radio listeners and newspaper readers can write letters of complaint or advice and can express their own points of view in radio phone-ins and television interviews. But these are nearly all ways of reacting to programmes or articles which have already been produced and decided upon. Comments from the audience usually come as the postscript to a presentation by the media rather than at the time when decisions are being made about what to include, what to leave out and what approach to take.

Of course, it would be well nigh impossible to involve all of the audience all of the time in discussions about the best methods of communication. And many of those responsible for the media claim that in their programmes and newspaper presentations they are 'giving the public what they want'. But exact information about 'what the public want' is very difficult to come by, and most television and radio companies have really very little detailed information about what people think about their programmes. Frequently their definition of 'what the public want' is based on motives more closely linked to making money than to satisfying the varied interests and needs of individuals.

The charges sometimes made that the mass media actually prevent communication by only providing a one-way flow of information is often held to be a technical inevitability. But in their study of 'The sociology of mass communications', McQuail and Enzenberger point out that 'every transistor radio is, by nature of its construction, at the same time a potential transmitter'. In other words, there is no electronic difficulty in making receivers like radios and television sets into instruments which could also be used to transmit messages back to the sources of information. However, the mass communications business, as we all know, has not developed like that. It has always been assumed that, with a few exceptions, mass communications will be largely a one-way process. In practice, those who own, control and work in the media decide what is news, who has something to say that is worth listening to, and how information, ideas, values and entertainment shall be presented.

A number of sociologists have speculated upon the reasons for this kind of development. It could be interpreted merely as a consequence of the division of labour in a complex society, in which not everyone can be equally involved in what is essentially a specialized and professional job. Or it could be seen as the way of ensuring that a very powerful source of influence is kept within the control of a few people who can use to inform and entertain others in ways which best serve their own interests.

The media business

The charge is often made that the mass media represent the interests of 'big business'. The interests of 'big business' are probably best served when people spend a lot of money on their products, learn to accept their station in life without complaining about injustice or inequality and believe what others tell them when it comes to formulating opinions about different social, political and cultural issues. In terms of the advertising industry this is not a difficult claim to substantiate but what about the other most important forms of mass communication?

As we saw in Chapter 8 the majority of national and local newspapers are owned by the same four companies (see page 230). In 1972 the five leading commercial television companies – London Weekend, ATV, Granada and Yorkshire Television – served 73 per cent of all homes in Britain. The top 5 paperback publishers – Pearson Longman, Granada Publishing, Collins, Thomson and Pan – controlled 86 per cent of the home market. EMI, Decca, Pickwick International, K-Tel and Ronco controlled 69 per cent of the market in mid-price LP record sales. Eighty per cent of the box-office takings at British cinemas went to five companies – EMI–MGM, Fox–Rank, Columbia, Warner, Granada and Laurie Marsh. In all of these instances the main aim of the companies involved is to make financial profits and keep the customers spending.

It is not just that most of the market for a particular media is controlled by a very few companies; most of the big companies have financial interests in a number of different media. EMI, for example, owns the country's biggest record company, second biggest cinema chain, a good deal of Thames television, numerous leisure centres and has significant interests in the production of industrial and consumer electrical equipment. Rank owns the largest cimena chain in Britain, Butlins, countless hotels and bingo halls, radio, television and hi-fi manufacturing companies and a large part of Southern Television. It would not be unusual in fact for you to switch on the television, go to a cinema, turn on the radio, put on a record or join in a game of bingo, and in every case be receiving information and entertainment from the same source.

Independent television and radio

Independent television and radio consists of fifteen different television companies and a growing number of local radio stations. They must all apply for contracts to produce programmes from the Independent Broadcasting Authority (IBA). The IBA was established by an Act of Parliament in 1954 and members of its board of governors are appointed by the government. The IBA grants contracts and transmission facilities to the various independent commercial companies who pay back part of their profits to the IBA in rent. The IBA has the right to ensure that companies provide television and radio which is 'informative', 'educational' and 'entertaining', to keep an eye on advertising standards and to make sure there is a proper balance in what is presented. So long as the various companies abide by their contracts with the IBA and do not get into financial difficulties, they have a good deal of independence, especially if they make a lot of money and can demonstrate that a lot of people tune into their programmes.

The main source of revenue for independent television and radio depends on advertising. Advertisers have no direct control over programmes, but just as they are prepared to pay more money to newspapers with large circulations, so too do they pay more money for advertising slots in popular programmes at peak viewing and peak listening times. This inevitably encourages the companies to concentrate on popular and entertaining programmes which are likely to have a mass appeal rather than serious or radical programmes which only attract a minority audience. In order to fulfil their contract with the IBA, however, all the independent companies, even local radio stations, have to provide informative and minority interest programmes. Some companies take this responsibility very seriously and produce excellent documentary, serious drama and news programmes, others prefer to do the 'public service broadcasting' late at night or early on Sunday mornings when few people are tuned in. And despite the claims of many local radio stations to be 'serving their local community', most discussion and 'serious' programmes are reserved for the evenings when listening figures are about one-fifth of those earlier in the day.

The government has given the go-ahead to a second ITV channel to begin broadcasting in 1982. Like ITV-1, it will depend on advertising revenue for its source of income but the government has made it clear that ITV-2 must be more educational, more experimental, less dominated by the 'big five' independent companies, and it must not place making money from advertising at the top of its list of priorities.

The BBC

The BBC was established in 1923 by royal charter as an independent, non-profit-making public company and like the IBA has a board of twelve governors appointed by the home secretary. The first director general of the BBC was Lord Reith who established early an educational and moral role for broadcasting. He believed that broadcasting should not pander to 'low popular taste' but should seek to educate, improve and elevate the tastes of those listening. He considered the development of broadcasting to be 'a mighty instrument to instruct and fashion public opinion, to banish ignorance and misery, to contribute richly and in many ways to the sum total of human well being'.

   Those who worked with him and succeeded him were very influenced by this kind of paternalistic and moral attitude to their work. Stories of radio news readers dressed in evening suits, the insistence on high standards of spoken English and the censorship of any kind of slang or vulgarity make quaint reading in today's more permissive atmosphere. But before the BBC had to compete for audiences with independent television and radio it could afford to be disdainful of popular, commercial and trendy presentations. Today there is much less to choose between independent television and radio and the BBC than there once was. The BBC is currently receiving a good deal of criticism for reducing its serious and current affairs programmes in favour of light entertainment and more trivial presentations. But its lack of dependence on advertising revenue, and the use of BBC-2 as an outlet for programmes of a more educational, experimental and serious nature, means that, at its best, the BBC still plays a responsible and pioneering role in producing good television which does not necessarily attract a large audience. Unlike independent television and radio the BBC depends on the state for money. Some finance comes from government grants and some from the sale of television licences. Clearly this dependency limits the independence of the BBC. The home secretary is legally allowed to prevent the BBC broadcasting anything which he considers to be detrimental to the government or to the interests of the country. More often, cautious directors cut out programmes which they fear might annoy the government.

   The independent companies are also vulnerable if they annoy governments too much. The IBA, a government appointed body can refuse to renew a company's licence to broadcast, and the amount of tax the company has to pay on advertising revenue could be increased to the point at which its profits were considerably reduced.

Socialization and the media

In a complex and rapidly changing society like ours the passing on of information, values, attitudes and opinions by word of mouth, in the family or even via education is only a part of the process of socialization. In a society in which over 93 per cent of homes has a television set and almost everyone has a radio, the media of radio and especially television are by far the most effective ways of getting a variety of messages to thousands of people in the intimacy of their own homes.

James Halloran, a sociologist who has done perhaps more research than anyone else in Britain on the impact of television, suggests that television is likely to be more influential when it is dealing with subjects or situations which are either very new to people or about which they have very little direct experience. People tend to believe what they see more than what they read, and compared to newspapers, for example, most people believe television to be more reliable and less biased in its presentation of information. Halloran suggests that this encourages many people to use television as their main source of evidence and as the basis of an increasing number of their opinions and attitudes. Certainly the state recognizes the influence of television in formulating opinion and the government, for example, is one of the largest buyers of advertising time. But if Halloran is right, then there is also a danger that television could help to misinform people as well as to inform them. If, for example, black Britons are only featured in programmes about the 'problems' of a multi-racial society, or used in so-called 'comedy' shows in a way which confirms prejudice and stereotypes about black people, then television could be seen as encouraging – and perpetuating biased and ill-informed attitudes among many of its viewers.

If Halloran is right and television is most influential in those areas in which people have little other evidence or experience to balance the opinions they glean from television, then young viewers are likely to be even more impressionable than adults. The fact that young people between 5 and 14 seem to watch more television each week than almost any other group, as Table 28 shows, has led sociologists and others to

Table 28 *Average number of hours viewed each week*

Age group	1975	1976	1977
5-14	24.0	22.0	22.0
15-19	19.3	18.4	17.6
20-29	18.2	19.1	18.2
30-40	18.4	19.0	17.9
50+	19.6	20.4	20.0

speculate upon the effects of television and sex and violence upon young viewers. The same kind of question is also asked about pop music in which an increasingly younger audience is possibly learning more in terms of attitudes and values than a superficial interest in pop stars and the pop charts might suggest.

Although there has been a good deal of research into the effects of the various media on people's reactions to sex, violence, consumerism and politics, the results are varied and as yet inconclusive. Some people believe that television commercialism breeds consumerism, others believe that the present generation is better educated and informed than any other generation has been because of the educational benefits of television. Some people point out that there is more real violence shown in news programmes than in television fiction, others claim that for many people television merely provides 'company' and a background noise which they do not really watch closely enough to be influenced by one way or the other. One thing is certain, though: businessmen, advertisers and politicians would not spend so much time and energy keeping control of television if they did not think it was a very influential method of communication.

The media and social class

Sociologists have also been interested to find out whether people from different social classes in society use the media differently.

In general, lower-middle-class and working-class people tend to watch television more frequently than middle class and professional people, as Table 29 shows. When ITV was first introduced in 1954 it was set up deliberately to appeal to working-class people and sociologists have found that, in general, middle-class people are more likely to watch BBC and working-class people are more likely to watch ITV. There are of course many exceptions to this generalization.

A similar pattern emerges when you consider newspapers. Middle class and professional people are more likely to read the *Daily Telegraph*, the *Guardian*, *The Times* and the *Financial Times*. Lower-middle and working-class people are more likely to read the *Daily Express*, the *Daily Mail*, the *Daily Mirror*, the *Sun* and the *Daily Star*. As we saw in Chapter 8, newspapers are also much more likely than television to be biased in support of one political party rather than another (pages 280-1). The *Daily Mirror*, for example, generally supports the Labour Party and is usually read by working-class people whose interests are probably best served by supporting the Labour Party. The *Telegraph* is a Conservative paper and is most frequently read by middle-class business and professional people who vote Conservative and whose interests are best served by the Conservative party. In terms of those who have power and

Table 29 *Average number of hours viewed each week*

Social class	1975	1976	1977
Professional/administrative (5% of the population)	14.0	16.7	14.4
Middle management/supervisory (25% of the population)	16.6	17.7	16.8
Working class (70% of the population)	20.0	20.3	20.1

control in society, therefore, it is interesting to speculate about what political influence papers with a conservative bias like the *Express*, the *Daily Star* and the *Daily Mail* have on their essentially working-class readers.

Because newspapers are also closely associated with the interests of 'big business' they are likely to be more Conservative than Liberal or Labour in their attitudes, and the fear that they use their influence over their readers to praise one party at the expense of another is a major cause of concern to Liberal and Labour supporters.

What is news?

Another aspect of television, radio and newspapers that interests sociologists is the way in which 'news' is selected. Each day there are an enormous number of things that happen in every part of the country and all over the world. Who decides which of these many events are newsworthy? And are the same news items considered to be equally relevant to all viewers, listeners and readers?

Well, clearly the selection is made by those who work in the media, and it is based to some extent on their decision about what is important and relevant, and also in relation to the opinions they have about their audience.

Because mass communications are designed to reach a maximum number of people rather than separate individuals in isolation, one noticeable tendency of the media is to stereotype their audiences – to think of them as large groups of people who are all more or less the same. This can lead, for example, to 'women's pages' in the press, and indeed women's magazines, which treat women as though they are all the same and as if all they are interested in is fashion, cooking, gossip, slimming and romance. It also means that television programmes and newspapers frequently oversimplify what they have to say – especially for working-class audiences – on the assumption that they are less well-educated and less intelligent than middle-class audiences.

Bias and stereotyping can happen in other ways too. There is the tendancy to go for stories that are 'sensational' and, as the Glasgow Media Study Group showed in their report, 'Bad News', there has been in recent years a clear anti-union bias in news reporting and a concentration on the damaging effects of strikes, quite out of all proportion to the number of strikes that actually take place. While it is the case that more working days are lost each year because of industrial accidents and as a result of industrial injuries than by strikes, the study group could find little evidence in the press of this information being made available.

Murdock and Golding, writing in 1973, made quite a detailed study of broadcasting. They found a noticeable tendency in the media to appeal to ideas of patriotism, the 'national interest' and 'togetherness', as a way of stressing conformity and isolating outsiders and those who do not conform. They also noted how British concerns, British exploits and British achievements are considered to be more newsworthy and important than events which happen in other countries.

Two other sociologists, Galting and Ruge, in a special analysis of foreign news, showed how:
1 Coverage of events in other countries stressed fighting, natural disasters and accidents rather than everyday events.
2 When countries are not considered to be very important only their very important citizens were considered newsworthy.
3 When ordinary people were portrayed it was usually only in circumstances of famine, war or political unrest.

The effects of this kind of news concentration, according to Galting and Ruge, is to emphasize 'bad news' and present a stereotyped image of countries in which the leaders are important and everyone else is stupid or starving.

It can't be all bad!

You may be feeling by now that all those involved in the media are unscrupulous people who, in giving the rest of us a 'good time', are really concerned to take advantage of us! Clearly that's only one side of the story.

No one can deny that in providing leisure activities, entertainment and pleasure for large numbers of people, the mass communications business does also perform a valuable service in society. The important thing to remember, though, is that those who provide the services have a variety of motives for what they do, and enabling people to enjoy themselves is not always their first consideration.

So far as radio and television goes, clearly no one should underestimate the important contributions they have made to popular education and to making people more aware of what is going on around them. And despite all the reservations outlined earlier, television particularlly has helped to bring drama, music, light entertainment, sport, knowledge and ideas to the attention of many more people than ever before. And despite the undue influence of advertising and government financing, there is enough evidence to suggest that conscientious journalism designed to expose corruption in high places and to give publicity to the plight of those who are often powerless to speak for themselves is also a part of the contribution that mass communications can make to a complex society.

2 Looking at the evidence

The characteristics of mass communication

1   Mass communications usually require complex organizations for them to be able to operate properly. The production of a newspaper or a television service involves the need for huge capital resources and calls for the employment of high skilled personnel. Everything has to be well organized, with a clear structure of authority and responsibility. Mass communication organizations, therefore, are very different from informal, face-to-face communications.

2   The mass media are directed towards large audiences. This results from the application of technology geared to mass production and widespread dissemination. The exact size of audiences or readership groups receiving mass communications cannot be specified but they are considerably larger than the audiences for other means of communication (e.g. a lecture or a theatre play), and they are large in relation to the number of communicators.

3   Mass communications are public – the content and distribution is open to all. But there is seldom the opportunity for complete open access because of constraints imposed deliberately or arising from the social structure.

4   The audience for mass communications is heterogeneous in composition. It is made up of people living under widely different conditions, under widely varying cultures, coming from different sections of society, engaging in different occupations and hence having different interests, standards of life, degrees of prestige, power and influence.

5   The mass media can establish simultaniety of contact with large numbers of people, at a distance from the source, and widely separated from each other. Radio and television achieve this result more completely than the print media, since the latter are likely to be read at different times and to be used more selectively. Two features of this immediacy of contact are important. The first is the speed, distance and immediacy of impact that is possible. The second is that it tends to produce uniformity in the selection and interpretation of messages.

6   In mass communications the relationship between communicator and audience is impersonal in that an anonymous audience is being addressed by people known only in their public role as communicators. Mass media are organized to allow communication flow in only one direction on the whole, and despite attempts to get to know about the audience by audience research, correspondence and the evidence of sales and box office returns, little is really known at the moment about an audience's response to the communications it receives.

7   The audience for mass communication is a phenomenon unique to modern society. It is made up of individuals who are focusing on a common programme, film, report or recording; taking part in an identical form of behaviour and likely to be directed towards similar responses. Yet the individuals involved are unknown to each other, have only a limited amount, if any, interaction, and they are in no way organized as a group or association. The composition of the audience is continually shifting, it has no leadership or feelings of identity.

Adapted from DENIS MCQUAIL, *Towards a Sociology of Mass Communications*

1   Explain in your own words the characteristics which make mass communication different to ordinary communications.
2   What kind of 'capital resources' would a mass communications organization need?
3   Suggest examples of 'deliberate constraints' and 'constraints arising from the social structure' which prevent the mass media being open to all.
4   What is meant by the term 'heterogeneous'? Does it matter that a heterogeneous audience receives the same communication? Do you agree that audiences are always heterogeneous?
5   What effects does the immediacy of mass communications have on the way they operate?
6   Why are the mass media 'impersonal' according to the writer? Do you agree with him?
7   Why is mass communications a 'phenomenon unique to modern society'?

The effects of the media

Does the mass media encourage more crime and violence? The chief constable of North Wales, speaking at a conference in 1978, firmly believed that it does. Mr Philip Myers linked the increase in violent crime to films and television programmes. He told the joint conference of police chiefs and local authority representatives, 'The violence portrayed today is alleged to be part of real life and likely to be copied.' He compared the crime and entertainment patterns of 1967 and 1977. 'In 1967 there were clear lines of what could or could not be shown on the cinema screen. Violence in the westerns of the day was removed from reality.' But, he said, 'Nowadays violence is such an integral part of adventure programmes that heroes have to continually display their physical superiority and sexual prowess. I don't think it's any accident that crimes of violence are on the increase.' When he was a child, he said, neither he nor other children hit people with bricks. He wondered if this was because he was not fed on violence from a television set in the living room so often that violence became normal to a six-year-old.

So far as sociological research shows, the effects of films and television on crime and violence are inconclusive. Here is what sociologist Denis McQuail has to say:

Mass communications research is probably most closely linked in its public reputation, with concern over the possible harmful effects of the media. The most persistent concerns have been with the danger to children, who cannot easily be protected from exposure to adult content in the cinema or on the radio and television. The rapid and seemingly uncontrolled growth in human activity has changed as a result of new developments in mass communications. It seemed hardly in doubt that some significant social changes must accompany the revolution in communications and that these changes would be outside the control of those who try to preserve public order and morality. However, such research as we have had into these questions has proved to be generally disappointing to those who welcome firmer policies of social control.

The expectation that crime and violence will be encouraged by mass media derives from the well documented fact that mass media tends to overrepresent the portrayal of acts of crime and violence. This has led to the speculation that mass media fans might come to accept crime and violence as 'normal', they might learn the techniques of crime, they might imitate what they see or read about, they might have deeply hidden emotions 'triggered off' or they might come to regard violence a perfectly acceptable way of getting what they want.

Research carried out in Britain by Himmelweit and others after the introduction of commercial television was inconclusive about the effects on children of TV violence, however. It was concluded that 'television is unlikely to cause aggressive behaviour, although it could precipitate it in those few children who are emotionally disturbed'. A more recent American study by Schramm largely confirmed the British findings. Whether or not children learn violence from television depends largely on what the child brings to television. Halloran does not altogether agree. He argues that portrayals of aggression are more likely to encourage rather than to release aggressive behaviour.

Adapted from DENIS MCQUAIL, *Towards a Sociology of Mass Communications*

Another widespread expectation about the mass media, and especially television, is some generally undesirable tendancies will be encouraged including 'passivity', 'escapism', 'unsociability' and 'loss of personal creativity'. This is what Denis McQuail has to say:

Again there are well documented observations to support this view; the mass media are popular and time consuming and their content is directed towards fantasy more often than reality. The question is whether an overconcentration of fantasy may reduce the individual's capacity to handle reality and whether by getting 'drawn to' the fantasy world of the media people lose their initiative and withdraw from personal action and social intercourse.

Again, studies on children have been the most common. And again the findings have been inconclusive. Himmelweit found that television had neither encouraged passivity not stimulated interest. Schramm found that it depended to a great extent on the personality characteristics of the child-viewer.

Belxon found a slight reduction in 'initiative' and 'interests' among 'new' adult viewers. His research into the effects of television on family life and sociability in Britain, despite the thoroughness of the research, found that whatever effects had occurred they were either slight, variable or both!

Adapted from DENIS MCQUAIL, *Towards a Sociology of Mass Communications*

1 Explain in your own words some of the commonly held fears about the effects of the media.
2 What sociological evidence is available to confirm these fears?
3 Make a list of the problems a sociologist would face if he or she was trying to discover whether television viewing encourages *(a)* passivity, and *(b)* violence.

ITV-2 – A channel with a difference?

Three years before ITV-2 is due to be opened, the Home Secretary, William Whitelaw, explains what he expects it to do:

The Government will not allow the fourth TV channel – which it has allocated to commercial television – to become 'just an ITV 2'.

The Home Secretary said that the Government would do this by preventing the Big Five ITV companies from dominating the new channel and by ensuring that the new channel – due on the air in 1982 – will have a positive bias towards programmes made by independent producers.

Mr Whitelaw said that the Independent Broadcasting Authority, which is to supervise the new channel, will also be charged with preventing the two commercial channels engaging in a battle for high ratings.

He said: 'The IBA will be expected to develop a distinctive service on the fourth channel. Within existing rules on taste, decency and the like, it should be designed to give new opportunities to creative people in British TV and to add new and greater satisfaction to those now available to the viewer.

'It will be expected to extend the range of programmes available to the public, to find new ways of serving minority and specialized audiences and to give due place to innovation.

'It will be expected not to allow rivalry for ratings between the two channels for which it has statutory responsibility nor to allow scheduling designed to obtain for each of these services the largest possible audience over the week.

'It will be expected to make arrangements for the largest practicable proportion of programmes on the fourth channel to be supplied by organizations and persons other than the companies contracted to provide programmes on ITV 1.

'It will be expected to provide an allotment of times for educational programmes both structured and informal on the fourth channel and for Welsh language programmes on the fourth channel in Wales.'

In his list of safeguards Mr. Whitelaw said that the IBA would be expected to ensure 'that the budget for the fourth channel is adequate to achieve the sort of service I have described and that a fair payment is made to all contributors on the channel.'

The main source of revenue for the fourth channel will be 'spot advertising' – the system used on ITV. But Mr Whitelaw surprised some by indicating that block advertising – the grouping of commercials in periods of 10 minutes or more – and sponsorship would also be permitted.

But the Home Secretary warned that 'competitive advertising on the two channels would inevitably result in a move towards single-minded concentration on maximising the audience for programmes with adverse consequences for both of the commercial channels and before long for the BBC as well.'

Hence the budgeting of the fourth channel would not necessarily be governed by the revenue earned from the advertisements shown on that channel. This implied that the IBA will be expected to propose taking enough money from the advertising revenue pool of both channels to provide the Channel Four service.

PETER FIDDICK, *Guardian,* 15 September 1979

1 Suggest reasons why the Home Secretary is anxious to prevent ITV-2 becoming too much like ITV-1.
2 How will the government try to prevent this happening?
3 Who is the IBA and what are its responsibilities so far as ITV-2 is concerned?
4 How will ITV-2 be financed? How does this compare with ITV-1?
5 Suggest why the home secretary believes 'competitive advertising' might have adverse effects for the BBC.

The press

Case study 1 Football hooliganism and the press

Media coverage of football hooliganism is worth singling out for special attention, for at least two reasons.

1 Since football hooliganism first began to attract public attention and concern – in the mid 1960s – it has received a very extensive press coverage. The nature and pattern of this coverage is a phenomenon worth analysing in its own right.
2 Despite appearances, only a very small proportion of the population has any direct experience of 'football hooliganism'. Most people have never seen, been

close to, or involved in a 'football riot', either at, on the way to, or from a football ground. The media provide the principal source of information about this problem for the vast majority of the public. It is therefore worth asking what the nature of that information is - how it is constructed, what it highlights, what it leaves out.

The press and their stories

It is very common to regard the press as, in fact, a more or less perfect mirror reflection of what is happening in the world. It's assumed that there is first a problem (fans rioting on the pitch; police and supporters brawl; supporters from one end putting the boot in to supporters from a rival end; innocent people caught up in a rampaging mob on the street leading to a ground; even, occasionally, a knifing or a fatal accident on a supporters' train or an underground) and then, second, the newspapers report on the problem, to tell us what happened. The analysis is considered in two separate and discreet parts - events first, reports second. But the question of the press coverage cannot be treated as an altogether separate and distinct process, easily distinguished from the events being reported. This is so for two reasons. First, press reports cannot be simply a straight reflection of what happened because there always intervenes a whole process of selection - which events to report, which to leave out; which aspects of an event to report, which to omit; and a whole process of presentation - choosing which sort of headline, language, imagery, photography, typography to use in translating what happened on Saturday afternoon into a story in Sunday's paper. Through the selection and presentation processes, the press plays an active and constructing role, not merely a passive and reflecting one, in relation to a problem like that of 'football hooliganism'.

This leads to a second consideration. The moment one advances the slightest criticism of the way the press handles an issue of public concern, especially when it has been defined as a violent social problem, it is immediately assumed that one is suggesting that the press made it all up; or that one is making excuses for what happened, laying all the blame at the door of the press. It's not my intention to do either. I do think there is a major problem about the way the press has selected, presented and defined football hooliganism over the years. But I don't think the press has simply made it all up; though there are instances where I believe a little 'creative journalism' has indeed been at work. The press has some responsibility, both for exaggerating and sensationalizing the character of the problem and for isolating the violent and sensational aspects from their proper social context. I believe that the press behaviour is (a) a problem in its own right and (b) that it has had the effect of increasing the scale of the social problem it sets out to remedy and contain.

News values and distortion

On most days - in sport as in any other domain of news - there are hundreds of potential news stories. Only some of them will find their way into the press. The key to the process is news values.

Newspapers thrive, not simply by printing the most newsworthy stories but by highlighting the most newsworthy aspect of a story. So there is a progressive tendency to rework and process stories, so as to isolate and identify for your readers the most dramatic angle. It follows, of course, that you can increase the news value of a not very dramatic story by adding a sensational touch or by selecting an unusual angle on a perfectly usual story. This value-added effect is especially strong in the fiercely competitive circumstances in which papers presently operate. Crucial circulation can be won or lost, depending on how successful a paper is in expanding the sum of the news values on each of its pages. When economic conditions are not favourable, as is the case at the present time, the temptation to inflate the news value of stories is particularly acute.

How the press stirs it up
Football hooliganism is not the only type of behaviour which the press exaggerates out of all proportion. But it is a good example of this tendency in the press in recent years.

If you look at the general press coverage of football hooliganism, riots and violence connected with the game since the mid 1960s, it is hard to sustain the argument that this treatment has been careful, judicious, measured, inquiring, attentive to the complexities of the problem, sceptical of exaggerated claims, anxious to calm unreal fears, or demystifying. Instead the treatment has been accompanied by graphic headlines, bold typefaces, warlike imagery and epithets, vivid photographs cropped to the edges to create a strong impression of physical menace, and the stories have been decorated with black lines and exclamation marks. Rather than a slow build up, the problem seems to enter the public arena each season, with expectations and prophecies of horrors to come. It would be hard to describe this press performance as one calculated to keep things in proportion.

The misleading use of language
Not every clash between supporters and the police justifies the language of 'Rampage' and 'Riot', 'Bottle Boys' or 'Thugs', which has by now become customary. Some incidents deserve dramatic language but this makes it all the more important to maintain a proper sense of scale and judgement, so as to avoid presenting hooliganism as a general feature of all major football games - which it isn't.

A further problem is that the language of violence is also part of the general language of sports reporting. The FANS GO MAD story (*Sunday People* 3.4.77) tells its own story; 'hundreds of fighting fans raced onto the pitch'. But on the preceding page, the even bigger 'CRUNCH' headline starts a story which is not about hooligans but about a tackle on the field that sent Howard Kendall off to have 'six stitches inserted below his right knee'. In a Birmingham-Newcastle game, 'Nulty charged like the Light Brigade. . .'. The *People's* 'TEARAWAY RICHARDS' is not a negative comment on some fan on the rampage but an positive description of the blinder John Richards played for Wolves. . . . So are a number of other headlines, reporting other hard games, in the same issue of that paper; 'FOREST'S BLITZ', 'POWELL BLAST SHOCKS STOKE', 'Hankin Makes Blues Suffer', 'RAY'S ROUSER: But Villa makes it mighty tough', and 'Doyle's Karate Gets Him Chopped'.

If the language of football reporting is increasingly the language of thrills and spills, hard tackles and tough games, of struggle, victory and defeat, studded with images drawn from the blitzkrieg and the military showdown, it is not so difficult to understand why some of what is going on on the pitch, and recorded with such vivacity in the newspapers, spills over onto the terraces.

Dismissive labelling
The label used to describe the supporters involved in violent incidents also merits some comments. 'Hooliganism' and 'hooligans' are, I suppose, by now so well established in the sports writers' litany that it would be difficult to reverse the trend. 'Thugs' has also in the last year or two become a required word of abuse. But increasingly the newspapers also use the term, 'animals'. 'RIOT! United's Fans are Animals' (*People* 29.8.75), 'SAVAGES! ANIMALS!' (*Mirror* 21.4.75). 'Another idea might be to put these people in "hooligan compounds" every Saturday afternoon . . . They should be herded together preferably in a public place. That way they could be held up to ridicule and exposed for what they are - mindless morons with no respect for other people's property or wellbeing. We should make sure we treat them like animals - for their behaviour proves that that's what they are.' (*Mirror* 4.4.77)

This verbal reduction of football hooligans to the level of animals, or the insane, has serious social consequences. We note here only two. First, it's the sort of language which suggests that there cannot possibly be any human rationale for, or reason behind, the actions of the 'thugs'. It also suggests a 'sort of' explantion for what is going on on the terraces and supporters' trains.

Explanations which reduce all threatening or deviant behaviour to animal-like insanity are quite common in our culture, and by no means exclusive to football hooliganism. But although we may not like social violence or its consequences, we have to acknowledge that some people have their reasons for behaving in such a way. Aggressive behaviour is by no means always irrational.

Using stigma
By labelling actions in this way, we stigmatize and degrade the actions of others. We implicitly flatter ourselves and our own 'rational', moderate and well controlled behaviour by comparison, and we legitimate any actions which we or the state might take in combating what we have so labelled.

The use of terms like 'animals' can all too easily become the description which we attach to those whose actions we are about to discipline and punish. The use of social stigmas frequently serves to legitimize punishment – which is often no more than meeting one kind of violence with another. It's as if we have to convince ourselves that these people must be animals (and therefore beyond the pale of civilization) before we can quite tolerate the idea of us 'moderate and rational folk' actually 'caging them in' or 'birching' or 'hosing them down'. Of course, if they are only animals, there's no way to teach them a lesson except by means of the judicious application of the whip.

Deeper explanations
It's much more difficult to explain what's happening in and around football if you assume quite the opposite starting point. Suppose these are not wild animals, thugs, hooligans, insane kids, running amok. Suppose they are the sons of those fathers who still make a trip to the terraces religiously every week, or stay in glued

to 'Match of the Day' every Saturday night; the children teachers teach, or have difficulties teaching; the lads in dead-end jobs or, increasingly these days, in no sort of job at all; not only 'United's' most disgraceful, but also 'United's' most fervent, most religious supporters. Suppose their aggressive acting-out arises, not from the withdrawal into passivity and rootlessness, but from their over-involvement and over-identification with the thrills and spills and the controversies and disappointments of the game. Suppose 'Man United Rules OK' is their only claim to cultural space and territory, their only claim to a place in the sun, the only compensating 'victory' for a lifetime of defeats.

Looking at things from this point of view leads, of course, to questions about society very far removed from the cut and thrust of the terraces. I can't help remarking that football hooliganism as a 'cause for concern' has grown directly in step with the severe deterioration in our economic situation - in a period of growing unemployment, public spending cuts and a sharpening political polarization, in which young working class people emerge as a particularly vulnerable group.

But then increasingly in our society, as things get tougher and bleaker for us all, the temptation grows to deal with any problem, first by simplifying its causes, second by stigmatizing those involved, third by whipping up public feeling into a panic about it, and fourth by stamping hard on it from above.

STUART HALL, *The Treatment of 'Football Hooliganism' in the Press*

1 Why is 'football hooliganism', as depicted by the media, worth studying by sociologists? Does it tell us anything else about the media other than their attitude to 'hooligans'?

2 Why is it incorrect to believe that newspapers merely 'report the facts'?

3 What are Stuart Hall's two main criticisms of the press in relation to reporting football hooliganism?

4 What does the newspaper world mean by 'news value'? Explain why economics has a lot to do with news value.

5 What types of techniques do newspapers use to dramatise stories and give them news value?

6 Do you agree that violent language is part and parcel of sports reporting in the press? What effects does the language of sports reporting have on the fans, according to Stuart Hall?

7 What do sociologists mean by the term 'labelling'? What are some of the effects of 'dismissive labelling' according to Stuart Hall? Can you find any evidence in the press to illustrate examples of 'dismissive labelling'?

8 What alternative explanation of 'football hooliganism' does Stuart Hall suggest? Why is this explanation not so 'popular' in the press do you think?

9 How far do you agree or disagree with Hall's analysis of how the press treats 'football hooliganism'? Give full reasons for your andwer.

10 Can you give any other examples of 'social problems' which are often exaggerated and distorted by the press?

Case study 2 Teenage magazines

If you want to indulge in a fit of desperation about the effectiveness of the women's movement, take a look at some of the new teenage weekly magazines - Pink, Mates, Blue Jeans, Oh Boy! and My Guy. They make a lot of money and get a wide circulation. The top one, My Guy, sells rather more copies than The Guardian.

Valentine, Romeo, and the like, full of gushy love stories that usually ended in wedding bells, are a thing of the past. This new genre aimed at the 11 to 16 year olds, is devoted almost entirely to boys, how to get them, how to entice them, what to do to them when you've got them. Reading through a stock of them this mono-mania is quite overwhelming and verging on the pornographic, far and away beyond the kind of material in traditional women's magazines. Nowhere is there a single suggestion that girls of this age might be even a little interested in anything else at all.

Take last week's My Guy, the best-seller. First page - jokey letters, and photographs of six spotty looking boys in a feature called 'Hi Guys!' 'If you want it - we can get it for you! So long as it's tasty fellas you're looking for . . .Help! Three hungry boys searching for three tasty girls. Fancy a bite! Well, take your pick from Ray on the left, Cyril in the middle, and Chris on the right.' That is followed by a photostrip about a girl going to a computer dating service.

Next comes a story in words about a girl picking up an Arab prince in a disco, a pop star gossip page, then a quiz, Love Test - Are You the One that He Wants? 'Do you ever catch him obviously thinking about something or someone else when he's kissing you? Does he kiss you in a crowded street? Does he mind if other lads think he's wet if he's paying you attention?'

Another photostrip story, exceptionally horrible, tells of a girl going out with a boy who turns out to be dying: he gets picked on by toughs: more next week. After that there is another quiz, Are his Talents Too Apparent? Sample question: 'Your Dad approves of him because: a. He's got the knack of keeping your Mum talking. b. He's an expert on real ale. c. He always calls him sir?'

Problem pages are staple fodder. The first one is 'You and Your Body'. Sample problem: 'When I'm wearing a bra, I'm a lovely shape. But as soon as I take it off, my breasts flop down to rest on the upper part of my arm. Is this because I always sleep on my stomach?' Then there's a 'My Guy Problem Story' also in photostrip, called 'His Body Makes Me Blush' about a girl with a skinny boyfriend. It is presented as a true story with a real girl, but it's fiction.

Then there's another problem page, called 'If you've got problems'. Sample problem: 'I am only 13 but I am in love with a 21-year-old married man and he loves me. We have to keep it a secret so his wife doesn't find out. The problem is I'm frightened he might ask me to have sex. What do I do?'

And that's it. That's what gets this huge circulation. In the early days it was a bit more overtly sexual, but Mary Whitehouse's complains made them water it down.

The little girls' comic market is now read by the 6-10 year olds. The eleven year olds are expected to gravitate to the My Guy category. Of the girls' comics the market leaders are Bunty, Misty, Jinty, Judy and Debbie. They are full of all those fantasies about girls who solve mysteries, win battles against apalling odds, trounce villains, and turn into stars or geniuses full of initiative, daring and stamina.

There's Little Miss Dynamite! Ping-Pong Champion! Myra Gold, Budding Ballerina! Tansy Tomkins, Skating Star; Gail Mason Cracks the Mirror Mysteries; Testing Time for Tania the Swimmer; Patsy and Kathleen, Girl Explorers in the Andes; and Chained to Her Racket, Jane Taggart Tennis Star!

These comics aren't art or education but at least the fantasies they encourage are lively, active, positive ones. Girls read them to identify with lives of excitement and achievement.

So what happens to their personalities at 11 or 12? What became of those heroines who showed so much promise? Wonderful Myra, Tansy, Gail and Tania have abandoned their high endeavours and have taken instead to giggling about boys and bras in coffee bars. They no longer live their own exciting lives but sit by the telephone and wait for Him to take them to discos. Their own ambitions have disappeared and they have settled for getting a boy who does exciting things instead.

The man behind this whole new genre of magazine is John Purdie, Deputy Editorial Director of the juvenile publications department at IPC which publishes four of the six main titles in the field. He is a small, dapper, elegantly dressed man in his mid forties who comes from a Scottish working class background. His journalistic career started at 21 when he left a whisky firm to work for DC Thomson in Dundee. He talks scathingly of the failure of 'academic dunderheads' in that organization, compared with the success of people like himself who 'had the common touch'.

At DC Thomson, John Purdie invented and launched Jackie, which was a great success, a milder version of his more recent magazines. He then moved to IPC where five years ago he launched Pink, and Mates, last year Oh Boy! and this year, My Guy.

The editors of his magazines are in the 21-24 age group. Each magazine appears indistinguishable from the others, all printed on the same cheap paper, with the same amount of colour and the same layout and designs. The photostrip was his big innovation and the next magazine he produces will be entirely photostrip stories.

I asked him how he justified selling young girls magazines without a single item suggesting that there might be anything for them in life except boys.

'We don't set the trends. We just follow what the kids want', he said. He blames advertising for making kids the way they are. 'Look, it isn't for us to educate. Why aren't teachers doing it, or parents? It's not my job to educate', Mr Purdie repeats. 'I entertain'.

But 'entertaining' these very young girls with a view of the world that is so grotesquely distorted amounts to sending out a shower of propaganda to those who are most vulnerable. He boasts about his problem pages, claiming them as a public service, but if any single person has contributed to the creation of those 'problems' it must be Mr Purdie and his sexist ethic. If a 12 or 13-year-old reads magazines that tell her that all that matters in the world is to get an attractive 'fella' hold on to him, and love him to distraction, is it surprising that she feels she has problems if she hasn't got a 'fella', doesn't want a 'fella', feels she's not pretty/developed enough to get a 'fella' is passionately interested in playing the violin, hockey, or chess, reading books, solving maths problems or mending bikes?

Mr Purdie then changed his ground. 'This is a matter of class. You middle-class people just don't understand what working-class kids are like. You want everything nice, the pictures and the stories showing nicely brought up young people. It's not like that in real life'. Of all the arguments for producing mindless rubbish to sell to the proletariat, that one is the worst.

It's supposed to be the show-stopper to silence prune-faced middle class people like me, who write for serious publications like The Guardian. But why, just because they are workers, should their children's minds be blown by such trivial trash? The magazines preach a stultifying message expressed in excruciating style, liberally smattered with 'geddit', ''cos', 'cept', 'fax' and 'fellas'. It is not snobbish or middle-class to believe impressionable girls, working-class or not, deserve better. Whatever Mr Purdie's class origins, how dare he create the basest and the lowest form of journalism and call it 'working-class'?

His next line was another familiar one. 'These magazines are just lighthearted fun. You probably aren't in touch with kids of today. The kids know it's all in fun.' He looked across at me as if I were utterly lacking in humour. 'They aren't to be taken seriously, you see,' he added for emphasis.

But what's funny? Where's the joke? The joke is that after all these years of battering on for a new deal for women, struggling with Equal Opportunities, Equal Pay, anti-sex discrimination, equal school curricula, striving to release young girls from the stultifying role stereotypes of the past, magazines like these are actually travelling fast in the opposite direction.

POLLY TOYNBEE, *Guardian,* 30 October 1978

1 Do you agree with Polly Tonybee that the new teenage mazagines for girls are 'exceptionally horrible'? Do you think her assessment of teen‑age magazines is a fair one?

2 Suggest reasons why the 'heroines' in girls' comics are different from the 'heroines' in teenage magazines.

3 What arguments does John Purdie offer to justify what he does? Do you think he is sincere? How might a sociologist interpret his arguments?

4 Why is Polly Toynbee angry about his assumption that magazines like his are for working-class girls?

5 Take a critical look at teenage magazines for yourself. Can you find any examples to either confirm or contradict Polly Toynbee's criticisms?

3 Questions and answers

In September 1979, the *Guardian* newspaper did a spot-check on the number of women presenting programmes on television and radio:

'Let's face it', said Anna Ford, 'there are no plain women on television. Character doesn't count as far as women are concerned. You have to have acceptable good looks.'

One of the main objections to women newsreaders in the past was that their voices did not carry authority. Anna Ford and Angela Rippon have put paid to that argument but they remain symbols. As Anna Ford put it, 'A token woman has to represent all womanhood. I am made into something special but lots of women could do my job. The problem is there are still very few women in the higher executive positions and it will take at least another 20 years to change that.'

A check through the *Radio Times* reveals a depressing picture. Radios 1, 2 and 3 list almost no women presenters since they are devoted mainly to music and sport. (There is only one well-known female DJ, Anne Nightingale.) But a three-day check on the listed speakers on Radio 4, the station that concerns itself with talk and is aimed during the day largely towards women, showed a daily average of nineteen women's voices to fifty-two men's. 'Women who are any good always get through', says Jim Black, head of presentation for Radio 4. 'We are inundated with women wanting to broadcast. When we advertise a newsreading position we have more women applicants than men.'

So does that show in their appointments? 'No. There has got to be a balance. You can't have an orchestra with more violins than trumpets. If you heard only women's voices it would seem unnatural. Just as it does if you hear only men's.'

A good deal of airtime, then, sounds unnatural. There were no women comedians on Radio 4 in the week we checked but the well-represented men included a weekly series of Hinge and Bracket's mimicry of women. The talk shows (one of which was called 'One Man, One Voice') consisted of either four men and a chairman or three men, one woman and a chairman.

We asked Carole Stone, producer of 'Any Questions', why her programme rarely deviated from the token woman format. 'Cross my heart and swear to die I am ready to class everyone as persons not as members of a sex. But I have to take people who are recommended to me and for every four men only one woman is suggested. I don't like to use up two of my precious women on one programme.'

Radio producers say they cannot afford to take risks. They use people who are already established; programmes therefore are weighted in favour of white, middle-class men, or to put it another way, the Establishment. The early radio newsreaders wore dinner jackets and bow ties. The atmosphere of the traditional posh dinner lingers on. It is not surprising that ladies, who were once expected to leave the table when the conversation turned serious, find it difficult to make themselves heard.

PENNY ALLEN, *Guardian,* 18 September 1979

To what extent do women in radio find it difficult to make their voices heard in your area? Make a study of either your local commercial or BBC radio station, or any of the national BBC stations if you prefer. Try to keep a check on their programmes for a period of two or three days.

1 Make a list of the programmes featured each day.
2 How many men and how many women are involved in the presentation of the programmes?
3 In discussion/documentary programmes, how many of the main contributors are men and how many are women?
4 How many news reports are read by men? How many by women?
5 How many of the programmes are directed mainly at men, mainly at women, at both sexes equally?
6 Discuss together the implications of your findings. What sort of questions would sociologists want to ask about these findings? What explanations might they give for the evidence you have collected?

Checkpoints

1 Which are the 'Big Five' independent television companies?
2 Which two organizations own the two largest cinema chains in Britain?
3 What is the name of the government appointed body which controls and co-ordinates the activities of independent television and radio?
4 When was commercial television first allowed to broadcast in Britain?
5 When was the BBC established?
6 How is the BBC financed?
7 Who was the first director general of the BBC?
8 Which age group watches the greatest amount of television on average each week?
9 What is meant by the term 'heterogeneous'?
10 What is the difference between 'spot advertising' and 'block advertising' in television?

O-level questions

1 The choice of newspaper a person reads may be a good example of the fact that an individual only sees or hears what he wants to. Discuss the point in relation to mass communications generally and the effect which they have on people's attitudes and behaviour.
2 According to television research each girl and boy spends on average more than two hours per day watching television. This is the equivalent to one-third of the time which 5- to 16-year-olds spend in school. We assume that school has some effect on the lives of its pupils, but what do sociologists know about the effects of television on the lives of children and young people?

3 Why do people often do what other people tell them to do? Illustrate
   your answer by giving examples about the influence of the mass
   media on people's lives.
4 'Attitudes and values can also be learned from television, and incorrect notions and stereotypes about life and other people and groups
   can be picked up. Children are particularly susceptible to stereotype
   presentations of groups, situations, occupations, etc., when they have
   little or no related knowledge or experience. Children (and for that
   matter adults) find it difficult to tolerate uncertainty and ambiguity,
   they look for meaning and they welcome definitions. Television can
   give meanings and definitions which the individual who finds himself faced with unfamiliar situations may find helpful and comforting.
   Short term personal adjustment is often gained at the cost of long term
   social disorganization. The role of television and the other media in
   the development of racial and ethnic stereotypes is a case in point, and
   one which requires urgent investigation. If the only time the media
   present immigrants is in crisis situations, ought we to be surprised if
   there is a widespread use of racial stereotypes?
      'It is in the areas of the unfamiliar, the uncertain and the unknown,
   then, that television may have its maximum effect on attitudes and
   values. Children are likely to be particularly vulnerable to outside influences, including the influence of television, if they have few guidelines, lack relevant experience, or if the family and other 'primary'
   agencies in the socialization process have not made their point of view
   clear or provided the necessary standards. If these conventional
   sources in the learning process are not available or are not felt to be
   adequate, then other sources including television are more likely to be
   used' (James Halloran, 'The social effects of television', in J. Halloran
   (ed.), *The Effects of Television)*
a Explain what the author means by 'stereotypes'.
b Discuss the point the author makes about adults and children.
c What does the author mean when he says, 'Short term personal adjustment is often gained at the cost of long term social disorganization'?
5 'Media and communiation which were at one time limited in their
   impact can now reach almost a whole population and may exert a
   tremendous influence upon people, their opinions, their attitudes and
   their way of life . . . at one end of the scale mass media can be used to
   provide sober factual information, and at the other can become a
   vehicle for political propaganda.' (Adapted from A. Hancock, *Mass
   Communications* 1968)
      What evidence can be put forward by sociologists concerning the
   effects of the mass media?
6 What evidence have sociologists offered as to the effects of television
   on any one of these: political behaviour, children, leisure activity?

Acknowledgements

The author and publishers are grateful to the following for their permission to reproduce the following extracts listed by chapter from copyright material:

2 Social class

Weidenfeld & Nicolson Ltd: *The Rise of the Working Class* by Jurgen Kuczynski; Longman: *From Birth to Seven* by Ronald Davie *et al.*; Arrow Books Ltd: 'The invisible ruling class' in *Education or Domination*, ed. Doug Holly; Longman: *The Middle Class* by John Raynor; Penguin Books Ltd: *Work*, ed. Ronald Fraser, © Penguin Books Ltd 1968; *Work 2*, © New Left Review 1967, 1968; *Guardian*: articles by Martin Wainwright and Melanie Phillips; ABP (UK) Ltd: 'Children and social class' in *The Sociology of Education* by P. W. Musgrave

3 The family

Michael Joseph Ltd: *Married Life in an African Tribe* by Isaac Shapera; Penguin Books Ltd: *Growing Up in New Guinea* by Margaret Mead; *Family and Kinship in East London* by M. Young & P. Willmott; Routledge & Kegan Paul Ltd: *Samples from English Culture 1* by J. Klein; Victor Gollancz Ltd: *The Feminine Mystique* by Betty Friedan; Feminist Books: *Wedlocked Women* by Lee Comer; Martin Robertson & Co. Ltd: *The Sociology of Housework* by Ann Oakley; *New Society*: article by Melanie Phillips; Wm Collins Sons & Co. Ltd: *Human Society* by Kingsley Davis; Penguin Books Ltd: *Coming of Age in Samoa* by Margaret Mead

4 Education and adolescence

Penguin Books Ltd: *Rights: A Handbook for People Under Age* by Nan Berger, © Nan Berger 1979; David Higham Associates Ltd & Rupert Hart-Davis Ltd: *The Home and the School* by J. W. B. Douglas; The C. A. R. Crosland Estate: *The Future of Socialism* by Anthony Crosland; Penguin Books Ltd: 'The public schools' by David Rubinstein in *Education for Democracy*, © David Rubinstein, Colin Stoneman & Contributors, 1970, 1972; The Critical Quarterly Society: 'Comprehensive inequality' by Tibor Szamuely in *Black Paper 2*, ed. Cox and Dyson; Caroline Benn: unpublished paper on 'Comprehensive not co-existence'; HMSO: *Children and their Primary Schools – The Plowden Report; Observer*: article by Auriol Stevens; Marshall Cavendish Books Ltd: *Who is the Adolescent?*

Marshall Cavendish Learning System; A. D. Peters and Co. Ltd: *Growing Up: A Practical Guide for Parents and Children* by Catherine Storr; *Guardian:* article by Polly Toynbee

5 The welfare state

A. D. Peters & Co. Ltd: *Meet Your Friendly Social System* by Peter Laurie; *Guardian:* article, 10.10.77; Fontana Paperbacks: *Social Welfare in Modern Britain* eds. E. Butterworth & R. Holman; Churchill Press: *Down with the Poor* by Rhodes Boyson; Nick Bond: *Knowledge of Rights and Extent of Unmet Need Among Recipients of Supplementary Benefit*

6 Work

MacGibbon & Kee Ltd: 'The future of work and leisure' by S. Parker in *Job Satisfaction*, ed. M. Weir; ABP (UK) Ltd: *Women at Work* by L. Mackie and P. Pattullo; *Guardian:* article by Julian Coles; Arrow Books Ltd: *Approaches to Work Place Organization in Industrial Studies* by Tony Topham; Penguin Books Ltd: *Work 2*, ed. Ronald Fraser, © New Left Review 1967, 1968; *Guardian:* article by Alec Hartley; *New Society:* article by Tom Forester; Penguin Books Ltd: *Work,* ed. Ronald Fraser, © Penguin Books Ltd 1968; Birmingham Community Development Project: *Youth on the Dole* (Report 4) by Roger Dicker & Allan Cochrane

7 Population in perspective

Oxford University Press: 'Between the generations' in *Change in British Society* by A. H. Halsey; *Guardian:* article by Judy Hillman; HMSO: *Social Trends;* Open University: *The Population Explosion*

8 British politics

Penguin Books Ltd: *Voters, Parties and Leaders* by J. Blondel, © J. Blondel 1963, 1965, 1966, 1967, 1969, 1974; *So You Want to be Prime Minister* by Des Wilson; *Guardian:* article by Peter Jenkins; Penguin Books Ltd: *Work 2* ed. Ronald Fraser, © New Left Review 1967, 1968; Routledge & Kegan Paul: *Women in the Community,* ed. M. Mayo; *Community Work 2*, ed. D. M. Jones and M. Mayo

9 Mass communication and the media

Cassell & Collier Macmillan Ltd: *Towards a Sociology of Mass Communications* by Denis McQuail; *Guardian:* article by Peter Fiddick; Inter-Action Inprint: *Football Hooliganism,* ed. Stuart Hall; *Guardian:* articles by Polly Toynbee and Penny Allen

Every effort has been made to ensure accurate acknowledgement. The publishers would be glad to know of any corrections for subsequent reprints.

Index

nature-nurture controversy, 51, 79
New Guinea, 53-6, 76-7
newspapers. 10, 229-30, 245, 257,
 261-3, 266-9, 274-9, 283

participant observation, 15, 16
pilot study, 12
Plowden Report, 86, 108-9, 115, 129, 130
political parties, 233-40, 257, 258
politicians, 20, 24, 95, 123, 227, 230-2,
 236-40, 244-5, 248-51
politics, 225-59
population characteristics, 191-223
poverty, 9, 35-8, 91, 119, 126-7, 128,
 129-30, 132-4, 145, 170, 199, 243
pre-industrial society, 11, 15, 48, 49,
 51-6, 75-7, 78, 79, 90, 96, 191-2, 193-6,
 203, 214-15, 218, 261
pressure groups, 122, 240-2, 252-7, 258
professions, 20, 23, 24, 26, 29-31, 42, 89,
 90, 125, 128, 150, 152, 156, 159, 170-2,
 238-40
public schools, 84, 87-90, 101-2, 115,
 237-8, 240

questionnaire, 11-12, 14, 16, 78, 216-18

Registrar General, 23, 26, 28, 41, 42
Rowntree, S., 35-8, 42, 119, 126, 133, 144

Samoa, 75-6
sample, 11, 12, 210, 213
secondary modern schools, 86-7,
 99-100
single parents, 46, 69, 70, 162, 252-4
soccer hooliganism, 9, 95, 274-9
social class, 10, 12, 19-42, 50, 63-4, 91,
 92-3, 94, 95, 98, 99-100, 103-4, 107-9,
 226-7, 242-8, 258-9, 267-8
social mobility, 24-5, 33, 41, 42, 153,
 203, 228
socialization, 46, 50-1, 71-7, 79, 80, 81,
 90, 236-7, 265-6

state, 7, 8, 63, 84, 88, 120, 136-8, 203,
 204, 208
statistics, 11, 12, 13-14, 213
status, 24, 42, 50, 91
streaming, 87, 93-5, 109-10
survey, 11-12, 14, 16, 104-6, 139-43,
 210-13, 216-18

technology, 7, 29, 147, 149-51
teenagers, 9, 62-3, 96-9, 110-14, 162-3,
 183-5
television, 230-1, 245, 261-70, 271-4,
 282-4
trade unions, 10, 13, 95, 97, 148, 151,
 152, 154, 158, 161-2, 169-71, 177-80,
 226, 229, 238, 254-7
tripartite system, 86-7, 91, 95, 99-100,
 115, 116

unemployment, 9, 23, 25, 36, 91, 95, 120,
 123, 130, 136, 150, 151, 154-5, 161-3,
 182-4, 199
upper class, 19-42, 84, 137, 226-8

voluntary organizations, 120, 213,
 252-4
voting behaviour, 84, 226-33, 242-8,
 258

wealth, 8, 14, 21, 24, 25, 34-5, 40, 42, 84,
 90, 119, 127, 198
welfare state, 7, 35-8, 47, 83, 129-45,
 173-5, 200-1, 208, 212-13, 252-4
women, working, 24, 47, 64, 70, 78, 91,
 156-60, 162, 167-76, 188, 204
work, 8, 47, 48, 57-60, 147-89, 200
working class, 19-42, 48, 56-7, 57-60,
 65-8, 78, 87, 91, 92-3, 94, 95, 99-100,
 104, 107-9, 119, 128, 177-9, 199, 204-5,
 226-33, 234-40, 242-8, 258-9,
 267-8